Ingrid Bergman

The Life, Career and Public Image

DAVID SMIT

McFarland & Company, Inc., Publishers
Jefferson, North Carolina, and London

10-17

#794708255

LIBRARY OF CONGRESS CATALOGUING-IN-PUBLICATION DATA

Smit, David, 1944–
    Ingrid Bergman : the life, career and public image /
David Smit.
        p.   cm.
    Includes bibliographical references and index.

    ISBN 978-0-7864-7226-0
    softcover : acid free paper ∞

    1. Bergman, Ingrid, 1915–1982.   2. Actors — Sweden —
Biography.   I. Title.
    PN2287.B435S54 2012
    791.4302' 8092 — dc23
    [B]   2012035336

BRITISH LIBRARY CATALOGUING DATA ARE AVAILABLE

Front cover image: Ingrid Bergman, circa late 1960s (Photofest)

Manufactured in the United States of America

McFarland & Company, Inc., Publishers
  Box 611, Jefferson, North Carolina 28640
    www.mcfarlandpub.com

Table of Contents

Acknowledgments

Throughout Chapter Three and in Chapter Seven of this book, I cite documents from the David O. Selznick Collection at the Harry Research Center at the University of Texas-Austin, where I spent an enjoyable two weeks in February of 2003 on a Big 12 Faculty Fellowship. My thanks to the staff at the Ransom Center for their gracious hospitality and for permission to quote from these documents. I would also like to thank the Provost's Office at Kansas State University for providing me the opportunity to make the trip.

Much of Chapter Three and a few paragraphs in Chapter Eight were published previously as "Marketing Ingrid Bergman" in the *Quarterly Review of Film and Video*, Volume 22, Number 3 (2005), pages 237–250, and are reprinted by permission of Taylor & Francis, (http://www.tandfonline.com). Several paragraphs in chapters five and six were previously published in "On Not Going Home: Ingrid Berman's Image in 50s America," in *Film and Television Stardom*, and are reprinted by permission from Cambridge Scholars.

I would like to dedicate this book to my wife Ann and my daughters Rachel and Joanna.

Preface

This book examines the life, career and especially the public image of Ingrid Bergman. It is divided into three parts. Part I, "The Idea of a Life," explores various ideas about the overall shape and meaning of Ingrid Bergman's life and career. Chapter One presents the background needed to understand the issues involved and the undisputed facts about Bergman's life. Chapter Two contrasts the very different Ingrids from the two major biographies — Laurence Leamer's *As Time Goes By* and Donald Spoto's *Notorious*— and presents the salient facts that might help us to decide which portrait is more accurate, more faithful to the facts as we know them.

Part II, "Other Ingrids," presents five in all: the Ingrid created by David O. Selznick's publicity machine and by Bergman herself, the Ingrid who confronted an existential crisis in her life in the late 40s, the Ingrid who suffered from the raw publicity over her affair with Rossellini, the Ingrid who reinvented her life when her marriage to Rossellini ended, and the Ingrid who in her interviews and autobiography shaped and molded her public image into that which survives today.

Chapter Three discusses Selznick Studios' creation and control of Bergman's image, which makes it so difficult to know her as a person.

Chapter Four explores the crises in Bergman's life in the late '40s, both in her marriage and in her career, that she tried to hide from the public. These two inter-related crises eventually led to the scandal with Roberto Rossellini in ways that Bergman always denied.

Chapter Five argues that the scandal was not as "epic" as Bergman and her biographers claim it to be; nor was it a clear indicator of postwar sexual morality as they also claim. Rather, the evidence suggests that the press accepted Bergman's interpretation of the affair and ignored alternative explanations.

Chapter Six presents an alternative to the usual interpretations of Bergman's later career. Most scholars and critics believe these years were simply unlucky for her, a consequence of her inability to find roles that would highlight her particular performance skills. I argue instead that Bergman settled for roles in undistinguished plays and films because she associated film "art" with Rossellini, whose methods and films she did not fully appreciate, and so she chose to live the life of an "entertainer" rather than an artist. In a sense, Bergman turned her own life into a performance.

Chapter Seven demonstrates that after her marriage to Rossellini, Bergman carefully controlled her image and the interpretation of her career through interviews and her autobiography.

Part III, "Appreciations," is an assessment of Bergman as an actor and star. Chapter Eight describes Bergman's performance skills and the components of her star image and argues that her best work is exhibited in Hitchcock's *Notorious*, Rossellini's *Voyage in Italy*, and Ingmar Bergman's *Autumn Sonata*. Chapter Nine extends this analysis of Bergman's contribution to these three films by showing that Bergman influenced Hitchcock, Rossellini, and Ingmar Bergman to make movies that were, for all practical purposes, inspired by or about her life and image, that Bergman was in these three films an "auteur."

The Epilogue concerns an aspect of Bergman's life we have no real name for: call it her basic beliefs and values, her way of life; the principles, philosophical or religious, that sustained her during the end of her life when she bravely battled cancer for years and struggled to maintain a normal working life until the very end.

PART I: THE IDEA OF A LIFE

One

Ideas About Ingrid Bergman

On March 14, 1950, Senator Edwin C. Johnson, Democrat from Colorado, also known as "Big Ed," gave a speech on the floor of the United States Senate. In the words of one observer, "Big Ed's voice quaked with indignant wrath. His mammoth head lifted in righteous purpose. Shoulders back, he stood proud and erect," index finger jabbing here and there, vainly trying to point out the object of his anger, a woman who was not in the Senate chamber at all.[1]

That woman was Ingrid Bergman. The cause of Johnson's wrath was Bergman's very public affair with Italian director Roberto Rossellini and the fact that Bergman had given birth a month before to a child out of wedlock. In the throes of his speech Johnson often seemed more angry about the publicity surrounding the movie Bergman had made with Rossellini during their affair — *Stromboli* — than he was at Bergman's supposed "moral turpitude." He saved the heights of his invective for RKO Studios and Rossellini for capitalizing on the couple's immorality in the advertising campaign for *Stromboli*. Posters for the film, vivid in orange and black, showed Bergman's name emblazoned over an erupting volcano. Additional text declaimed:

> This is it.
> Stromboli
> Raging island — raging passions
> Under the inspired direction of Rossellini

Although Johnson held Rossellini responsible for Bergman's downfall — he called Rossellini a "love pirate" and a "home wrecker" — his anger seems to have been fueled by a deep sense that Bergman had personally betrayed him. He described her as a sweet, understanding, and attractive person who captivated all those who met her or saw her in the movies. He identified her as his favorite actress of all time, a person who inspired love and even reverence, a person who caused her fans "to have implicit faith in her," an actress who seemed most effective when she portrayed "a serious saintly person."[2] Clearly, what outraged Johnson about Bergman's "unconventional free-love conduct" was his intense disappointment that she had not lived up to the ideal she obviously was: "Had some friendless streetwalker pulled such a stunt, it would not have meant so much, but we have here the pin-up girl of millions; Hollywood's sweetheart; a celebrated international figure, who has started a crusade against the holy bond of matrimony."[3]

During his speech, Johnson clearly indicated he had never met Bergman personally. Yet he thought he knew who she was.

It never seems to have dawned on Johnson that Ingrid Bergman was not necessarily the woman he had seen on screen or read about in the newspapers. It never seems to have dawned on him that the woman he so admired may have been different from the characters she portrayed on screen or the woman reported on in the press. Perhaps the most egregious assumption Johnson made was that of the many roles Bergman had played until the scandal with Rossellini, the parts which most clearly reflected her own personality were those in which she portrayed "a serious saintly person." Johnson is probably referring to Bergman's roles as Sister Benedict in *The Bells of St. Mary's* and Joan in *Joan of Arc*, but she had also played sincere and wholesome women who suffer from love or abusive husbands in *Adam Had Four Sons*, *Rage in Heaven*, and *Gaslight*. Ironically, what Johnson dismisses are all those films in which Bergman portrayed women who were engaged in extra-marital affairs (*Intermezzo*, *Casablanca*), women who were promiscuous (*For Whom the Bell Tolls*, *Saratoga Trunk*, *Spellbound*, *Notorious*) or women who were outright prostitutes (*Dr. Jekyll and Mr. Hyde*, *Arch of Triumph*).

Still, Johnson thought he knew who Ingrid Bergman was.

Now, half a century after Johnson's tirade, we know much more about Ingrid Bergman, but who she was and the significance of her life and career are as difficult to determine as ever. Bergman published her autobiography, *My Story*, co-authored by Alan Burgess, in 1980. *My Story* gives us some sense of Bergman as a person, but in many ways the book hides more than it reveals. The Bergman of *My Story* is the Bergman of the David O. Selznick Studio publicity machine and her public interviews. She is honest and forthright about what she very carefully chooses to be honest and forthright about, and as a result, she reveals very little about her inner life.

Since Bergman's death, two major biographies have been written about her: Laurence Leamer's *As Time Goes By*, published in 1986, and Donald Spoto's *Notorious*, published in 1997.[4] The two biographies mostly agree on the facts about her life, but they paint two very different pictures of her as a person. In fact, it is possible to read the two books and wonder at times if they are really describing the same person at all. Leamer's Bergman is egocentric, selfish and so consumed by her career that she is willing to sacrifice everything, including family and friends, for the glory of stardom. Spoto's Bergman is generous, wholesome, sincere, a great actress who desperately tried to balance the demands of family and friends with those of her lovers and her career.

These differences should not surprise us. At least since the rise of the "New Biography" at the turn of the twentieth century, literary biographers, as well as scholars and critics of the genre, have recognized that biographies are not complete and impartial narratives of who people are, but fragmented, biased accounts which share many techniques with fiction. Biographers select and arrange details to fit a distinctive point of view. They infer aspects of characters from phrases dropped in conversation or recorded in letters. They embellish details to heighten the effect of crucial moments in their subject's life. They invent detail for the scenes in which those moments occur based only on pictures of what the room looked like during the period or what the weather must have been like at that time of year. They even occasionally go so far as to portray the thoughts and feelings of their subjects based only on reports of what their subjects said and did.

And perhaps these techniques confirm what we have come to understand about human nature in general. Now it is generally accepted — as perhaps we have always known — that people have multiple identities and are not so easy to pin down, label, and classify. Some of our multiple identities are determined by the accidents of birth — gender, race, nationality, basic temperament, family upbringing, childhood circumstances — and some, influenced by a host of factors, are more or less freely chosen: lovers, spouses, careers, religious affiliations, hobbies, leisure activities, and contributions to politics and charities.

The difficulty of comprehending a person's life is illustrated by Johnson's speech. In that speech Johnson was using a certain "idea" of Ingrid Bergman for his own purposes. Johnson's ostensible legislative purpose for giving the speech was to propose that the government of the United States license actors, producers, and films in order to control the "moral turpitude" of the film community. However, it was rumored later that Johnson was not as scandalized as he seemed, that in giving the speech Johnson was really conducting a test run of an issue on which he might be able to campaign for the presidency. Or, as an editor in *Variety* speculated, at a minimum, Johnson was using the speech to signal his political opponents back home in Colorado not to encourage Frank H. "Rick" Ricketson, President of Intermountain Theaters, to run for governor.[5]

Today, Johnson's speech is remembered, if it is remembered at all, primarily because it was used by Bergman herself — and her co-author Alan Burgess — in her autobiography as part of an argument and interpretation about the shape of her life and career. Bergman and Burgess cite the speech as one of a series of episodes that provided a major turning point in her life. Later, Bergman's first biographer, Laurence Leamer, would also begin his book on Bergman with the story of her affair with Rossellini and cite Johnson's speech as evidence of the affair's cultural importance. And so both Bergman herself and her later biographers would use Johnson's speech in ways that he had never intended.

Ideas about public figures become known in order to further the interests of particular people in particular circumstances; these ideas circulate, get embellished in the re-telling, accumulate rumor and half-truth, and often emerge at the end of an era as full-blown legend, or even myth. Commonly accepted ideas about public figures take on the color and the biases of all the people who helped to circulate those ideas.

Sorting through the ideas, the embellishments, the rumors and half-truths, the legends and myths, it is often difficult to know just what to think about Ingrid Bergman.

During the late '40s Bergman was the most celebrated actress in Hollywood and on Broadway. She received her first Academy Award in 1945 for her work in *Gaslight*. In fact, *Life* magazine declared 1945 to be "Bergman's Year." The magazine put her on the cover in November and devoted a four-page spread to her three newly-released films: *Saratoga Trunk*, *The Bells of St. Mary's* and *Spellbound*. A joke made its way around the country that someone had actually seen a movie *without* Ingrid Bergman. A year later she received over twenty awards for portraying the lead in Maxwell Anderson's *Joan of Lorraine* for six sold-out months in New York City. *Newsweek* put her on the cover as the "Queen of Broadway" and reported that she was making more than any other theater actress at the time: 15 percent of the gross, or about $129,000, for her stint of half a year. In 1949, 272 women journalists surveyed by *Pageant* magazine voted Bergman one of the "The Most Powerful Women in America," along with Eleanor Roosevelt, Bess Truman, Princess Elizabeth, Margaret Chase Smith, Sister Elizabeth Kenny, Emily Post, Helen Keller, Eve Curie, Kate Smith, and, of all people, Rita Hayworth.[6]

In other words, in the late '40s and early '50s, before and during the Bergman-Rossellini scandal, Americans lived with certain ideas about Ingrid Bergman. She was a household name, and not just among movie fans. News magazines, commentators, and intellectuals alluded to her beauty, her popularity, her career, the Rossellini affair, as standing for something about the times, as standing for the way the lives of the famous, their images on the screen and in advertising, the stories and interviews in the tabloids and popular press, influence the culture at large.

During the scandal, the media told Bergman's story as if it had a moral:

her life was about how a beautiful, wholesome, honest woman had thrown away her popularity and acclaim, even her standing as an actress, all for love. It was for that reason she had been banished to Europe and did not dare return. Producers were afraid that she was no longer good box office and that too many of the public would stay away from her films out of moral principle. And as part of her punishment, it was also understood that the films she made in Europe, all but one of them with Rossellini, who became her husband, were artistic disasters.

When Bergman resurrected her career in America in 1956, with her starring role in *Anastasia*, the media reconfirmed their original story but with a different moral: now the story was that after six years in the wilderness, Bergman had suffered sufficiently for her indiscretion, had paid the necessary penance, and a gracious and forgiving American public had accepted her back to the promised land. The Academy Award she received in 1957 for playing the lead in *Anastasia* was a sign that the larger public was now willing to forgive and forget.

But something interesting happened as Bergman continued to work: she seemed to gain in stature and prestige, even as the plays and films she appeared in were judged mediocre at best. However, when she did appear in serious work, she was recognized for her achievements. She received her third Academy Award for a very small part in *Murder on the Orient Express*. She received an Emmy for her portrayal of the governess in a TV production of Henry James's *The Turn of the Screw*. Critics proclaimed her last two films, Ingmar Bergman's *Autumn Sonata* and the made-for-TV life of Israeli prime minister Golda Meir, *A Woman Called Golda*, perhaps her best work ever. Bergman received an Emmy Award posthumously for her work in *Golda*. Film critics and scholars began to consider the possibility that Bergman's career had not peaked in the late '40s but that she had continued to grow and mature as an actor all her life. To this way of thinking, her career was truly climactic. By the 1980s, having lived with Bergman's career in films for forty years, Americans began to develop new ideas about what that career meant.

The publication of Bergman's autobiography in 1980 furthered the legend and burnished Bergman's image as a truthful and honest woman. With a disconcerting charm, Bergman confessed to an affair with the great war photographer Robert Capa and the difficulties of her marriages to Petter Lindstrom, Rossellini, and producer Lars Schmidt. Bergman's life seemed to be an open book.

After her death, something equally interesting happened. American film scholars rediscovered Roberto Rossellini and resurrected the claims of a number of French critics during the '50s that Rossellini's films with Bergman were landmarks in the history of cinema, that in the words of critic Alain Bergala,

"With his Bergman films Rossellini was in the process of inventing nothing less than the modern cinema."[7] *Voyage in Italy* is regularly voted one of best films of all time by the influential French film journal *Cahiers du Cinéma*. In retrospect, then, Bergman's involvement with Rossellini took on a whole new meaning. After all, it was Bergman who had initiated contact with Rossellini by sending him a telegram, asking him to consider her for a role in one of his films, even though the only words she knew in Italian were "*Ti amo*," "I love you." It was Bergman who always claimed that she wanted to work with Rossellini because she fell in love with the art of *Open City* and *Paisan*. It was Bergman's life and career that were the inspiration for the films Rossellini made with her. And so film scholars began to wonder if Bergman's affair with Rossellini was more than just a matter of passion. They began to wonder whether Bergman herself was the occasion for something of major significance in the history of cinema. The idea of Ingrid Bergman became even more interesting, and it was not so easy to talk about her in the terms of the standard narratives.

The publication of the two biographies after her death called into question whether the wholesome image she had maintained all her life bore any relationship to reality. Filled with testimony, rumor, and innuendo about Bergman's alleged liaisons with a multitude of lovers, her rocky marriages, and her possible neglect of her children, Bergman's life no longer seemed like an open book. Scholars pondered whether Bergman was really an honest and wholesome woman or whether she deliberately cultivated that image because she had a great deal to hide. They entertained the possibility that Bergman was a mistress of the media, setting the agenda and determining for the press the little they could learn about her.

Because of Bergman's mastery of the media, we know a great deal about her life, but what we know does not necessarily tell us a great deal about her. Certain facts are not in dispute.

Bergman was born in Stockholm on August 29, 1915. Her parents were Justus Bergman, the owner and manager of a camera shop, and Frieda Adler, a German woman Justus had first met when she came to Sweden on vacation from her home in Kiel, near Hamburg. Justus was introspective, imaginative; a dreamer and an amateur painter, and he was fascinated by that popular invention, newly accessible to amateurs: the motion picture camera. During her childhood, Bergman may have been the most photographed person in Sweden.

Frieda died when her daughter was two. For much of her early life, Bergman was raised by her father's sister Ellen, whom she called Mama. During the summers until she was almost twenty, Bergman visited her mother's family in Germany: her grandparents, the Adlers, and her aunts Elsa and

Luna. The Adlers were much more staid, orderly, and conservative than her father, and so Bergman was attracted to the more fun-loving Elsa, who taught her German, encouraged her to read good books, and indulged her interest in putting on plays. Bergman came to call Elsa Aunt Mutti ("Aunt Mommy").

When Bergman was about seven, her father took on a housekeeper named Greta Danielsson. Eventually Greta became her father's mistress, even though she was eighteen and he was fifty-one. Aunt Ellen moved back to her old apartment a few blocks away. Although Greta treated Bergman as a younger sister — they often went to movies together — she was now the third mother-figure in Bergman's life.

In 1929, after considering traveling abroad without Greta, Justus Bergman took sick with what was assumed to be the flu, but was later diagnosed as stomach cancer. Justus, a bohemian to the end, went off to Germany with Greta to get a second opinion. The diagnosis was confirmed and Justus came back to Stockholm to die. Bergman and Greta nursed Justus on his death bed. Bergman was thirteen.

Nine months later, Aunt Ellen died in Bergman's arms, from an apparent heart attack.

Bergman attended Stockholm's Lyceum for Girls from the ages of seven to eighteen, from the autumn of 1922 to the spring of 1933. The curriculum was similar to other schools of the time: in the early grades, Swedish language and history, Scandinavian geography, handwriting, arithmetic, German, singing, drawing, sewing, and physical education; in the later grades, biology, chemistry, French, and cooking. Bergman was especially good at German; she did not do well in cooking.[8]

Upon graduating from the Lyceum, Bergman applied to the Swedish Royal Dramatic Theater Academy, whose performances she had attended with her father. She was accepted, and so for one year she studied theater history, voice and diction, stage movement, dance, and what was then called body culture: how to sit, stand, enter and leave a room. The summer after her first year at the Royal Academy Bergman did not join the rest of her class in a theater tour of Russia, but instead took a part in the film *The Count of Monk's Bridge* (*Munkbrogreven*), perhaps because she was having an affair with the star of the film, Edvin Adolphson.[9] The Swedish film community appreciated her work, and Bergman was quickly offered and accepted another role that summer and one promised in the future, to be directed by the famous Gustav Molander. The curriculum for the Royal Dramatic Theater Academy ran for three years, so Bergman bravely resigned from the school in order to risk her stage career for possible stardom in films. During the next six years, she made eight films in Sweden and one in Germany, a variety of roles that demonstrated her emotional range and versatility.

While still at the Royal Theater Academy, Bergman had met an aspiring dentist named Petter Lindstrom. The relationship survived the affair with Adolphson, and Bergman married Lindstrom on July 10, 1937. Bergman's first daughter, Friedel Pia, but always called Pia, was born fourteen months later on September 20, 1938.

The success of one of her Swedish films—*Intermezzo*—attracted the attention of the David O. Selznick Organization, which after intense negotiations brought Bergman to America in 1939. Bergman's career was carefully nurtured by Selznick personally, and after a series of moderately successful films, beginning with an American version of *Intermezzo*, she blossomed into fame with performances in *Dr. Jeykll and Mr. Hyde*, *Casablanca*, and *For Whom the Bell Tolls*. By 1946, Bergman was possibly the most famous actress in the world.

But Bergman's increasingly acclaimed career put a great deal of stress on her marriage. Lindstrom had followed her to America in late 1940 and had decided to further his career by becoming a surgeon. After considering the University of Southern California, the University of Chicago, the University of Rochester, and Yale, Lindstrom chose the University of Rochester, and so he, Bergman and Pia moved to Rochester, and Bergman commuted back and forth from Rochester to Hollywood. Away from her husbands she had either affairs or intense emotional relationships with her co-stars Spencer Tracy, Gary Cooper, and Gregory Peck and with director Victor Fleming. Increasingly, perhaps because of the strains on her marriage, perhaps because of the pressure of stardom, she became alienated from life in Hollywood and longed to escape in ways that she could not articulate to herself.

During World War II, Bergman toured and performed for the USO, gave radio talks for the Office of War Information, and produced at least one patriotic film for the war effort: *Swedes in America*. On tour in Europe she met entertainer Larry Adler and the war photographer Robert Capa, and for years she had an on-again, off-again affair with Adler and an intense affair with Capa, who followed her to Hollywood for the shooting of Hitchcock's *Notorious* and to New York, where she rehearsed and then performed in Maxwell Anderson's *Joan of Lorraine*.

Lindstrom eventually became aware of Bergman's affairs. The couple discussed divorce but then negotiated a tentative peace and stayed together. Still, Bergman had an affair with — or resumed her previous relationship with, depending on the sources — Victor Fleming, the director of the film version of Anderson's play. Under intense pressure from Hitchcock to do another film with him, Bergman followed *Joan of Arc* with *Under Capricorn*. Both films were difficult personally, perhaps because of the intensity of her relationships with the directors.

Because of her success, Bergman formed her own production company and starred in *Arch of Triumph*, but she was not happy with the production and had little hope for it.

Despairing over the emotional turmoil of her love life and the failure of her latest pictures, Bergman made a list of some good directors who might make her enjoy making films again and resurrect her career. But she only sent a letter to one: Roberto Rossellini. Rossellini replied to Bergman's letter with gusto, came to America to negotiate the deal, and swept Bergman off her feet. When Bergman left for Italy in 1949 to make *Stromboli* with Rossellini, she began the scandal that many people would take to be the defining moment of her life. She quickly became pregnant with Rossellini's child, negotiations with Lindstrom over divorce broke down, and as a result she gave birth to son Robertino out of wedlock.

Bergman's marriage to Rossellini lasted from 1950 to 1956. She was divorced from Lindstrom and married to Rossellini in early 1950. She gave birth to Renato Roberto (called Robertino) on February 2, 1950, and the twins Isabella and Isotta Ingrid on June 18, 1952. Rossellini was a jealous, possessive husband and would not let Bergman work with other directors. During her life with him Bergman made six films, four of them—*Stromboli*, *Europa '51*, *Voyage in Italy*, and *Fear*—so closely related in theme and subject matter that film scholars call this the "Bergman period" in Rossellini's career.

The marriage was difficult from the start but began to become really strained by the mid-fifties. After touring with Rossellini's production of the oratorio *Joan at the Stake* and making a film based on the piece, Bergman had had enough. She left to make a film with another director, Jean Renoir, *Paris Does Strange Things* (*Elena and Her Men*); she then acted in a Parisian stage production of Robert Anderson's *Tea and Sympathy*, during which she had an intense emotional relationship or possible affair with the playwright. She went on to make the film of *Anastasia*, which resulted in her triumphant return to America in 1957. Bergman's decision to work without him enraged Rossellini, and so Bergman spent much of the years 1957 to 1958 consumed by the divorce from Rossellini and negotiating the custody of their three children.

Bergman did find one source of consolation in all this. She met and was wooed by Swedish producer Lars Schmidt. They married on December 21, 1958. The marriage lasted for seventeen years, but it was over long before that. As she had with Lindstrom, Bergman was always on the road, performing in plays or making films. In 1970, Schmidt took a mistress. Bergman swallowed her pride and held on to the fiction of the marriage until 1975. During her marriage to Schmidt, rather ironically, she increased her stardom in a long line of conventionally undistinguished films that began with *Anastasia* and included *Indiscreet*, *The Inn of the Sixth Happiness*, *Goodbye Again*, *Murder on the Orient Express, The Visit, Cactus Flower,* and *A Walk in the Spring Rain.* But age did not seem to diminish her need for romance. While shooting *Goodbye Again,* Bergman may have tried to seduce Tony Perkins, and she may have had affairs with Anthony Quinn during the shooting of *The Visit* and *A Walk in the Spring Rain.*

Bergman's stage work was more ambitious than her film work. It included roles in *The Turn of the Screw, Hedda Gabler, A Month in the Country, More Stately Mansions,* and *Captain Brassbound's Conversion,* but none of these plays was a critical success, and they are remembered primarily because Bergman appeared in them.

In 1973 during the run of *The Constant Wife,* Bergman noticed a lump in her breast. She was worried but not enough to take her doctor's advice to have the tissue of the nodule biopsied. She finished the run of the play and completed her part in *Murder on the Orient Express.* Only then, after noticing that the lump in her breast was larger, did she submit to a biopsy. She was immediately diagnosed with a massive breast cancer and suffered a mastectomy. Several years later the other breast had to be removed. The mastectomies did not stop her from acting in the play *Waters of the Moon.* Knowing she was in the last years of her life, Bergman agreed to work with her countryman Ingmar Bergman on *Autumn Sonata,* a film about a pianist returning to visit her daughters after a long absence. The life of the lead character bears a remarkable similarity to Bergman's own life and is often interpreted as Bergman's last great gift to the world. Certainly dying now, Bergman agreed to do one last part, something totally new for her, the re-creation of a contemporary figure, Golda Meir, in the TV movie *A Woman Called Golda.* For this role, another triumph, she was awarded an Emmy posthumously.

Bergman died on her birthday, August 29, 1982, at the age of 67.

Despite this broad outline of Bergman's life, mysteries remain, ambiguities abound, and the significance of her life and career is open to a great deal of speculation and interpretation. We know little about her love life, about the crisis in her life and career in the late '40s, about the real reasons she left America to work with Rossellini, about her relationship with her husbands and children, or about the discrepancy between her outward cheerfulness and the pain and suffering she endured throughout her life, from the loss of her parents as a child to her brave battle with cancer in her 60s. We know little about the sources for her art, and there is no critical consensus about what constitutes her best work. What we can safely say is that the charming woman of the interviews and the autobiography is not necessarily who she was at all.

We may be living with Ingrid Bergman, with the complicated idea of who Ingrid Bergman was, for a very long time.

However, we live with the idea of Bergman, she is clearly a cultural icon, a metaphor of her times, perhaps more representative of mid–twentieth century culture than many other major female stars that were prominent during her career. Bergman's life and career may have greater significance and cultural resonance than her peers Katharine Hepburn, Lana Turner, Rita Hayworth, and Bette Davis in the '40s; Marilyn Monroe, Audrey Hepburn, and Doris Day in the '50s, and the many lesser lights that followed them until Bergman's death in 1982. Bergman's public romance with Rossellini played out on the international stage more than the indiscretions of other female stars, with the possible exception of Marilyn Monroe. But except for this one lapse, Bergman's ability to protect her privacy and control the media makes her the model of mid-century career women, women in transition. Bergman is the traditional woman, caught between the competing demands of family and career, but she is also the post-modern woman, creating a life beyond the scrutiny of the public, beyond the image she so deftly projects, where she can live the life she wants — creatively, sexually — on her own terms.

Certainly it is possible to think of Bergman's accomplishments as comparable to or even superior to those of her peers.

Consider the following.

Ingrid Bergman spoke five languages — Swedish, German, English, Italian, and French — and performed in plays and films in all five.

Ingrid Bergman moved seamlessly from screen to stage and back again, appearing in major stage productions of *Anna Christie, Liliom, Joan of Lorraine, Tea and Sympathy,* and *More Stately Mansions.* For her work, she received three Oscars, one Tony, and two Emmys.

Ingrid Bergman starred in what may arguably be called the most popular American film of all time, *Casablanca.*

Ingrid Bergman worked with the major film directors of her time, both American — George Cukor, Alfred Hitchcock — and European — Roberto Rossellini, Jean Renoir, Ingmar Bergman — and with the legendary stage director José Quintero. Three of these film directors are now considered to be modern masters and Bergman appears in some of their best work: Hitchcock's *Notorious,* Rossellini's *Voyage in Italy,* and Bergman's *Autumn Sonata.* Moreover, these three pictures were specifically written — with Rossellini, the better word might be "improvised"— with Bergman in mind, and so more than with most films, her persona and image, what she brings to the screen, were inherent in the very conception of these films. Bergman may be the only actor to give a name to a creative period in a director's career. It is common among film scholars to refer to the six years that Bergman worked with Roberto Rossellini as his "Bergman period," and indeed four of the films Rossellini made with Bergman can be understood as a meditation on her life and the culture she represents.

Ingrid Bergman counted as friends or was courted by major artists and intellectuals of the period. Eugene O'Neill wanted her to be in a repertory company he was planning for his last great cycle of plays dramatizing the history of America. Maxwell Anderson wrote *Joan of Lorraine* for her. She discussed Joan over tea with George Bernard Shaw. Ernest Hemingway called her "daughter." She had an affair with photographer Robert Capa. Paul Claudel and Arthur Honegger were deeply grateful that she appeared in their oratorio *Joan at the Stake*.

Woody Guthrie wrote the lyrics of a song about her in 1950. (He may also have written the music but that has been lost.) In any case, Billy Bragg put Guthrie's words to music in 1996 and recorded it with a group called Wilco in a CD entitled *Mermaid Avenue*. The narrator of the song focuses on the Rossellini scandal, praising Bergman's beauty and lasciviously suggesting through a series of metaphors that any man would be enflamed by her good looks, eager like a mountain to feel her "touch its hardrock," lusting after her to the point of exploding like a volcano.

Bergman has a rose named after her, a hybrid tea with a gorgeous deep red color and long stems, suitable for cutting and display. The plant is also hardy and reasonably resistant to disease.

Consider this book then a celebration of the life and career of Ingrid Bergman. But it is not a biography. Rather, consider it a series of critical essays on the problems of understanding Bergman, her art, her life, her career. Consider this a book about living with the *idea* of Ingrid Bergman. Living with the idea of Ingrid Bergman is living with the idea of what we can reasonably know about public figures through the craft of biography, the business of press coverage, the image-making of Hollywood, and the politics of film scholarship. Bergman's life and career say something about the status of women during her lifetime and how one woman created a life for herself among the competing demands of love and ambition. Her life and career tell us about the contribution actors play in the making of theater and film, the nature of the imagery produced by the Hollywood dream factory and its influence on the culture. Because of the contradictory interpretations of her career, Bergman's life and career can also be the occasion for us to contemplate the nature of interpretation itself and the way we look at a life and determine its shape and meaning. And in her dying Bergman may give us the opportunity to ponder what we really value when we talk about art, sex, and beauty, what we value when we ponder death and the end of our lives.

Living with Ingrid Bergman is living with a person, a career, a way of life, forms of art, issues of truth and beauty, and the meaning of life and death.

Two

The Two Ingrids

"Not only do biographies suggest that things as difficult as human lives can — for all their obvious complexity — be summed up, known, comprehended: they reassure us that, while we are reading, a world will be created in which there are few or no unclear motives, muddled decisions, or (indeed) loose ends."
— John Worthen, "The Necessary Ignorance of a Biographer"

Biography is the worst possible excuse for getting people wrong.
— Mrs. Swan in Tom Stoppard's *Indian Ink*

In 1997 Donald Spoto, the biographer of such Hollywood personalities as James Dean, Elizabeth Taylor, Marilyn Monroe, and Alfred Hitchcock, published another biography. This one was about Ingrid Bergman, and it was entitled *Notorious*. Although the title suggests a hint of scandal, Spoto makes clear even in the opening epigraph that he has not written a steamy expose: the epigraph cites *The Oxford English Dictionary* that the word "notorious" comes from the Latin *notus* (known); that is, famous or celebrated, and only secondarily, known for something not generally approved. The Ingrid Bergman in *Notorious* is indeed famous and celebrated. Spoto clearly worships Bergman personally for her beauty and honesty, for her dignity, discretion, and graciousness, and he worships her professionally for the artistry that characterized her lifelong work on stage and in film. In fact, it is often difficult to determine why Spoto called the book *Notorious* at all, considering that today we use the word almost exclusively to mean "known for something not generally approved." Spoto seems to want to capitalize on the one major scandal of Bergman's life, her very public affair with Roberto Rossellini and her becoming pregnant by him while still married to Petter Lindstrom, even though he dismisses it as an example of misplaced public outrage and a sign of the immaturity of the times. There is little in Bergman's life of which he does not approve.

Spoto depicts Bergman as straightforward, down-to-earth, humble, and honest, a person whose life was apparent for all to see; to Spoto, Bergman's public image was the essence of who she was in private. That public image was not terribly complicated. Bergman was basically a good person. She was a devoted wife, whose three marriages did not last for reasons not her fault. In each case, she made the best of a difficult situation. True, Spoto concedes that Bergman had a number of affairs, but not nearly as many as have been rumored. In each case, there were good reasons for her to seek solace with other men because of difficulties in her marriage or in the circumstances of her life. Despite the difficulties created by her marriages and the demands of working in film and theater, Bergman was for the most part a loving mother. She did what she could for her four children, considering that she had to be away from them so much. Although they had periods of doubt and resentment, eventually the children came to understand and appreciate the nature of Bergman's life.

In all her personal relationships, Spoto's Bergman was gracious. He cites Bergman's third husband, Lars Schmidt, who told him that Bergman did not speak harshly, she did not bear grudges, she did not dwell on past unhappiness; rather, she always met the world with immense good will.[1] She was sensitive to the needs of others: she sent flowers, she wrote effusive letters of thank-you and apology.

To Spoto, Bergman was the consummate professional. She was an intuitive actress with great talent who played a wide range of roles. In fact, she went out of her way to seek demanding roles that played against her type as a wholesome beauty, the girl-next-door: the prostitute Ivy in *Dr. Jekyll and Mr. Hyde*, the Romanian-Italian singer Joan Madou in *Arch of Triumph*, and the dowdy missionary Greta Ohlsson in *Murder on the Orient Express*. Although Bergman may have gotten emotionally involved with co-stars such as Gary Cooper and Anthony Quinn, she did not indulge in affairs while working. She took acting seriously and always knew her lines and was cooperative on the set. She may have questioned directors occasionally in order to improve her performances and the play or film as a whole. And in her later stage career she did make mistakes: missing entrances, fluffing lines, ignoring blocking. She occasionally covered for these errors by addressing the audience directly. The audience loved it, and despite some mild tisk-tisking and eye-rolling from her fellow actors, Spoto believes she covered for herself the best way she could.

Moreover, Spoto's Bergman was apolitical, but not any more so than most people, and when she was made aware of social issues, she made the appropriate statements of support for liberal causes to the press. She may have made films in Nazi Germany and crossed picket lines, but she also contributed a great deal in support of America's involvement in World War II: she toured extensively for the USO, entertaining the troups, and she made films, most notably *Swedes in America*, and did radio broadcasts in support of the war effort for the Office of War Information.

The reviews of *Notorious* turned Spoto's aria of admiration for Bergman into a chorus of praise. David Denby's review in *The New Yorker* is in one sense typical and yet goes beyond other reviews in recognizing qualities in Bergman that make her life exemplary. From reading Spoto's book and seeing Bergman in films, Denby finds her the least egocentric star in Hollywood's middle period. As an actress, she was dedicated to her craft and took her work seriously. As a person, she was not "actressy, remote or queenly," but the kind of woman people thought they could converse with like a neighbor. Denby's final judgment of Bergman's life is that it was always "honorable": she was "a woman of generous beauty and talent who did what she wanted to do, was waylaid by public sanctimoniousness, and never complained." Bergman "made out of the common fate of women an art that remains a singular triumph of will."[2]

In their general acclaim for Spoto's biography in 1997, reviewers did not realize or willfully ignored the fact that it is haunted by a predecessor. In fact, Spoto very deliberately does not mention the earlier book, even though his book can be read as a refutation of it. In 1986, Laurence Leamer published the first major biography of Bergman, *As Time Goes By*, and the Bergman in that book is not the same person at all. To Leamer, there was always a split in Bergman's personality between the shy "child woman" and the cunning creator of a public persona at odds with much of her personality. The public image of a wholesome, honest woman allowed her to have a secret second life filled with flings and affairs and to cover up aspects of her personality that were considerably less than wholesome.

Leamer's Bergman is cold, calculating, and manipulative, a person who hid behind her public persona in order to accomplish her own selfish ends. She claimed that the men early in her life trained her to be dependent on them — for example, in her mind, first husband Petter Lindstrom was so "helpful" during their marriage that she felt "tied down." For the rest of her life, she was helpless without men to give her advice and instruction. Still, Bergman always managed to get what she wanted from men.[3] Leamer's Bergman is also superficial. Other than acting, she loved to shop, attend plays and movies, go out for coffee and drinks, live the life of a grand dame; she considered her one major stint as a housewife in Rochester, New York, a prison. She was not terribly perceptive or insightful, even of her own behavior. She did not understand how good the films she made with Roberto Rossellini were. She did not see the connections between her life and the lead role in Ingmar Bergman's *Autumn Sonata*.

According to Leamer, Bergman always put her own career before her husband and children or other relationships; she left her first daughter Pia behind to run off with Rossellini and did not meet with her in person for six years; she was a distant mother, leaving the children with nannies or relatives; true, she fought for custody of the Rossellini children but then conceded custody to Rossellini in the end. During her marriage to third husband Lars Schmidt, to make her own life easier, she suggested that first daughter Pia help take care of the Rossellini children.[4]

After her marriage to Schmidt and well into middle age, Bergman continued to have affairs but maintained the illusion of a happy marriage, as she had with her two previous marriages. When the marriage to Schmidt faltered, she found herself increasingly alone — at times content, at times regretful of the choices she had made — but always alone. To compensate for the lack of an immediate family, near the end of her life Bergman gathered around her a loving group of substitute caretakers who became in effect her surrogate family, a family who could support her in the life she had to live. These included Griffith James, a stage manager, and Margaret Johnstone, a masseuse and cook. Free of any obligation to family now, Leamer's Bergman indulged her tendency to act like a prima donna, grandly bestowing her gifts upon an overly respectful base of fans, a tendency reigned in only by the strenuous direction of Ingmar Bergman in *Autumn Sonata* and the humbling face of mortality in *A Woman Called Golda*.

In Leamer's eyes Bergman was a professional all right, but she used affairs with co-stars to improve her performances in love scenes: the affairs with Spencer Tracy in *Dr. Jekyll and Mr. Hyde*, Gary Cooper in *For Whom the Bell Tolls* and *Saratoga Trunk*, Gregory Peck in *Spellbound*, and Anthony Quinn in *A Walk in the Spring Rain* were for her own benefit, and when the filming was over, she walked away from these men and never looked back.[5] Late in her career she reveled in being a grand dame of the theater and acted more like a star than an actress on stage. With her missed entrances and flubbed lines, which she excused by making light of them directly to the audience, she made herself the focus of the performance rather than the play.

Leamer's Bergman was apolitical to the point of ignoring the larger world around her. She deliberately made films in Nazi Germany after she had been warned that to do so would make her seem sympathetic to the Nazi cause. She had to be persuaded to make a statement against acting in a segregated theater in Washington, D.C.[6]

The reviewers of *As Time Goes By* did not use the occasion of the book's publication to sing Bergman's praises as the reviewers of *Notorious* had. They clearly admired Bergman as an actor, but they were disappointed in Leamer's revelations about the discrepancy between her image and her life, especially her sexual history, and felt let down somehow. Some of the reviewers thought that the sexual revelations were irrelevant to Bergman's significance. Some of them thought this information was necessary for a biography, although they did not like learning about it. None of them questioned the accuracy of Leamers's account. Mary Gordon in *Ms.* magazine expressed dismay that Leamer did not seem to like Bergman and confessed that she wished she had not read the book. After calling Leamer "an earnest well-meaning writer and a fine researcher," Patricia Bosworth in *Working Woman* concluded that Bergman's life suggests "richness and mystery" and took Leamer to task for not adequately capturing her "infinite perverseness." Anne Edwards in the *Washington Post Book World* may have raised the great question: "If Bergman was the shallow, passionless, self-absorbed woman of Leamer's book, perhaps she was not a worthy subject for reexamination or an 'in-depth' biography (as his publishers claim this to be), for we are not told whether her performances or her life had any real value (I think both did)."[7]

In other words, if biographies cannot account for their subject's significance—as Edwards claims that Leamer's does not—then why read them? This may be a valid question for biographies of writers, painters, royalty, politicians, statesmen, major figures in history and minor figures who participated in important events. As biographer Robert Skidelsky puts it, "We are curious to know about such people because they have done extraordinary things; we expect their biographies will help explain how they came to do these things, and illuminate the achievements for which they are remembered." But Skidelsky concedes that the trend in modern biography, since the glory days of Victorian hagiography and the mythmaking of important figures, is toward the tell-all biography of people who have not done great things but simply led "interesting or unusual lives": "But now the example is the life itself, not what the life enabled the person to achieve. Or, more precisely, the life is the achievement; what used to be called the achievement is only one accompaniment, possibly a minor one, of a style of living."[8]

Spoto's book on Bergman participates in the Victorian tradition of biography as the discreet treatment of a significant figure as moral exemplar. To Spoto, Bergman's artistry is the result of a keen and developed sense of observation, intuition, and hard work. Leamer's book is more contemporary: it treats Bergman's life as gossip, interesting in and of itself. Leamer's only attempt to illuminate Bergman's art is reductionist. To Leamer, Bergman's portrayals of love and devotion are not acting but her true feelings captured on the screen. Leamer turns Bergman's performances in *Dr. Jekyll and Mr. Hyde, For Whom the Bell Tolls, Saratoga Trunk, Spellbound,* and *A Walk in the Spring Rain* into documentaries.

Edwards' demand that biographies of Bergman illuminate her artistry may apply particularly to biographies of film stars. Stardom confuses the actor's life, the actor's image promoted by the studio and the gossip industry, and the actor's image on the screen. Whether Leamer or Spoto intended it or not, we read their books to help sort out Bergman's life, to help us distinguish who she was from the image in the TV spots, in the magazine interviews, and on the screen. We want to know if the Ilse we adore in *Casablanca* bears any relationship to Bergman the actress and if her personality in real life accounts for her power over us on the screen.

We read biographies of Bergman first and foremost to learn who she really was. We want an idea about her life.

And we are most impressed by biographies that are thick and heavy, definitive and comprehensive. Leamer's *As Time Goes By* runs to 423 pages, counting a list of Bergman's performances, notes, a selected bibliography, and the index; Spoto's *Notorious* reaches 474 pages, counting the notes, a bibliography and an index (but it has bigger type). These are standard lengths for biographies of celebrities. Literary biographies by the acknowledged masters of the genre, works that set the standard for all biographers and can be considered works of art in and of themselves, can be much longer. Richard Ellman's *James Joyce* is 842 pages long, including all of the back matter. Leon Edel's magisterial biography of Henry James is five volumes long.

Leamer's and Spoto's biographies of Bergman may be a conventional length for biographies of popular figures, but they each implicitly claim to be definitive and comprehensive. They each offer a coherent picture of who Bergman was. Leamer and Spoto and their research assistants have consulted letters and diaries, newspapers and magazines, memoirs and biographies of Bergman's family and the people she worked with; histories of America, Europe, Sweden, Italy, and Hollywood. They have interviewed scores of people. *As Time Goes By* takes 26 pages to cite all of its sources; *Notorious* takes 22. Leamer and Spoto have seemingly viewed all of Bergman's films, and Spoto has consulted books that Bergman read and valued for clues to her character. Both biographies can be frustratingly vague about certain aspects of Bergman's life. Neither provides a convincing chronology of the late 1940s, when Bergman was undergoing a crisis in her marriage and professional life, and neither provides a great deal of detail about Bergman's relationships with her three lovers during this period. Nevertheless, barring new evidence that may eventually be released by the Ingrid Bergman Archive at Wesleyan University in Middletown, Connecticut, it is difficult to imagine what more the biographers could have done to provide a more thorough picture of Bergman as a person and as a professional.

And yet Leamer and Spoto disagree on the most fundamental issue to which we entrust biographers. They disagree on the very idea of Bergman's life: who she was as a person, the nature of her relationship to those closest to her, the fundamental motives that guided her behavior, and the basis of her art.

All biographies are necessarily subjective and personal. They involve the selection and arrangement of evidence, the ability to evaluate the credibility of sources, and the construction of a coherent narrative that seems to sum up a pattern that was inevitably there in the subject's life waiting to be found. But evidence, even the testimony of diaries and letters, is biased. Diarists always present themselves in a certain light, if only to themselves, and often diarists write as if they were already shaping their own thoughts for posterity—writing, as it were, as if their future biographers were reading over their shoulders. This is certainly true of Bergman. Near the end of Bergman's life, daughter Isabella asked her why she saved so many letters, photos, and diaries. Replied Bergman, "I always knew I was going to be famous."[9] Bergman's diary, at least the entries that have been published, is often eloquent, even literary, but it is also very controlled and often not terribly revealing. Often Bergman sounds as if she were addressing posterity, not herself.

Letters may tell us no more than diaries. As biographer Victoria Glendinning points out, letters "are written in different moods and for different purposes. A letter shot off in a foul temper to someone who has irritated you may not reflect your more permanent feelings about that person. All it proves is that the writer of the letter is capable of expressing foul temper."[10] Still, a series of letters to the same person may reveal a pattern that provides a clue about the relationship between the letter-writer and the recipient. But even that pattern may be called into question by the letter writer's behavior. Bergman's letters to daughter Pia, while the two of them were an ocean apart during the long custody battle with Lindstrom, are anguished and full of love and grief, but they are contradicted by Bergman's curious unwillingness or inability to see her daughter for six long years, even when she first returned to America and Pia was available for a meeting.

And of course, the testimony of family and friends, lovers, acquaintances, co-workers, secretaries, housekeepers, onlookers of every sort, is necessarily limited, biased, a view from a very narrow window overlooking a broad panorama. For his assessment of Bergman's character, Leamer relies a great deal on the memory and opinion of Lindstrom, who was by many accounts a very bitter man after his divorce from Bergman. In addition, Leamer relishes the gossipy tidbits he picks up from a wide range of acquaintances and spectators to the drama of Bergman's marriages and her behavior during play rehearsals or on the film set. Spoto, enthralled by his personal meetings with Bergman, uses his sense of her as a person to interpret her contribution to her many films. He conducts considerably fewer interviews than Leamer and relies on the mature outlook of Bergman's children, who seem to have forgiven their mother for their itinerant childhood, watched over by a series of relatives, nannies, and makeshift governesses. Interviewed by Leamer ten years earlier, Pia and Isabella were much more frank about how they felt about their mother's absences. Spoto enjoys rebutting the rumors of affairs that Bergman had with certain co-stars by boldly asserting that no single source has ever come forward to substantiate certain claims, but he carefully avoids the suggestions from a wide variety of sources that, if nothing else, Bergman did not disguise her passion for certain of her leading men.

Perhaps most significantly, life is messy and chaotic and has no pattern, but we expect biographers to impose patterns on source material that is, in Richard Holmes's words, "inherently unreliable." Holmes continues: "Memory itself is fallible; memoirs are inevitably biased; letters are always slanted towards their recipients; even private diaries and intimate journals have to be recognized as literary forms of self-invention rather than an 'ultimate truth of private fact or feeling. The biographer has always had to construct or orchestrate a factual pattern out of materials that already have a fictional or reinvented element."[11] There is a real sense in which all biographies are fiction, transparent attempts to impose an order and a meaning on material that is inherently unreliable to begin with.

And yet biographers persist in writing biographies as if they had indeed seen into their subjects' souls, had captured who their subjects really were, their essential selves. This is a convention, a kind of institutional white lie. Get a group of biographers together to talk about their craft, and they will freely admit that their creation of unified coherent personalities who seem fully known is at best an interpretation of unreliable data.[12]

Neither Leamer nor Spoto constructs or orchestrates Bergman's life into a pattern as coherent as a novel, but each has an implied thesis. Leamer's Bergman, greatly influenced by the loss of her doting and permissive father as a child, comes to resent male authority and gradually discovers how to get what she wants from the men in her life who are not as permissive as Daddy. Promoted as a wholesome spiritual beauty by her first producer David O. Selznick, Leamer's Bergman learns to use her public image to hide her true nature, to carry on a life of wanton self-indulgence, personally and professionally. Spoto's Bergman is modeled after a book Bergman recommended to lover Larry Adler as capturing who she was: Marcia Davenport's *Of Lena Geyer*, a popular novel in 1936. Just as Lena Geyer rises from a childhood of poverty to become a world renowned soprano through the thoughtful support of a number of mentors, so Spoto's Bergman rises from humble beginnings through the help of a succession of male directors and co-stars to become a famous film star. Just as Geyer sacrifices the one great passion of her life to the ascetic demands of the world of opera, so Spoto's Bergman sacrifices her husbands and children to the demands of her art.

Who Ingrid Bergman was depends on the diary entries we find authentic, the letters we find revealing, the testimony we find reliable. Who Bergman was depends on the images we want to hold on to, the stories we want to believe in, the narrative coherence we want to impose.

We may read a chronology of Bergman's life as if it should inherently reveal something about her as a person, give us a clue about who she was. But the mere facts of a life reveal very little. From a chronology of Bergman's life, we could construct any number of personalities for Bergman. We may expect biographies to deliver what Ida Nadel calls "the essential person ... a core personality, the 'real Me,'" but that does not mean that biographical subjects necessarily *have* an essence, a core personality, a real self.[13]

All human beings are a mix of complex biological and psychological systems. Our minds, our personalities, no less than our bodies, are complex structures that have adapted and developed over time to particular circumstances, but again there is no necessary connection between our circumstances and how we develop. The child is not necessarily the mother to the woman: the child did not have to become a particular sort of woman.

We may want to believe in the notion of a real self, a unified and coherent self that is easily inferred from our words and actions, but we are constantly reminded of the tenuousness of this belief. Every time we learn about the identity of a serial killer or read about a student who took a gun to school and shot his classmates and teachers before he turned the gun on himself, we are shocked, *shocked*. The serial killer who lived next door seemed so normal, he was so polite; he voluntarily shoveled the snow off widow Johnson's sidewalks. The raging suicidal student was so quiet, so reserved; yes, he often seemed angry but not *aggressively* so.

And even if people did have a real self, a true self, a unified and coherent self, we would not have direct access to it. We would have to infer that self from the subject's words and actions. Family and friends, acquaintances and bystanders, memoirists and biographers would each have access to different information, different anecdotes and incidents, and each would interpret his information differently. We are back to the fundamental ambiguity of what we can know with any certainty about our fellow human beings. Believing in a person's real self, her true self, is just that, an act of faith, much like believing in the inerrancy of a sacred text. Even if the sacred text were the unmediated word of God, believers would still have to determine how to take those words and what they mean: are the anecdotes history, legend, or myth? Are they to be taken literally or figuratively, or even allegorically? Are the moral precepts applicable only for that cultural moment or binding for all time?

In her essay "The Art of Biography," Virginia Woolf suggests that it is the job of biographers to work through the historical record in order to develop a sense of who their subjects are, and in sifting through the enormous amount of information generated by a life, the biographer must learn to separate the gravel from the gold, the ordinary fact from "the creative fact, the fertile fact; the fact that suggests and engenders," the fact that resonates with larger implication and meaning.[14] Of course, this is a very subjective undertaking, and the only proof that the biographer has accumulated the appropriately fertile facts is the persuasiveness of the biography itself, whether the facts do indeed seem to suggest and engender a convincing interpretation, whether the facts do resonate with a sense of authenticity and truth.

To know who Ingrid Bergman was, Woolf suggests, biographers must distill the evidence of her life into some sense of the essentials: biographers must ascertain the fertile facts — notes in her diary, key passages in her letters, images captured by friends and colleagues, and stories that can function as representative anecdotes. Biographers must assemble these fertile facts, these clues to her character, and impose a narrative order that does justice to the facts of her life, as the biographers know them. And yet Bergman may still elude her biographers.

Bergman's two major biographers have relied on different sets of fertile facts. They have given priority to different evidence, different testimony.

Consider: Bergman never disguised her naked ambition to be a famous actress and do "great" films. In *My Story*, Bergman admitted that becoming pregnant with Pia would not stop her from making films. She was adamant that being in Swedish films was not the height of stardom and that the only place where she could work with talented directors on big budget movies was Hollywood.[15]

"Success," Bergman wrote in her diary after *Jekyll and Hyde*. She had been praised for the film by the New York critics. Yet she was disappointed that she wasn't even nominated for an Academy Award. Now she did not want to even hear the words "Academy Award" mentioned until she could hold the statuette in her hand.[16]

None of her marriages was truly happy after the first few years, and one major reason seems to be Bergman's ambition. Bergman's primary interests were not in family life or traditional wifely activities. After moving to Rochester, New York, to be with Lindstrom while he went to medical school, their first home together in America, Bergman quickly became restless and bored, and no amount of mothering Pia could compensate for her being away from the film set.

In a letter to Ruth Roberts, she complained of feeling trapped and stifled. She was torn because she had everything a woman was supposed to want: an active life, a home with a loving husband and daughter. Still, she wondered if a home and family were all that life was about. She thought of life in Rochester as an unending series of lost days, as if only part of her was alive. She felt as if she had been stuffed into a bag and was slowly suffocating. In her autobiography, her co-author uses an even more drastic metaphor: he calls Bergman's life in Rochester "a living death."[17]

Bergman was frank with her children about her love of acting, and all of the children in their own way seem to have come to terms with the fact that their mother longed for a life away from them. In her memoir, daughter Isabella concedes Bergman's preoccupation with her career and admits that it took her some time to get over feeling hurt that she was not the first thing in her mother's life. She recalls that if her mother were asked to name the most important thing in her life, Bergman would get red and act nervously, but she would not lie. She would always answer, "Acting." Isabella liked to think that Bergman wished she could have said "Family" to spare their feelings.[18]

Pia took it the hardest, of course, when Bergman left her and her father for Rossellini. The divorce and custody battle for Pia was extended and bitter. Lindstrom was convinced that if Pia went to Italy, Bergman would find a way to keep her there, perhaps even kidnap her. Rossellini would not allow Bergman to go to America. He was a jealous man and afraid that Bergman would be seduced by her daughter and not return to Italy. It took extraordinary negotiations for Bergman and Pia to meet in neutral London for a three-day visit, closely monitored by Lindstrom, who had to be persuaded to let Pia go to the movies alone with Bergman. Bergman recalls that during their meetings Pia was calm, even serene. During these meetings, Bergman told Pia that she loved her but that Pia might love her father more because she had to care for him. Still, Bergman got no sense that Pia would object to visiting her in Italy.[19]

Bergman says that she wrote Pia regularly during the early period of their separation but that the letters were rarely answered. She did not know if Lindstrom was allowing his daughter to read them. Still the wrangling over visits with Pia continued, and in 1952, Bergman filed a suit in Los Angeles requesting that Pia be allowed to visit her in Italy accompanied by an escort other than her father.

Required to testify in court in June of 1952 as part of that suit, Pia admitted in response to questions from attorney Gregory Bautzer that she did not love her mother — she only liked her — and she did not miss her, that she did not have any desire to see her and preferred to live with her father. Perhaps the most damning assertion in Pia's testimony was that Bergman had not seemed very interested in her before she left for Italy. It was, she said, only after Bergman had gotten remarried and had other children that she wanted Pia back.[20]

The judge denied Bergman's request that Pia visit her, blaming both Lindstrom and Bergman for treating Pia as their personal property, passed back and forth between them "to satisfy their pride, convenience and desires." Still the judge went out of her way to say that whether Bergman wanted to admit it or not, Bergman herself was responsible for her alienation from Pia.[21]

After their meeting in London Bergman may not have seen Pia again until 1957, six long years later. In her autobiography Bergman blames Rossellini for not allowing her to visit Pia in America, and the letters she wrote are full of love and devotion. But Pia responded at least to one letter in a way that set Bergman back. The letter is only summarized in the autobiography: the gist is that Pia resented Bergman's promoting the scandal to make her father look bad. She wanted to know why if he was so bad, Bergman had married him in the first place. Pia ended the letter by telling her mother in no uncertain terms that Bergman had three other children to worry about, that she should devote herself to them, and that she should leave Pia and her father alone.[22]

Bergman was deeply hurt by this letter, but she could see no way to win back Pia's affections. And so she responded, pouring out her heart. She wrote that she certainly loved Pia as much as she loved her other children, that she would always be near Pia even if Pia did not see her there in person. She denied that she was promoting the scandal and told Pia not to believe everything she read in the papers. No matter what the papers said, she loved Pia with all her heart.[23]

When Bergman returned to America in 1957 for two days to accept the New York Film Critics' Circle Award as best actress for *Anastasia*, she telephoned Pia, then a student at the University of Colorado, late on the second day, the night before she left. Her excuse for not arranging to see Pia was that she was caught up in a tight schedule of events and that she was being shadowed so thoroughly by the press, any meeting would simply reopen old wounds and give rise to renewed public speculation about their relationship. Moreover, she simply could not handle the meeting emotionally. Nevertheless, the two did meet six months later in Paris. Pia was in Europe, accompanying her father, his new wife, Agnes, and her step-brother Peter on a trip to Sweden.[24]

Bergman could never understand why Pia felt so abandoned. Rossellini's niece, Fiorella Mariani, the daughter of Rossellini's sister Marcella, was good friends with Bergman during her marriage to Rossellini, even though she was twenty years younger. Fiorella told Leamer that she and Bergman were like sisters, despite the fact that she was much younger. Fiorella thought of herself as more mature than Bergman because she has suffered from the divorce of her parents and she found Bergman's inability to understand Pia's feelings childish. She had to remind Bergman again and again that it was Bergman herself who had left Pia, that for a child there is no excuse for being abandoned. Bergman became very upset when Fiorella told her these things.[25]

Spoto cites Bergman's care of Isabella during her bout with scoliosis as evidence for her devotion as a mother. In caring for Isabella for about a year and a half—from the spring of 1966 to the summer of 1967—Bergman left for only one major professional assignment: to do a television version of Jean Cocteau's *The Human Voice* in London. She was only gone a few weeks.

Isabella's treatment was painful. To prepare for surgery her entire torso from the neck down was placed in a plaster cast, and she was stretched with her head pulled back, all this without anesthetic so that the doctors could monitor how well her spine was responding.

However, it is not clear just how much nursing Bergman actually did. In *My Story*, she tells a moving story about sitting at Isabella's bedside while the girl is still in the hospital waiting for the plaster of the body cast to dry. A nurse informs Bergman that she can help provide a small measure of relief after the plaster has dried by gently pulling on Isabella's head. And so Bergman sat there for hours, holding her daughter's hand, waiting for the plaster to dry. And when the plaster was finally dried, she began to pull Isabella's head to stretch the spine. Bergman did not find the process easy, and even though she tried to be brave, she found herself in tears. She simply couldn't help crying because both she and her daughter were in such pain.[26]

But Bergman quickly goes on to say that Isabella seemed to recover and learned to live with the limits of her cast. Bergman does not mention any other direct care of Isabella, but she does give an account of moving Isabella to a clinic in Florence and then, more dramatically, of the operation, during which, in order to relieve the stress Isabella is under, Bergman washes her hair. Clearly in these circumstances Bergman is moved and concerned, and she recognizes that being away from him for that long is a terrible strain on Schmidt.

Isabella told Leamer that Bergman's care for her during this period changed her perception of her mother. Until then Isabella thought of herself as her father's daughter. But the bonds the two established during Isabella's illness became the norm for their later relationship. Still, Isabella admits that she doesn't know whether Bergman regretted that she hadn't spent more time with her children.[27]

Of these anecdotes, which contains the fertile fact, the clue to Bergman's personality, torn between being an actor and a mother?

Consider: Because Bergman was so discreet about her private life and because she may have inspired a comparable discretion from her possible lovers, we know little about her love affairs. Leamer's assertion that Bergman was sexually promiscuous and used affairs with her co-stars to improve her performances relies on two key pieces of evidence: Lindstrom's bald assertion of the fact — "Ingrid told me often that she couldn't work well unless she was in love with either the leading man or the director" — and the gossip and innuendo of stage hands and observers on the sets of a number of Bergman's films.[28]

Spoto grants that Bergman had any number of affairs. In fact, he says that Bergman told both Lindstrom and Schmidt about a lover that Leamer missed: Edvin Adolphson, a handsome, married middle-aged actor, who was popular in both plays and film. Bergman met Adolphson before Lindstrom on the set of *A Crime* (*Ett Brott*) while she was still in the Royal Dramatic Theater School in Stockholm and he apparently swept her off her feet. But Spoto denies that Bergman had affairs with co-stars and argues that Robert Capa was most likely her first lover since her marriage and that the affairs with Capa, Adler, and Fleming were the result of her failing marriage with Lindstrom and a new confidence in dealing with men. Moreover, Spoto argues that Capa, Adler, and Fleming were in effect mentors for Bergman, "men of ideas" who helped Bergman refresh her creative instincts, something that from then on she valued not only in husbands and lovers but in companions and friends.[29]

In the broad sweep of Bergman's career, there is little evidence that Bergman was promiscuous. There are no rumors that she even flirted with co-stars Leslie Howard, Robert Montgomery, Humphrey Bogart, Bing Crosby, Charles Boyer, or Cary Grant, to name just the major figures she worked with during her early years in Hollywood. The evidence that Bergman slept with Spencer Tracy, Cary Cooper, Gregory Peck, and Quinn is based on the reports of bystanders, what the men themselves don't say, or in the case of Anthony Quinn, what he leeringly implies.

John Houseman, the director and actor, spent some time on the set for *Dr. Jekyll and Mr. Hyde*, and he told Leamer that he had "watched" Bergman's relationship with Tracy, but it was "not uncommon" in show business. On the other hand, Billy Grady, an MGM executive supervising *Jekyll and Hyde* told Tracy's biographer Larry Swindell that Tracy was too discreet to be involved with Bergman, and, besides, he knew that Bergman was simply unavailable, so he settled for a professional relationship. Much later, Tracy himself told another biographer, Bill Davidson, that the only thing he and Bergman ever did was "to have hamburgers at a drive-in in Beverly Hills."[30]

Much of the assumed affair between Bergman and Cooper is based on Cooper's reputation as a womanizer. If he slept with Clara Bow, Marlene Dietrich, and Patricia Neal, he must have slept with Bergman.

On the set of *For Whom the Bell Tolls*, Bergman and Cooper spent a great deal of time together, rehearsing, eating, going on long drives. Bergman was starstruck with Cooper, and Leamer makes much of the way Bergman describes Cooper's physical characteristics and personality in her autobiography. Bergman called Cooper's personality "enormous" and "overpowering," and found his eyes and face more expressive than he was given credit for: his features were "delicate and underplayed." But Leamer deliberately ignores the fact that in using these words, Bergman is describing Cooper's image on screen, not in real life. These sentences occur after a description of how Cooper seemed to be so expressionless in person. Bergman follows up her paean to Cooper's overpowering personality by saying that it wasn't noticeable until you saw Cooper on the screen. In film, Cooper's power came from being so very understated and natural.[31]

Bergman was so happy working on the film that she wrote Dan O'Shea to give Selznick the news: she was so happy she could not keep her eyes from dancing even in the saddest scenes. Ruth Roberts was bothered enough by Bergman's behavior to warn her that she really had to stop looking at Cooper as if she were in love with him.[32]

Leamer also assumes that Cooper took the lesser part of Clint Maroon in *Saratoga Trunk* so that he could renew his affair with Bergman. Producer Hal Wallis told Leamer that Cooper wanted to do the film because the romance that had started on *For Whom the Bell Tolls* had carried over to *Saratoga Trunk*. Wallis didn't mind because he thought the chemistry between the two would help the film. And Bergman and Cooper were seen about town together, cruising down Sunset Boulevard. They called each other pet names from the film: Cooper's name for Bergman was "Frenchie." Bergman called Cooper "Texas." All of this fostered a great deal of gossip.

Leamer's clinching piece of evidence is that Cooper later told an interviewer that he had never seen a woman so much in love with him as Ingrid had been, but the day after shooting *Saratoga Trunk* ended, she wouldn't answer his phone calls.[33] Cooper's biographer Jeffrey Meyers relies entirely on Bergman's comments in *My Story* and Leamer's account, but Spoto eloquently and without qualification denies the affair. To Spoto, gossips tend to see what they want to see, and people who wanted an affair between Bergman and Cooper convinced themselves that they were seeing one. Neither Bergman nor Cooper nor anyone else involved in the two films they made together, Spoto argues, ever provided any concrete evidence that there had been "a realized romance" between Bergman and Cooper.[34]

About the affair with Gregory Peck, Leamer was told by an unnamed cast member of *Spellbound* that one day Bergman and Peck arrived on the set "late, all disheveled, and there was a lot of speculation."[35]

Peck told interviewer Gregory Speck, "I think you fall in love a little bit with a woman like Ingrid Bergman, and I don't think there's any way to avoid it, for she was incredibly beautiful, and a very sweet person.... Her lovely skin kind of took your breath away, and her whole radiance was something to behold." Comments biographer Gary Fishgall, "Peck didn't talk that way in public about many women."[36]

In 1987 Peck told interviewer Brad Darrach of *People* magazine, "All I can say is I had a real love for [Bergman], and I think that's where I ought to stop.... I was young. She was young. We were involved for weeks in close and intense work."[37] Here Peck is using his gentlemanly persona to basically imply that he in fact did have an affair with Bergman. A simple denial would have put all the rumors to rest.

Finally, there is the case of Anthony Quinn, who does not have Peck's image of decency and rectitude. In his memoir Quinn cannot help but leeringly imply all sorts of things about his relationship not only with Bergman but with her daughter Pia when she had come of age. Reflecting on his work with Bergman in *The Visit*, he says that he "fell momentarily in love with my sublime costar." The two had known each other for years, but it took "the cocoon of a motion picture set to bring us together." Then Quinn offers these two curious sentences: "It was Ingrid who taught me that you can tell an actress she is a lousy cook and she will forgive you; you can tell her that she is lousy in bed and she will explain it away; but God forgive you if you question her acting. I did not question the gift of her company, however, even as I questioned myself for returning her affection." Quinn's questioning his affection for Bergman is prompted by the fact that he was not yet separated from his wife, and his mistress was pregnant with their second child.

Tooling around in a new red Maserati, Quinn meets daughter Pia, who expresses intense admiration for the car and, giggling, accepts Quinn's offer of a drive in it after securing permission from her mother. Whereupon in his anecdote Quinn again becomes alternately coy and leering: "A few minutes later, we were speeding off, bound for adventure — and, inevitably, for each other, thus beginning a rather complicated relationship, laced with a strange mother-daughter competition. Pia was constantly asking about her mother — did she do this? Oh, and what about this? — but the bounds of propriety kept me from responding." In the next paragraph Quinn says that he "took up" with Bergman again on the set of *A Walk in the Spring Rain*, when Bergman "reheated the rivalry. I did not think much of it at the time, only that it was an unusual thing. And it was."[38]

However, from another point of view, whether Bergman actually went to bed with these men is beside the point. Yes, it is an empirical matter whether Bergman actually slept with them, and the facts of each case may concern some of us for whom sexual morality is severely constrained by religious convictions about purity and the sanctity of marriage. However, whether she slept with them or not, what she clearly *did* do was pay intense attention to them as co-stars. Says Joseph Steele, her long-time publicity agent, "She scouts her leading men the way a football coach scouts an opposing team, by seeing them in action. In the Selznick projection room she ran all of Charles Boyer's pictures before commencing *Gaslight*. Cary Cooper, Robert Montgomery, Humphrey Bogart, Spencer Tracy and others were subjected to the same microscopic examination."[39]

And Bergman did become emotionally involved with them. In the closed world of the film set, she freely demonstrated her affection and deliberately ran the risk of scandal. But when the films were over, she walked away from these emotional involvements perhaps too easily. She tended to walk away and not look back. This suggests that Bergman needed intimacy and romance, but that she also held something back. All the while as she was gazing longingly at Cooper and gushing over Tracy and Peck, she was also keeping some part of herself in reserve. She may have wanted romance; she may even have manufactured it. But she was also detached and distant; she felt no need for commitment.

Of these anecdotes, which contains the fertile fact, which implies the appropriate way to think about Bergman's romantic life with her co-stars?

Consider: Bergman disagreed with martinet W. S. Van Dyke, II, the third director brought in by MGM to save *Rage in Heaven*. She insisted on doing scenes over and over until she thought she had gotten it right. Van Dyke, a director famous for controlling temperamental actors and bringing his films in on time and under budget, wanted to live with the scene he had shot and move on. Bergman complained at least once in front of the crew that they were moving too fast. Bergman herself remembers that she confronted Van Dyke in her dressing room, telling him to his face that he should have stayed in the army because of the way he enjoyed marching up and down on the set and yelling at people. Perhaps, she suggested, he should wear roller skates, since he seemed more interested in getting from one place to another than helping the actors with their roles. She went so far as to accuse Van Dyke of not caring about people's feelings, especially women's feelings. According to Bergman, Van Dyke was so taken aback, he threatened to have her fired, but she shot back that being fired was all she really wanted and he should fire her as quickly as possible. Van Dyke stormed out of the dressing room, but came back later all meekness and supplication, wanting to know if he was as really as bad as Bergman had said he was. Bergman was firm and told him that he certainly was, she had never worked with anyone else who was so unpleasant. Whereupon Van Dyke promised to change, to do better.[40]

Like a great many of Bergman's stories, this one is suspect, but it probably does indicate that even early in her career she was entirely professional and generally accommodating, but there were limits to her tolerance and good will. Over time and with increasing fame, she became more temperamental and combative.

In 1967 Bergman appeared in a TV production of Jean Cocteau's *The Human Voice*, a one-person show, a fifty-minute monologue in which a woman reveals her existential grief and longing over the telephone. The character rages, she reflects, she flirts, she becomes lost and anguished, she is finally resigned. According to director Ted Kotcheff, Bergman seemed intimidated by the material. Working with a new translation by David Exton, during rehearsals she frequently stopped to complain about how the dialogue was inappropriate, difficult to understand, and too clumsy to say effectively. At first Kotcheff tried to be patient and understanding, promising that further work might resolve the problems with the text and, besides, he would not tape the show until Bergman was satisfied. She was not mollified and continued to complain about the script. Finally, Kotcheff had had enough and shouted out that Bergman should stop being so hysterical. He demanded that Bergman continue with the rehearsal, reading the lines as he had indicated; they could resolve their differences later. Certain that he had lost Bergman's trust, Kotcheff called the producer David Susskind to resign. But the next morning, Susskind contacted Kotcheff to tell him that he had talked with Bergman and she was not upset at all, that she admired him, and that she would forthwith be more cooperative.

Husband Lars Schmidt told Kotcheff that if he had allowed Bergman to continue with her temperamental outbursts, she would have lost all faith in him. Only when Kotchoff asserted himself forcefully did he win Bergman's respect. Spoto insists that Bergman's behavior was the result of her insecurities and that her occasionally badgering and disagreeing with directors was the only way she could be confident in their abilities. Generally she was not moody or even particularly demanding. She simply respected her own instincts and abilities and needed her directors to reassure her so that she could do her best.[41]

But Bergman herself confessed that she made life miserable for director José Quintero on the set of *More Stately Mansions* later in 1967. One key moment was when Quintero announced that for her first entrance Bergman should walk all the way down to the front lip of the stage at the Ahmanson Theater in Los Angeles, pause for a moment, and then sit on the steps going down to the auditorium. Quintero thought that Bergman's character should come flying in and establish her dominance by taking the stage down front. What Quintero did not admit publicly was that such an entrance would also be a tour de force and boldly announce Bergman-the-star's return to southern California. Bergman, however, was appalled by the idea and insisted that she should stay upstage until she could "get her breath" and allow her pounding heart to calm down. She proclaimed her anxiety about being that close to the audience, who would be able to see how nervous she was and how old.

Bergman confessed in a letter to Schmidt that this minor disagreement caused a major uproar. Quintero lost all control and dressed her down in front of the cast and crew. Bergman's disagreement had been so low-key that at first she did not realize that Quintero was yelling at her. She finally realized that she was the source of his tirade just before he said that he couldn't deal with her anymore. Quintero and Bergman quickly made up, and in *My Story* she details her realization on opening night how "absolutely right" Quintero's staging of her entrance was and how "absolutely wrong" she had been. It is curious, however, that in the autobiography Bergman justifies her behavior by confessing to her insecurities, but in the letter to Schmidt she notes that at first she did not even realize who Quintero was yelling at because she was so sure of herself.[42]

In 1971, Bergman performed in *Captain Brassbound's Conversion*, where she was late to the first day's rehearsal and once the play was in performance had trouble keeping to her blocking. Co-star Joss Ackland, who played Captain Brassbound, complained that Bergman could only portray characters in which she found something of herself. She was simply incapable of adequately portraying the nineteenth-century English woman in Shaw's play because that character was outside the range of Bergman's experience.[43]

In 1975, Bergman performed in a London production of *The Constant Wife*. Stage manager Griffith James, an intense admirer and later caregiver, noted that Bergman never seemed to get nervous before the show. Rather ironically, during the run of the play, Bergman discovered a lump in her breast and was pressed by her husband to see a doctor. Bergman, however, would have none of it. She did not want to disappoint her fellow actors or her audience, or perhaps, she wanted to avoid this threat to her mortality. In any case, either because of her raging ego or the nagging fear of cancer, she often wound up drawing attention more to herself as a star than to her character. She indulged in erratic line readings and did not stick to rehearsed patterns of blocking. One evening, talking to Griff offstage, she missed an entrance and did not even bother to cover the error: she swept on stage and announced to the audience, "I am sorry I'm late. I was talking to Griff." During another performance she was alone on stage when the curtain did not come down at the end of the act. Once again, instead of covering for the mistake, she simply announced to the audience, "The curtain should have come down." Breaking the illusion of a rigorously realistic play is one of the great sins of stage acting.

After *The Constant Wife* moved to New York, Bergman twisted her ankle and could not walk. Her foot was put in a cast, but she insisted on performing anyway. The play had a butler, so she arranged to act the part at first by having the butler push her around the set in an office chair on casters. For the last act, the stage manager found a wheelchair, so that Bergman could maneuver her way around the set on her own. But of course, because of these ad hoc arrangements, the actors could not follow the rehearsed blocking patterns. The blocking became chaos. Actors ran into each other. Bergman constantly bumped into things, and once on an exit, she missed the door so badly that books fell off shelves and the set tottered as if it might fall down. The audience found all this immensely amusing; they laughed and cheered. And so Bergman acted in the wheelchair for five weeks, and even when the cast was removed and her doctor gave her permission to walk, she was so enamored with using the wheelchair that she insisted on using it for several more weeks.[44]

During the run of *Waters of the Moon* in 1978 co-star Wendy Hiller had real concerns about Bergman's inability to keep to her blocking or follow the script exactly. It was really quite awkward, Hiller told Leamer, trying to tell "an international star for God's sake keep still." And after a performance in which Bergman blew her lines, Hiller called the director Patrick Garland. "You must come in," Hiller said. "She's speaking Chinese again."[45]

But we must remember that the stories critical of Bergman in rehearsal or on stage cover a forty-five year career in theater and film. Scores of co-workers, from Cary Grant to Goldie Hawn, praised Bergman's preparedness, her ability to learn her lines, her willingness to work with others to achieve the best possible performances for everyone involved in the production. Jimmy Lydon, who played Pierre d'Arc, Joan's brother in *Joan of Arc*, may be more representative of what people thought of Bergman's work. He exclaims, "The quality of this woman!" and tells the story of the day she came in late for suiting up in the fake armor used in the battle scenes. She was terribly apologetic. She apologized to Fleming and to the entire cast and crew. She gave no excuses: the alarm went off, and she just went back to sleep. She said that she was terribly sorry any number of times.[46] And we must also note that the most damning recollections of Bergman's behavior on stage are from her last two stage shows, when she learned about and then began battling her cancer.

Of these anecdotes, which contains the fertile fact, the clue to Bergman's professionalism as an actor?

Consider: Lindstrom says that he argued against Bergman's signing a three-picture contract with UFA, a major German film company, but she signed the agreement anyway. While she was in Germany making *The Four Companions*, Bergman accompanied her director Karl Frohlich to a Nazi rally where she did not participate in a Nazi salute. However, this was not a political statement: Bergman claimed she did not understand the political implications of what she had done. She also claimed that she did not understand why she should play up to Goebbels if his office invited her to tea. Lindstrom asserts that this is disingenuous. Bergman knew who Goebbels was and admired one of his speeches. Lindstrom says that he had to finagle to prevent her from going back to Germany to make another movie after the birth of Pia.[47]

Bergman herself admitted to John Kobal in an interview that she took the part in *The Four Companions* only because she knew German; she had no intention of staying in Germany at all; she had her eyes set on Hollywood and was waiting for the right opportunity. Still, upon reflection she realized that because of her lack of interest in politics, she didn't know what she was doing. If she had known anything about politics, she "would have had more sense than to go to Germany to make a picture in 1938." During the production of the film she sensed "there was something brewing" and "the fear was something unbelievable. But I wasn't interested and just went there to make a movie."[48] Even a sympathetic biographer like Spoto finds this a bit much to take. He documents how the Swedish government enforced its neutrality by banning the wearing of Nazi insignia, closing down a Nazi office in response to Germany's censorship of mail from Sweden to Germany, and jailing eleven Nazis for participating in banned military groups. The Swedish government conducted an active campaign to make Swedes aware of the brutalities of Nazism. Bergman would have had to be deaf and blind to not be aware of what was going on in Germany after Hitler's rise to power in 1933. In fact, late in her life, while she was playing the role of Golda Meir in *A Woman Called Golda*, Bergman told the *Los Angeles Times* that she was very "subborn" for going to Germany to make a movie in 1938, that looking back she had to say in all honesty that she "had no reason for objecting to Hitler then."[49]

Larry Adler told Spoto that Bergman crossed a picket line during a strike by a Hollywood union during the filming of *Notorious*, which seriously affected the morale of those on the line. When Adler confronted Bergman with this insensitivity, she replied that she was only an actress and actors had nothing to do with strikes. Her only duty was to make the movie.[50]

In 1946 *Joan of Lorraine* was scheduled for a tryout performance in Lisner Auditorium on the campus of George Washington University in Washington, D.C. As in many cities at the time, the theaters in Washington were segregated and there was a national campaign by the American Veterans Committee, a leftist alternative to the American Legion, and the NAACP to stop the practice. Before the cast even appeared at Lisner Auditorium, their performance of *Joan of Lorraine* was being picketed by the Southern Conference for Human Welfare and the American Veterans Committee. Bergman recalls that she was indignant when Maxwell Anderson informed her of these circumstances and vowed to say something in a press conference when she had the chance. But at the press reception the day before the play opened, no reporter asked "the right question," the question and answer session proceeded as scheduled, and the publicity people for the play began to breathe a sigh of relief. Then, Bergman says, she dropped her bombshell. Amidst a flurry of polite goodbyes and thank-yous from the reporters, Bergman announced that she would never perform in Washington, D.C., again. That put the reporters back in their chairs, giving Bergman the opportunity to make her statement. Why wouldn't she come back to Washington, the reporters clamored to know. Because, Bergman said, she never would have even entered Lisner Auditorium, much less performed there, if she had known that the theater was segregated. Because of her contract she was legally required to continue with this show, but she would not come back until everyone, white people and black people, could come to see her. Her shows were for everybody! Bergman claims that this statement made its way into the newspapers, causing Anderson a fit of hysteria and many people outside her stage door to spit at her and call her "nigger lover."[51]

In Bergman's memory, her declaration of principle was a spontaneous moment of moral witness, something Saint Joan might have done. Joe Steele, her publicist, recalls a different version that basically confirms the story without the spontaneous moral fervor. According to Steele, while the company of *Joan of Lorraine* was still rehearsing in New York, he received a letter from the NAACP informing him that Blacks would not be allowed to see the play in Lisner Auditorium. When he informed Anderson and business manager Victor Samrock, Anderson felt no obligation to be supportive. Segregation was traditional in Washington, D.C., he argued; it was to be deplored but there was nothing they could do about it. When Steele informed him that Bergman would hit the ceiling, Anderson suggested that they finesse the issue by offering a separate performance for Blacks on Sunday. Bergman was furious when she found out about the situation, and immediately agreed to do the extra performance. But the NAACP rejected the offer on the obvious grounds that the extra performance would obviously reinforce the segregation that existed. Anderson, Samrock, and publicist William Fields then agreed that if they or Bergman issued a statement unsolicited this early before the performance it would not only cause further difficulties with attendance but encourage the protesters. Instead, they planned to postpone any statement until the press conference Fields had set up for Bergman upon her arrival in the capital, hoping that Bergman would be asked about the issue.

Steele's version of the press conference contains the gist of Bergman's recollection without the dramatic refusal to return to Washington until the end of segregation. In Steele's memory, when the press conference was over and reporters were heading for the exits, Bergman said something to this effect: Please, one more thing before you go. I have been expecting you to ask me a particular question, but since you have not asked it, I am going give you the answer anyway. Never in my wildest imagination would I have thought that theaters in Washington were segregated. When I finally discovered that Negroes were barred from coming to my show, the contracts had already been signed. If I had known about the situation earlier, I would have not even considered performing in this city.[52]

However, according to Lindstrom, Bergman learned from Joe Steele about the segregated theaters in Washington and told Lindstrom, Steele, and Anderson that she was in the city to play Saint Joan and she was not concerned about theater rulings. She had to be talked into making a statement by Steele, and according to Lindstrom, it was a statement formulated under Steele's guidance that Bergman announced to the press and eventually appeared in the newspapers. The published version of Bergman's remarks is quite similar to both her and Steele's recollections.[53] The discrepancies among the stories about Bergman's anti-discrimination statement concern her motivation and the circumstances in which she did so. We may never know whether Bergman actually initiated her protest against segregation in Washington, D.C., or had to be talked into doing it.

In any case, Bergman's performing in Washington, D.C., did not detract from her national reputation. On April 5, 1948, President Truman awarded Bergman the Women's National Press Club Award for her outstanding achievement in the theater. After accepting the award and perhaps influenced by her viewing of Rossellini's films, Bergman proceeded to talk about how difficult it was to make honest pictures in America at the time, what with the film industry's self-censoring credo in the Motion Picture Production Code, government meddling, and the demand for what Spoto paraphrases as "shallow, escapist entertainments."[54]

At the National Press Association presentation in 1972, Bergman was asked if an actor could be interested in more than acting, politics for instance. She replied that she was an entertainer and tried to live in a way that would help other people. She was not interested in politics, only in humanitarian issues, such as orphans and prisoners of war.[55] But there is little evidence that she actively or extensively worked for charitable causes.

Of these anecdotes, which contains the fertile fact, the clue to Bergman's politics?

Other than acting, acclaim for her performances and a certain amount of romance, it is difficult to determine just what Bergman wanted out of life.

Isabella claims her mother was practical and down-to-earth, advising her as a child to learn both English and how to type, because with those skills she would always be able to find work.[56] But from her late teens, Bergman had a job, was well remunerated, and had to fill in the time between performances somehow. Her husbands and children were not enough.

In her early life in Hollywood, Bergman had simple tastes: she enjoyed throwing small dinner parties with lots of conversation. She was not overly concerned about fashion and preferred practical clothes she could buy off the rack at department stores. She was frugal. At home, she did not like to cook but she was a fanatic about cleanliness and despite the help of maids, she often did much of the cleaning herself. She enjoyed drinking more than her publicity let on, but there is no record that she was ever drunk in public. While she did not smoke when she arrived in America, she eventually became a smoker. However, it was not until she had long been established as a star that she was ever photographed in public with a cigarette.

During her life in Rochester, Bergman escaped to New York as much as she could, often accompanied by her press agent Joe Steele. The life she wanted in New York was unpretentious and fairly simple: she attended the latest plays, saw newly released movies, and went for long walks, especially along Fifth Avenue. She enjoyed modern art, chocolate ice cream, and hamburgers. Back in Hollywood, she sometimes saw a double-feature, had dinner, saw another double-feature, and took in a late show: five movies in a day. For dinner she preferred the Beachcomber for its South Seas décor, its rum drinks, and its rumaki, spiced chicken livers and water chestnuts wrapped in bacon. She did not pay much attention to clothes or jewelry or the latest fashions. She enjoyed going out and about in simple slacks and a peasant blouse, and being anonymous. She would take long walks, go window-shopping, or stand happily in lines for theater tickets without being recognized. Bergman's ideal life when she was not on stage or caught up in a passion seemed to involve an escape from family, indulging simple tastes — plays and films, museums, shopping, eating out — but they were simple tastes she often enjoyed alone.[57]

Escaping from Rossellini was more difficult because he was controlling and easily bored, so their life together, often a carnival swirl of parties and vacations, was closer to her ideal than it was with Lindstrom.

In the marriage to Schmidt, the two quickly reached an accommodation and often went their own ways, so Bergman was free to indulge herself in the kind of life Steele so eloquently describes.

After her divorce from Schmidt, Bergman's preferred way of life was a small two-bedroom apartment with lots of storage space. For transportation, she took buses and taxis. For silverware she had an elegant wooden rod with six screws circling it, each for a small set of utensils: forks, spoons, and knives.

Isabella thinks of the silverware rod as an example of her mother's "philosophy of life."[58] That philosophy included the maximum freedom to do as she wanted.

In an interview with critic Tom Shales during her book tour for *My Story*, suffering from her double mastectomies and still smoking Marlboros, Bergman was reflective. She said that she had gotten her strength from her parents, as well as good health and a sense of humor. The ability to laugh at herself, she said, helped to sustain her. And, she said, laughing, she had many friends, more than she could count on one hand — she could count her good friends with both hands — and thus she did not need to talk to psychiatrists.[59] Here Bergman acknowledges her limited circle of friends at the end of her life, not just fewer than five as some have implied but as many as ten. It is significant that she does not mention her children, her ex-husbands, or her lovers as the main source of her support. Leamer would call Bergman's final reliance on a very small circle of friends, a non-traditional family, most of whom were from the theater world and adored her, a sign of her loneliness and her selfishness. Once again, this judgment may have some truth to it, but it may be too severe.

We are tempted by the idea that if biographers simply knew more, if they knew enough — if they could discover one more letter or diary entry, if they could interview one more intimate acquaintance of the subject — then, *then*, we would know the subject definitively and comprehensively. If only biographers could apply the most appropriate psychological principles, if they could intuit the most apparent narrative devices, then the subject's sudden, instinctive, or inexplicable behavior would make coherent *sense*.

On the evidence of the two biographies of Bergman, clearly Leamer has interviewed many more people and accounted for more of Bergman's life, especially the controversial aspects of her life — the custody battle with Lindstrom, the gradual estrangement of the marriages, the affairs she never acknowledged even though she promoted the image of herself as honest and forthcoming. Although Leamer relies entirely too much on the random observations of stage hands and others on the fringes of Bergman's life, the sheer number of stories about her indiscretions and what we might generously call the prickly side of her nature are hard to ignore. As a result, Leamer's biography, despite its gaping holes in chronology, seems to be more data-based, more thorough, and more kaleidoscopic than Spoto's. Spoto's refusal to acknowledge few if any imperfections in his heroine calls his judgment into question, and he relies entirely too much on an analysis of Bergman's films as an indication of her appeal. Despite what Spoto implies, those films are not necessarily clues to Bergman's character.

And yet, Leamer seems to have missed something essential about

Bergman, a quality that Spoto has captured: despite what Leamer demonstrates as the unseemly side of her life, Bergman was also a woman who could brighten any room she entered, a woman who could command the complete allegiance of family, friends, and lovers, a woman to whom a host of people were intensely devoted. It is difficult to believe that a woman with such a devoted following could be as petty and devious as Leamer suggests. It is easier to believe in Spoto's Bergman: a woman who was larger than life out of sheer will and determination, the woman she wanted herself to be, the woman she wanted the world to see.

Even if Leamer and Spoto had given us all the information we could know about Ingrid Bergman, we would not have to choose between them. We could choose the Bergman we want to believe in.

But we don't have to believe in just one Ingrid Bergman. There are other Ingrids to consider. And we can believe in as many Ingrids as we can imagine.

PART II: OTHER INGRIDS

Three

The Studio Creation

"I could understand why everyone likes her in her pictures; she's a great actress. But I couldn't understand why they [soldiers] all thought of her as a sweet girl that they would all like to take home to their mothers when she had played somewhat of a bitch in all her pictures.... But there was the answer to why they all like her — Ingrid has had damn good *publicity.*"
— Letter from Lieutenant Cecil Barker to David O. Selznick.

When Bergman first arrived in Hollywood in 1939 to film the American version of *Intermezzo*, she impressed everyone with her apparent wholesomeness, honesty, and simple values. Says Irene Selznick about first meeting Bergman, "Her lack of affectation was monumental. Simple and direct, she had a totally refreshing quality. In fact, she didn't seem like any other actress I ever knew."[1] Ake Sandler, Swedish journalist and professor, who visited her on the set of *Intermezzo*, said that he had seldom seen someone with such an "innocent face." To Sandler, Bergman radiated a sense of purity and charm.[2] Film critic Bosley Crowther in the *New York Times* was equally impressed. During the publicity tour for *Intermezzo*, he asked his readers to imagine a Viking maiden, fresh from her bath, sitting on a cliff high above the surf below, eating peaches and cream on a warm spring day.[3]

In her autobiography, Bergman tells a vivid story about how she first met David O. Selznick, the producer who brought her to America in 1939. According to Bergman, when she first arrived at Selznick's house after her trip from Sweden and a two-week layover in New York, she was welcomed by Selznick's wife Irene, but Selznick himself was not at home. Irene offered his excuses: Selznick often worked late at the office. However, Irene had arranged to take Bergman to dinner at the Beachcomer with several friends, among them Marian Hopkins. So during her first night in Hollywood, Bergman had a pleasant dinner with several current Hollywood stars, but all through dinner, she worried about why Selznick had not met her himself.

41

After the dinner, the group retired to Hopkins' house to see a new film. Bergman was very impressed with the private screening room where the guests lounged on floor cushions, the screen came down from the ceiling automatically, and the projection room was hidden behind a painting. This kind of opulence she had not experienced in Sweden. But as the movie started, Bergman could not take her mind off Selznick. She continually asked Irene where Selznick was, and to which Irene would always reply, "Oh, don't worry. He'll be here shortly."

Just as Bergman became engrossed in the film, she felt a hand on her shoulder and a male voice whispering in her ear, telling her that Selznick had arrived and was in the kitchen, eating. He was waiting for her. Bergman politely made her way out of the screening room and down the hall to the kitchen. It was one o'clock in the morning.

Entering the kitchen, Bergman was shocked to discover a man, presumably Selznick, sprawled across the table, shoveling food into his mouth. Without any opening civilities, Selznick demanded that Bergman take her shoes off. Self-conscious about her height, Bergman replied that removing her shoes wouldn't help: the shoes had flat heels. Selznick groaned, and then mustering his manners, asked how her trip from Sweden had been. Before she could answer, he blurted out that her name was impossible. "Ingrid," he said, was too easy to mispronounce as "ein-grid" and "Bergman" was too Germanic. "Lindstrom" might be better. It sounded like "Lindbergh," the name of Charles Lindbergh, the famous aviator. Would she accept "Lindstrom" for a stage name?

Bergman bristled and gave Selznick a lecture on how proud she was of her name. He seemed mildly surprised as her resistance, but after another mouthful of food, he dismissed her objections: they would talk about it in the morning. He stared at her, as if she were a mere object, or perhaps a work of art. Then he announced that Bergman's face would need some work: her eyebrows were too thick and her teeth were bad, among many other things. He would personally take her to the make-up department in the morning to see what they could do for her.

To this, Bergman really dug in her heels. She told Selznick in no uncertain terms that she was who she was and she would not change anything. If he continued to badger her about changing her looks, she would go back to Sweden. Perhaps, she said hotly, he "shouldn't have bought the pig in the sack." Selznick stopped eating and continued to stare at her. Then, after a prolonged silence, he got a look in his eye and announced that he had gotten a great idea, an idea that was so simple and yet no one in Hollywood had ever done it before. Selznick would not try to alter anything at all about Bergman. She could remain herself. She was going to be the first "natural" actress.[4]

As a result of her protest, according to Bergman, Selznick put his plan into effect very forcefully with the makeup man and publicity people who attended her first screen test the next day. She repeated the story at length in a letter to Spoto in 1975.[5]

However, for the rest of his life, Selznick claimed that *he* originated "the revolutionary instructions" to minimize Bergman's makeup and leave her "alone in all [her] pristine beauty." Selznick has been described as "overbearing, egocentric, aggressive, exhausting, and impossible." Looking like a boxer from the Bronx with wire-rimmed glasses, Selznick was a pugnacious fighter of causes, both financial and artistic, as the head of the studio that bore his name. A demanding workaholic who took Benzedrine to help with an overactive thyroid, he worked long hours, involved himself in every phase of the films he produced, and as a result he was always late to meetings, dinner engagements, public ceremonies. If he was less than forty-five minutes late, he felt no need to apologize.[6]

It was not out of character, then, for Selznick to take all the credit for the success of Bergman's career. After Bergman had left Selznick Studios to make films with her own production companies, Selznick learned that her publicist Joseph Steele was writing a brief biography of Bergman for *Photoplay*, and Selznick was concerned that Steele give him and his studio proper credit. He wrote Paul MacNamara, his Director of Advertising and Publicity, asking that MacNamara check with *Photoplay* to be sure that Steele's story was accurate in conveying "the fact that never in the history of the business has there been so extraordinary a job of star discovery and star building as what we accomplished with Ingrid Bergman, which is conceded by everyone in Hollywood even though they are not familiar with all the facts...."[7]

After the difficult contract negotiations in which he lost Bergman, Selznick was so anguished that he composed a nine-page, twenty-eight-point memo pretending to be Bergman, a memo to himself from Bergman, in which she lists all the things that Selznick has done for her. Point fifteen is this: "For seven years, you worked personally on every phrase of my publicity, including the approval of my still photographs, and the designation of the dignity with which I was to be treated. You laid out an entirely different approach to the publicizing of a new-comer, and then to the publicizing of a star. This was followed scrupulously, under your direction, by the member of your publicity department, including Joseph Steele."[8] The memo was never sent.

Selznick did not treat Bergman any differently than he did his other female stars: he involved himself equally in the details of the publicity campaigns for Joan Fontaine and Vivian Leigh, among others. But Selznick's control of Bergman's image presents special difficulties in understanding who Bergman was. Selznick not only controlled how Bergman looked on the screen and in publicity stills; he also controlled the way she presented herself to the public in personal appearances and interviews. When Bergman first arrived in Hollywood, she may very well have been the person Selznick thought she was, the wholesome innocent Swedish beauty who projected a sense of naturalness, wholesomeness, and dignity. But the more Selznick controlled her image, the more opportunities Bergman had to go her own way and live her life any way she chose. By the time of the intense publicity campaign to promote *For Whom the Bell Tolls*, Bergman's image had taken on a life of its own, and what appeared in the press was increasingly at odds with the life that Bergman actually lived.

Whatever the truth of Bergman's anecdote about how she met Selznick, the news of how to market her apparently did not reach all parts of the studio, at least at first. Leslie Howard, Bergman's co-star in *Intermezzo*, wrote a memo to Selznick a week after Bergman discussed her image with Selznick, which suggests that Howard did not know the studio had decided to promote Bergman's naturalness. In the memo, Howard says that he had seen the tests of Miss Bergman for *Intermezzo* and he is "absolutely convinced that from every point of view, hair and appearance, the one marked 'no makeup' is the best." Howard goes on: "Without makeup she looks much more natural and much more attractive and much less Hollywood. Her skin has a natural sheen and apparently she has a perfect complexion. Also, the lips, instead of looking absolutely fakey [*sic*] and made up, seem to be very natural and attractive in the test without grease paint. The whole effect is really startling. Also, since I myself wear no grease paint in black and white photography we may much [*sic*: match?] better. Incidentally, this might be a good publicity point."[9] If Selznick started promoting Bergman's naturalness right away, no one told Leslie Howard.

Nevertheless, it is clear that a month after Howard's memo, Selznick had become preoccupied, even fanatical, about capturing the "natural" beauty of Bergman's face in the first rushes of *Intermezzo*. Ironically, he thought her naturalness needed to be made up and photographed a certain way in order for the camera to capture it adequately. This is, of course, a paradox, the packaging of naturalness to make it seem even more natural.

In June of 1939 Selznick expressed his dismay to Harry Stradling, the first director of photography on *Intermezzo*, that the studio had not yet found the best way to photograph Bergman, that the rushes for the picture were just as "frightening" as Bergman's original screen tests. He emphasized to Stradling that photographing Bergman correctly was extremely important because in her case the camera made all the "difference between great beauty and a complete lack of beauty." If they couldn't make Bergman look "divine," the entire film would fail to impress audiences. The studio simply hadn't yet learned the appropriate angles from which to shoot her or how to light her face, and Selznick urged Stradling to do another series of tests and solve the problem as quickly as possible. Solving the problem of how to photograph Bergman would make the difference between a successful picture and an unsuccessful one.

Selznick took credit for making Hedy Lamarr a star "purely by photography." He recognized that Lamarr, unlike Bergman, was comparatively easy to photograph — her beauty was much more obvious — but Bergman's stardom was "equally dependent upon photography, especially because we know her capabilities as an actress." Selznick was simply shocked that his team had not yet found a way to capture Bergman's "curious charm," her "exciting beauty and fresh purity."[10] In this memo Selznick sounds almost panicked at Stradling's inability to photograph Bergman appropriately.

But about two weeks later, and with a new director of photography for the film, Gregg Toland, he came up with some principles for photographing Bergman. In a memo to Gregory Ratoff, the director of *Intermezzo*, copied to Toland, he articulates these principles: that properly photographing Bergman "depends not simply on avoiding the bad side of her face; keeping her head down as much as possible; giving her the proper hairdress, giving her the proper mouth make-up, avoiding long shots, so as not to make her look too big, and, even more importantly, but for the same reason, avoiding low cameras on her ... but most important of all, on shading her face and in invariably going for effect lightings on her."[11]

Here we have it. Selznick's bill of particulars on how to capture or enhance Bergman's "natural" beauty:

- avoiding the bad side of her face;
- keeping her head down;
- giving her the proper hairdress;
- avoiding long shots and low camera angles; and
- shading her face and using "effect lighting."

In this and other memos Selznick elaborates on how he thinks Bergman should be photographed. Notice that it is not just a matter of limiting the amount of makeup Bergman wears. For the rest of the filming of *Intermezzo*, Selznick had reminders typed up for him to consult with Toland and Ratoff about photographing Bergman. These reminders cover all aspects of photography, but at the top of the list for the July 28 reminder is this: "1. Angles on Bergman's good side."

Later, in the long June 9, 1939, memo, Selznick says that Bergman needs makeup to make her lower lip seem less "unattractive," and the "effect lighting" can include such things as "shadows across her face, unique angles, or rim lighting."[12]

And under other circumstances makeup is absolutely necessary. In response to the suggestion that Bergman wear no make-up in her test for *The Bells of St. Mary's*, Selznick says, "It is dangerous to use no make-up on Miss Bergman until and unless a test is made with Crosby. With Crosby wearing no make-up she may look awful without it...."[13]

Selznick's concern for how to photograph Bergman continued through her entire career at Selznick Studios. In March of 1940, he tells Daniel O'Shea, then his vice-president of the studio, to be sure in any contracts in which they loan out Bergman, "we provide approval of cameraman and other photographic safeguards ... as many as you can devise, but not less than their agreement to spend at least one day, when the picture is finished, on retakes of any close-ups that are not satisfactory to us; at least one set of tests by the cameraman in advance of starting the picture, hopefully with our right to approve the cameraman withheld until we see the tests, but certainly with our having at least the right to view these tests and confer with the cameraman."[14]

Several months later, Selznick tells Victor Fleming how to photograph Bergman for *Jekyll and Hyde*: he urges Fleming and his camera crew to look at *Intermezzo* to see how Gregg Toland photographed her. However, aware that this suggestions might be insulting, Selznick softens the suggestion by saying the Bergman couldn't get "better photographic treatment" than Fleming and Ruttenberg can provide but "Toland did such wonderful things with her that you might as well all get the benefit of seeing the picture."[15]

To prepare Bergman for her screen test for Paramount Pictures in July of 1942, the test to see if she would be suitable to play Maria in *For Whom the Bell Tolls*, Selznick sent a list of 15 instructions. It is not stated to whom the instructions are addressed. In a follow-up memo Selznick addresses his secretary Francis Inglis, and the studio files contain a telegram from Raymond A. Klune, Selznick's production manager, to Sam Wood, the director of *For Whom the Bell Tolls*, so perhaps Selznick was addressing Klune. In any case, the tenth of Selznick's instructions expresses his standard concern about Bergman's eyebrows and lipstick. Point 12 is this: "Miss Bergman knows how to favor the better side of her face, but be sure the cameraman does this also; and warn [Joseph] Cotton [who would be in the screen test] so that he will cooperate, as he will."[16]

Occasionally Bergman did not cooperate with Selznick's ideas for her and did use certain kinds of makeup for publicity stills that he found unacceptable. This violation of his principles usually sent Selznick into a fit. In a memo to Victor Shapiro, he offers the usual complaints about eyebrows, lipstick, and eyelashes in the publicity stills taken by Howard Strickland and

The Selznick glamour shot used by director Gregory Ratoff to photograph Bergman in *Intermezzo*, during the scene in which Anita Hoffman (Bergman) first goes out with her future lover Holger Brandt (Leslie Howard). The shot conveys what Selznick called Bergman's almost spiritual sense of devotion and love (Selznick International Studios, 1939).

then goes on: "This is no whim of mine. We discovered early in the game that this was her great charm, and hundreds of thousands of people throughout the country went mad about her partly because of this naturalness. Editorials were written about her lack of artifice, and her great natural beauty. I am amazed that Ingrid would wear this kind of makeup in stills, since she is so averse to it on the screen; and I would appreciate it, if you would personally speak to Ingrid and say that I would be grateful if in the future she would not have any different ideas about makeup for stills than she has for the screen."[17]

So it should be no surprise that Selznick's requirements for photographing Bergman's naturalness became a common way of photographing her during her career in Hollywood, at least before she ran off with Rossellini. In *Intermezzo*, in most of the crucial scenes between Anita Hoffman (Bergman) and her lover Holger Brand (Leslie Howard), Bergman is photographed with a high-angle shot of the left side of her face, usually with a great deal of contrast that puts part of her face in shadow and gives her eyes her signature dewy look. When she submits to the inevitability of love in the scene in the tavern, she leans back on the bench and into Howard, making her submission even more obvious.

This way of photographing Bergman is constantly repeated in her early Hollywood films. There are clear indications that Fleming took Selznick's advice for *Dr. Jekyll and Mr. Hyde*. When Jekyll (Spencer Tracy) first meets Ivy (Bergman), Fleming photographs Bergman in medium shot from the right, but after Jekyll deposits Ivy on the bed in her flat and Ivy begins flirting with Jekyll, Fleming resorts to the same high-angle, high-contrast, soft focus shot on the left-side of Bergman's face, the shot recommended by Selznick.

Michael Curtiz uses similar shots in all the key scenes in *Casablanca* when Ilsa expresses her love and devotion. He photographs Bergman's left side in all but one of the close-ups when she first enters Rick's, and when she first confronts Rick after all their years apart, Curtiz uses the Selznick-recommended high-angle, high-contrast, "effect" lighting shot. He uses similar closeups when Ilse informs Rick in their Paris apartment that she was once married to another man but that he is dead; in La Belle Aurore when she says that he need not pick her up to go to the train station to escape the Nazis; after the flashback, when Ilse explains to Rick how she fell in love with Victor Lazlo as a young girl; and most importantly, in two key scenes at the end of the film: in the scene when Ilse confronts Rick in his café apartment, demanding that he help Lazlo escape, pulling a gun to emphasize her sincerity, and when Rick calls her bluff, breaking down and confessing that she has always loved him; and in the finale while Ilse listens to Rick's "I'm no good at being noble" speech and realizes what he is doing. In short, Curtiz uses the Selznick-recommended shot in almost all those situations when Ilse expresses her spiritual sense of love and dedication.

Sam Wood uses the same shot in the scene in *For Whom the Bell Tolls* when Pilar gives Maria (Bergman) to Robert Jordon (Gary Cooper), saying she is "a gift to any man," but not, interestingly, in the two sleeping bag scenes. In these scenes Wood shoots Bergman from the right in profile or in the final sleeping bag scene, from the left at low-angle. But the convention of photographing Bergman in high-contrast and soft focus in intense romantic moments continued, even if the shots were more straight-on than high angle. Good examples are the bedroom scenes in *Gaslight* and *Spellbound*, and the final rescue scene in *Notorious*.

What we might call the "Selznick shot" of Bergman is a major reason for her image as natural and wholesome. The shot literally highlights Bergman's beauty: the soft focus bathes her in light and shadow and captures

Top: The Selznick glamour shot used by director Victory Fleming to photograph Bergman in *Dr. Jekyll and Mr. Hyde*, during the scene in which the prostitute Ivy (Bergman) tries to seduce Dr. Henry Jekyll (Spencer Tracy) by pretending that she has been hurt. The shot conveys, rather ironically, Bergman's image of wholesomeness and innocence. *Bottom*: The Selznick glamour shot used by director Michael Curtiz to photograph Bergman in *Casablanca*, during the scene in which Ilsa Lund asks Sam (Dooley Wilson) to play "As Time Goes By." The shot conveys what Selznick considered Bergman's radiant, natural beauty (Warner Bros., 1942).

the light in her eyes. Her look of longing and devotion, her posture of sub-mission, all suggest something beyond the mere physical, something that cap-tures the depths of romantic love, something that Selznick thought of as "spiritual."

Selznick was equally infatuated with Bergman's personality. He found her demeanor "fresh and unspoiled," "something that just floated off a cloud," "dignified and remote," a sort of "quality" and "nobility," not inherently glam-orous but capable of glamour if it was required of her; he thought she possessed the simple values of frugality, hard work, conscientiousness, and humility. Implied in all this but never quite stated was the idea that Bergman lived a conventional life, that she was faithful and dedicated to small-town values and a doctor-husband and child, far away from the bright lights of Hollywood, which may have been the truth, at least at the beginning. Bergman's apparent personality reinforced the image of her wholesomeness and helped to reassure her male fans that she was the kind of girl they could take home to meet mother and not a woman with a lurid past, such as Maria, Ivy, or Alicia. Selznick's construction of Bergman's image did not disturb the fantasies of her male fans.

But because Bergman was in many ways open and candid about her opinions, but not her private life and because she could blurt out all sorts of things that might be taken by the press and her public the wrong way, Selznick limited access to Bergman and tried to control what she said to the press. He limited her endorsements, and he limited what he called "leg art."

Selznick got the idea to promote Bergman's simple values just a few months after her arrival in America. In a memo to William Hebert, his Direc-tor of Advertising and Publicity, Selznick praises Bergman's conscientiousness, her frugality, and her lack of affectation, and suggests that these qualities be the basis for a publicity campaign. He is impressed that while Bergman is engaged in making a film, she focuses exclusively on her work and does noth-ing personally or professionally that distracts her. In addition, he says, she is "simply frantic" about not spending the studio's money, and in being so ded-icated and frugal, she is "completely unaffected." Selznick is so impressed that he wants to start a publicity campaign based on these qualities in order to turn her into a legend. Such a campaign would also have a more pragmatic reason: it would distinguish Bergman from Greta Garbo, Marlena Dietrich, and other "exotic" foreign actresses with whom she might be compared.[18]

In order to build Bergman's "legend," Selznick developed a number of strategies. The most important was the principle that everything associated with Bergman be dignified and not associated with crass commercialism. In a memo to Howard Strickling, Selznick arranges for someone to do a publicity drive for Bergman, but only on these grounds: "The one thing I definitely don't want to do with her is anything cheap. Our policy on her has always been to avoid most of the things that are done generally in the way of publicity, and ... I still feel violently against any trick stills of [an] undignified nature, tie-up with soaps, cosmetics, etc.— in fact commercial tie-ups of almost every kind. [new para.] Generally I feel that she ought to be handled in the same way that you would handle any really dignified and important artiste."[19]

The strategy for promoting Bergman mentioned first in this memo is Selznick's control of still photography. Selznick was particularly sensitive to Bergman's costumes and questioned Bergman's own taste in the costumes she chose for publicity. In a memo to Russell Birdwell, Director of Advertising and Publicity, Selznick says that he is appalled by the photographs taken of Bergman for *Life* magazine largely because of the "hideous costumes." He goes on to say that he would rather kill the layout if the photographers are not willing to make a new set. He wants Kay Brown to approve the new set of photos and he wants final approval of the costumes in all future still photos of Bergman. For all future photo shoots, he wants Bergman to check with Kay Brown in New York, or he himself when Bergman is on the coast, because he doesn't think "Miss Bergman has the right perspective on what costumes she should use in accordance with the dignity and important way in which I wish to handle her, and in accordance with what would be right for American publication."[20]

Selznick sends Brown copies of the memo to Birdwell and calls the costumes "hideous." He goes on: "Ingrid's taste continues to confuse me. Sometimes she looks divine and sometimes her clothes look as though they were selected by Margaret Pemberton — even worse. [new para.] If she makes any photographs in New York, let's for God's sake borrow some costumes for her."

In a memo three days later, Birdwell tells Selznick that he has killed the layout on Ingrid for *Life* magazine. And in a follow-up memo to Selznick on the same day, Kay Brown takes the blame for the clothes in the *Life* layout. According to Brown, Bergman saw the clothes at Brown's house and ordered similar ones for herself. Brown goes on: "I agree they did not look well in the photos. I had no idea she would use them for that purpose." She says that she has talked to Bergman about clothes, going so far as to arrange "a special price at Hattie's," but Ingrid "isn't keen to buy. She has never had clothes other than those especially made for her. She doesn't quite understand our system and doesn't like the possibility of duplication by purchasing at Hattie's." Brown suggests a strategy: "Don't have her buy anything here.... Wait until she gets back to the Coast. Make out a list of things she *must* have in her private wardrobe. I will get her to the point of realizing she must buy immediately a basic and simple complete wardrobe." Brown says that she didn't see the *Life* proofs but can imagine the clothes: "There just wasn't anything to put on her. Her wardrobe resembles her make-up kit — a large-sized tube of toothpaste."[21]

A few days later, Selznick writes a memo to Brown, expressing his aversion to "most women in slacks — particularly when they are big women like Ingrid, particularly when the slacks are not particularly attractive, particularly when we are trying to establish her as something that just floated off a cloud."[22]

Selznick Studios also attempted to limit Bergman's commercial appearances and her endorsements of commercial products in order to promote a sense of her dignity. In the Selznick Archive are a number of telegrams from Leo Mishkin to various people in the Selznick Studio about planting Bergman in magazines without fashion credits.[23] And there is a letter from Daniel O'Shea to Jack Benny, c/o Myrt Blum, granting permission for Bergman to appear on the "Lucky Strike–Jack Benny Program" on either October 14 or 21, 1945, for her to attend rehearsals, and for her name and likeness to be used to promote the program, "that such use will in no way constitute an endorsement of the product." In addition, Bergman will not be required "to participate in any way whatsoever with the commercial advertising of the product on said radio program."[24]

Selznick Studios also tried to limit the content of interviews and control the overall media coverage of Bergman. In a telegram, Al Wilkie tells Bergman's publicity man Joseph Steele about a prospective interview with columnist Earl Wilson. Because Wilson has done two previous very successful interviews with Bergman, the telegram reads, "HE UNDERSTANDS FULLY THAT HER MARRIAGE AND NON-PROFESSIONAL LIFE ARE NOT TO BE DISCUSSED."[25]

A few years later, in a memo to Joe Steele and Harriet Flagg, Selznick's east coast representative, about a prospective article in *Time* magazine covering the opening of *For Whom the Bell Tolls*, Selznick insists that Steele sell the idea that "Hollywood has not changed [Bergman's] habits in the least. She does not smoke. Her drinking is confined to an occasional eggnog at home with friends, and the fancy rum drinks when she goes to the Beachcombers." She is called Miss Bergman on the set and has "an innate dignity which prevents all but a very limited few even to call her Ingrid." She herself addresses all but a few people as Mr., Mrs., etc. Hollywood crews are "notorious for their expressed bawdy dreams and ambitions about most Hollywood stars," but one electrician, after watching Bergman for a week, said, "I'd like to kiss that woman's hand."[26]

Selznick was especially adamant that Bergman not be allowed to produce "Leg Art." In a memo to Whitney Bolton, he complains about the Studio's lack of control over Bergman's interviews, as well as her "hideous photographs" and then says this: "Also I don't know who let her in for the type of interview where reporters would try to raise her skirts for 'leg art,' etc. Ingrid in any case should not have group interviews, and shouldn't be photographed under such conditions."[27]

There is no evidence that Selznick knew that Bergman's marriage was foundering or that her behavior on the set of *Dr. Jekyll and Mr. Hyde* was causing rumors about her relationships with Fleming and Tracy. Later the same rumors — this time about her relationship with Gary Cooper — surfaced on the sets of *For Whom the Bell Tolls* and *Saratoga Trunk*. Selznick thought he was promoting Bergman's personality as he understood it. It may have just happened that his strategy to promote her wholesomeness and dignity and to severely limit any revelations about her personal life gave Bergman the opportunity to develop a life of her own that was significantly different from her public image.

Finally and most decisively for Bergman's image, Selznick promoted her professionalism as an actress. Rather ironically, he seems to have arrived at this goal out of necessity. At the beginning of her career in America, Selznick had Bergman under contract for seven pictures and she insisted on working as much as possible. He found it difficult to find pictures suitable for her image, so he wound up having to allow her to act in the theater. Selznick gave considerable thought to the problems of how to handle Bergman's sputtering career. The reviews of her appearances in *Adam Had Four Sons* and *Rage in Heaven*, in which she played the same basic type — a love-struck young ingénue — were respectable, but the films themselves were not major hits. In the end, Selznick stumbled upon an appropriate strategy to account for her work in the theater: he would actually promote the fact that Bergman had theatrical training, which made her an "artiste," not just a star. As a result he actually trumpeted Bergman's stage work and promoted the fact that not only Bergman but two other female stars in his studio — Joan Fontaine and Vivian Leigh — were trained in the theater and active on the stage, thereby implying that they were more skilled and talented than the stars of other studios.

At first Selznick resisted Bergman's desire to work in the theater. Kay Brown suggested that Selznick Studios employ Winifred Lanahan, who played Joan of Arc for the Theater Guild Production, to help Bergman with her English and work on an interpretation of Joan, a part Selznick had been promising Bergman since he had signed her to work for his studio. Selznick responded emphatically that he was "much opposed" to this idea: "I am terrified that Ingrid's natural talent and unique method of achieving effects will be spoiled and stylized by contact with any specific school of theatrical acting or any particular interpretations." He thought their future problem would be finding directors who would "know how to bring out what is Ingrid's naturally, and I don't want this complicated by having to tear down an impersonation by Ingrid of somebody else's interpretations, however good that person might be." Besides, Selznick wasn't sure that his studio would even do a film about Joan of Arc and "the very worst thing we could do, in my opinion, would be to inure her fresh and unspoiled quality and invest her with Theatre Guild ideas, good or bad." Selznick noted that Katherine Cornell was successful as Joan, and he didn't want Ingrid "to come in contact with [Cornell's interpretation]."[28]

Brown quickly apologized for suggesting Lanahan, but asserted that she, Brown, *did* understand and appreciate "Ingrid's type of acting." She went on to say that she chose Lanahan mostly because she could fill Ingrid in on the background material on Joan — and Lanahan and Bergman could study Shaw's version of Joan mostly to practice English, not act.[29]

A week later, Selznick informed Brown that he had hit on an idea to promote Bergman's image as an actress. By then Selznick had already given in to Brown's urging that he allow Bergman to appear in a Broadway production of *Liliom* to cure her boredom from lack of work. He announced that he had asked Russell Birdwell to publicize the fact that the studio has "made" three stars in a row in three successive pictures — Leigh, Bergman, and Fontaine — and "we are the first studio, and I am the first producer to preach the value of players working on the stage, to learn about sustaining scenes, timing, audience reactions, etc...." And he wanted it known that he has given permission for all three to do stage work.[30]

Once he had the idea, Selznick was not shy about promoting Bergman's work on stage. Before the opening of *Liliom*, he sent a memo to Birdwell, asking if Birdwell could plant an attached excerpt from a Dorothy Kilgallen column "reprinted for the benefit of Hollywood producers — perhaps in Hoffman's column?" The excerpt from Kilgallen's column from the *New York Journal and American* of Friday, March 1, 1940, speculated on "how long it will be before the Broadway stage finds another great 'flash' like Katherine Cornell" or others. Said Kilgallen, "If I had to make a guess at who'll be the next dramatic standout, I'd choose Ingrid Bergman, the young Scandinavian actress."[31]

Perhaps as a result of Selznick's relentless publicity campaign, Bergman may have needed to have her acting skills promoted. Her roles in her first three films were very similar, and she may have been in danger of being stereotyped as a wholesome beauty who could only suffer for love. The year after she appeared in *Liliom*, Bergman appeared in John Houseman's production of *Anna Christie*. Bergman herself reports that when she walked out on stage as the whore in Eugene O'Neill's play and called out to the barman, "Gimme a whiskey and make it a double," "the audience collapsed — laughing. They expected, I suppose, for me to say, 'Give me a glass of milk.'" Bergman's memory of the line may be faulty: in the text, the line reads, "Gimme a whisky — ginger ale on the side. And don't be stingy, baby" — but her general impression of the incident is probably reliable.[32] Clearly, Bergman had to convince the audience that she could play against type. And this she did: she got excellent reviews, and O'Neill's wife Carlotta approved of her in the role.

After his decision to promote Bergman's theatrical training, Selznick's publicity campaign emphasized not just Bergman's star qualities but her abilities as an actress. After the run of *Anna Christie*, Whitney Bolton, Selznick's Director of Advertising and Publicity, sent a memo to Selznick, reporting that *Screen Guide* magazine's piece on Bergman would include two faced pages of art and text and the heading across both pages would be "The Screen's Greatest Actress."[33]

But Selznick did not think the headline was enough. In a responding memo four days later, he complained, "If you will forgive me, I don't think the material generally gets over enough of her extraordinary qualities." Why not quote Spencer Tracy (with whom Bergman had just worked on *Dr. Jekyll and Mr. Hyde*) on his having worked with many actresses of note, including Helen Hayes, "and he regards Bergman as the greatest of them all" — or get from Tracy something similar or equally good, and also try to get Mr. or Mrs. Eugene O'Neill, unless John Houseman doesn't like the idea, to give him a quote about Bergman being "the greatest Anna Christie of all times, etc."

In fact, Selznick was so delighted with his strategy he said in passing in a letter to Petter Lindstrom that he knew he would lose money by letting Bergman appear in *Anna Christie* but felt that the part was important "from the standpoint of building Ingrid's prestige."[34] Of course, Selznick's comment is to a certain extent self-serving. Selznick and Lindstrom were constantly at loggerheads over Bergman's contracts and salary, and his comments can be interpreted as a bargaining strategy. Still, there can be no doubt that Selznick was committed to building Bergman's prestige as an actress. Her prestige would help further his own interests.

The degree to which Selznick would use the notion of Bergman as an actress to promote her larger "pure and spiritual image" is clear in the way he handled Bergman's playing the prostitute Ivy in Fleming's *Dr. Jekyll and Mr. Hyde*, a role she insisted on when everyone in the film community thought she was better suited for the role of the doctor's long-suffering wife. Selznick was concerned to explain away the fact that *Jekyll and Hyde* is "loaded with sex" and that Bergman's appearance as Ivy was an indication of her acting ability and not true to her composite image as a simple, natural, wholesome, dignified woman who brought distinction to any role. In a memo to Victor Shapiro, Director of Publicity and Advertising, Selznick attached notes to a rough press release on how he wanted "the Bergman story handled," especially "a banner out of [gossip columnist] Louella [Parsons] on it." The draft of the release is headlined "Ingrid Bergman to Co-Star with Spencer Tracy in Jekyll and Hyde" [all in caps]. The second paragraph of the release read as follows: "The role will mark a departure for Miss Bergman, since, in the words of Victor Fleming, it is 'loaded with sex' ... etc., etc. (suggest you get quote from Fleming). Miss Bergman, who created such a definite impression in Selznick's 'Intermezzo,' has heretofore been identified in this country with roles of a very pure and spiritual type, having just completed a part of this kind as the star of 'Legacy' [*Adam Had Four Sons*], and is now completing another one as Bob Montgomery's co-star in 'Rage in Heaven' at MGM. [new para] However, in her native Sweden, Miss Bergman played a wide variety of parts — one of her last pictures there being the very heavy emotional role in 'A Woman's Face,' which Metro has purchased for remake with Joan Crawford."[35]

A year later in a memo to Kay Brown, Selznick pondered the issue of how to balance Bergman's portrayal of Ivy with more sympathetic roles which would promote her image of dignity and nobility. It was, he said, a matter of picking the right roles in the right sequence, so as to "capitalize on the quality she suggests of nobility, at least for a few pictures, rather than following 'Jekyll and Hyde' with another unsympathetic portrait."[36]

By 1943, Bergman's image was set in the public eye. Which is why Lieutenant Cecil Barker could write to his friend Selznick in the letter that is the epigraph of this chapter and report that no matter the rank, when army men talk about actresses, he could not "remember a time that Ingrid Bergman wasn't the topic of conversation one time or another during the evening. And everytime it was the same thing: what a great actress she is, what a nice girl she must be, what a real human quality she has that other actresses don't have, etc." But Lieutenant Barker was more sensitive than most people to the source of Bergman's popularity: he could understand why everyone appreciated her as an actress; he could not understand why people thought they knew what she was really like, " a sweet girl" that army men would all like to take home to their mothers. Then he saw an article in *Look* magazine and he knew: Bergman had had "damn good *publicity* [underlined in the original]."[37]

Bergman's publicity at the beginning of her career followed the Selznick script with remarkable fidelity. The articles about her work in *For Whom the Bell Tolls* reflected all of the basic ideas that Selznick had been promoting about Bergman from the beginning. An article in *Life* magazine by Thomas Carlile and Jean Speiser in July of 1943 played up her naturalness and naiveté when she first arrived in Hollywood, her lack of demands, and a brief history of her childhood. But after establishing her basic personality, the piece went on to describe her "settled home life," the little stucco house in Rochester,

New York, the doctor husband and single daughter, "the quiet life they pre-ferred." And the article ended with praise for Bergman's work not as a star but as an actress. Her last few roles demonstrated to Carlile and Speiser that Bergman had "greater versatility than any actress on the American screen," that "her roles have demanded an adaptability and a sensitiveness of charac-terization to which few actresses could rise."[38]

The cover story for the August 2, 1943, issue of *Time* magazine calls Bergman the person "most likely to salvage the picture [*For Whom the Bell Tolls*]" and "the best artist in the company," the one "most sensitive to an artist's job." And in the process of singing her praises, the article recycled the old Selznick stories, that Bergman didn't want "anything to do with bathing suits and plucked eyebrows," that she was interested in acting and not in being a star.[39]

In September of 1943, Donald Culross Peattie in an article in *Reader's Digest* called Bergman the "first lady of Hollywood" because her performance in *For Whom the Bell Tolls* wasn't "glamour" or "just entertainment"; "it's the kind of performance you'll tell your children you saw" (39). Peattie went on to describe Bergman as a "glutton for work" and the fact that she went home every night to "a modest five-room apartment that is not listed in the guide map to the movie stars' homes." This was the home to which Bergman's family moved in the summer of 1943 and where Bergman "turn[ed] into Mrs. Peter Lindstrom, wife of a young Swedish doctor and mother of four-year old Pia," even though Lindstrom was spending most of his time in a residency in surgery in San Francisco. Peattie ended the article with more Bergman lore from Selznick's office — stories about Bergman putting on her own makeup, refusing to pose for leg art and refusing to wear "startling evening gowns," "never per-mitting her face or name to be used to advertise anything," rarely going to Hollywood parties — and a paean to Bergman's artistry: the range of her roles, the fact that she worked on both screen and stage.[40]

Even the venerable *New York Times Magazine* followed the Selznick script. In an interview with Bergman entitled "In, But Not Of, Hollywood," S.J. Woolf began with the standard portrait: the lack of "publicity escapades"; no temper tantrums on the set; no controversial appearances in nightclubs; her marriage to a doctor and her devotion to her young daughter; her being "unassuming, serious-minded." And then after recording the interview, in which Bergman talked about her preparation for her part in *Gaslight*, he offered a brief biography, ending with the fact that Bergman was "still the housewife and her husband the master of the house." Woolf concluded his piece as a whole with a review of Bergman's wholesome traits, her dedication and energy, her healthiness in skiing to the location of an Office of War Infor-mation film in Minnesota, and then this quotation from Bergman herself: "I work so hard before the camera and on the stage that I have neither the desire nor the energy to act in my private life. There I prefer to be myself and forget all about audiences and look after my family."[41]

Everyone agrees that Bergman was dedicated to her work, polite, and respectful to everyone on the set, even technicians. She acted modestly and did not often make demands or throw tantrums on the set, although, as we have seen, she did quarrel with W.S. Van Dyke on the set of *Rage in Heaven*. And she did fight for the parts she wanted such as Paula Alquist in *Gaslight* or Clio Lane in *Saratoga Trunk*. Obviously, she was ambitious, but not for money or the usual notion of fame. Although she and Lindstrom engaged in extensive and intricate contract negotiations with Selznick, it was Lindstrom who seemed concerned with whether Bergman was adequately compensated. Bergman herself did not want to be rich. True, she did want to be a success and famous, but she wanted these things because they were indicators of her accomplishments as an actor. Above all, she simply wanted to be kept busy *acting* and she wanted to be good at it.

During the fight with Selnick for the part of Clio Dulaine in *Saratoga Trunk*, Bergman was happy to be involved in the fray: she wrote Ruth Roberts that she did not care about her image or reputation as much as Selznick did, and that she could transform the part, which seemed more suitable for Vivien Leigh, and wasn't it going to be fun and interesting to see what she could do with the part, her line readings, the talk, the walk, what she could do with her hands and feet. The letter is exuberant with Bergman's girlish enthusiasm for the fundamental stuff of acting.[42] Above all, her major ambition was to play the heroic part of Joan of Arc. Perhaps Bergman's enthusiasm for acting and her goal to be Joan of Arc are enough to confirm her studio image.

During the years Bergman was under contract to Selznick Studios, the Selznick publicity machine ground on and on, and Bergman's image became fixed in the public mind: her beauty and spirituality captured in the close-up photography Selznick preferred, her dignity and candor projected by Selznick's control of her still photography and her public appearances, and her performance skills recognized and shaped in the public media by the Selznick organization.

The problem is that during her years of work for Selznick Studios, Bergman's life resembled her public image less and less. She had created another life. She had things to hide.

Four

The Existential Heroine

"For the first time I have broken out from the cage which encloses me, and opened a shutter to the outside world. I have touched things which I hoped were there but I have never dared to show. I am so happy for this picture. It is as if I were flying. I feel no chains. I can fly higher and higher because the bars of my cage are broken."
— Entry in Bergman's diary, January–March, 1941

In June of 1945, Bergman arrived in Paris at the beginning of a USO Tour of Europe. She stayed at the Ritz Carleton, which was the major hotel in town for the American press corps. The afternoon after her arrival, she found a six-point memorandum under her door. The subject line read, "Dinner. 6.6.45. Paris, France." The first point noted that the memo was a "community effort" of Bob Capa and Irwin Shaw. Subsequent points noted that the two men were short on cash and had been forced to choose between sending Bergman flowers or taking her to dinner. They had decided on dinner. They offered to pick her up at 6:15. Point seven read, "We do not sleep." The memo was signed, "Worried."

Bergman had never heard of Robert Capa and Irwin Shaw, but she found the memo amusing. When the men rang her room at 6:15, she went down to the lobby to meet them and learned that Capa was a war photographer and Shaw a soldier who wanted to write. She got on well with both of them and had a wonderful time. They went out to eat, and the two men introduced her to their friends. They laughed and danced.[1]

Bergman was particularly struck with Capa. He was darkly handsome with slicked black hair and worn, baggy eyes. He had a quiet, composed, world-weary manner that was vaguely dangerous. He seemed to have been everywhere, done everything, exulting in the moment and enjoying himself immensely. Often he erupted into fits of enthusiasm, tossing off opinions and telling stories about the famous men he had met and the events he had covered: battles in Spain, the invasion of Normandy, the liberation of Rome. Still, he took time to look at her, tilt his head, grin slyly and compliment her beauty, her films, and imply somehow that meeting her was one of the high points of his life. Bergman was deeply flattered at his attention.

In her autobiography, Bergman says that after her dinner with Capa and Shaw, she left Paris with the USO and toured with Jack Benny, pianist and harmonica player Larry Adler, and actress Martha Tilton. By coincidence she met Capa again in Berlin. The two of them toured the ruins of that great city, and Capa took pictures of her, one in particular: it was a picture of Bergman in a bathtub, fully clothed in a long coat and with a scarf around her head. Capa was so excited to get the shot, according to Bergman, that he raced back to his office to develop the film, but when he arrived, he discovered that somehow the negative had been ruined. Bergman was amused: poor Capa wouldn't have his scoop of the famous actress in the bathtub to sell to the magazines.[2]

Bergman suggests that the bathtub story is an intimate moment between two close friends. And so when the USO troupe returned to Paris, she met Capa again, and that was when she "supposes" that she began to fall in love with him.[3] The major revelation of Bergman's autobiography is her love affair with Robert Capa. It is the only love affair she ever confessed to.

Bergman tells the story of her affair with Capa with a great deal of reticence and Hemingwayesque understatement, and for good reason. Her affair with Capa occurred at the beginning of the most difficult period in her life: her marriage was foundering and within two years, her career would be in jeopardy. Capa was both a cause and an escape from her difficulties. On the one hand, Bergman's version of her relationship with Capa hides more than she reveals. She does not acknowledge that despite the intensity of her love for Capa, she may have had affairs with two other men during her relationship with him. On the other hand, Bergman reveals more than she intended. Capa introduced Bergman to a life outside the bounds of the conventional: a life of risk and danger. For most of her life, Bergman maintained the image created by Selznick Studios, an image of honesty, wholesomeness, and decency, a woman deeply committed to family values. Already involved with men outside of her marriage, Bergman responded to Capa's influence by throwing discretion to the winds. Capa prepared her to risk everything for Roberto Rossellini and for a new and different sort of art.

Since coming to America for *Intermezzo*, Bergman had been apart from her husband more than she had been with him. She had gone back to her family in Sweden after *Intermezzo*, but the four months in America had changed her relationship with Lindstrom: they were awkward and prickly with one another. Later Bergman would wonder whether her marriage ever really recovered from that first separation. After making the Swedish film *June Night*

(*Juninatten*), Bergman returned to America, this time with Pia. Lindstrom found this absence convenient because he had volunteered to supervise a series of short films on dentistry for the Swedish Army. The following June, Lindstrom visited Bergman during the run of *Liliom* on Broadway, but the couple had trouble reestablishing their old rapport. Bergman arranged for Pia and her nurse to stay in the country and booked herself and Lindstrom into a room on the 34th floor of a hotel, overlooking Central Park, but Lindstrom was not seduced by this attempt at romance. All that Bergman recalls about the visit were Lindstrom's complaints. He found New York unclean. He thought the room too high and disliked having to look so far down at his surroundings. He complained about the filthy carpet in the room. The visit, Bergman says in the autobiography, "was not a success."[4]

Nevertheless, when it became clear that Bergman was determined to stay in America, Lindstrom decided to give up dentistry and become an American doctor. He arrived to stay during Christmas of 1940 and quickly began the process of applying to medical schools. After considering the University of Southern California, in Los Angeles, the University of Chicago, the University of Rochester, and Yale, Lindstrom chose Rochester.

But while Lindstrom was visiting schools, Bergman was acting the role of the prostitute Ivy Petersen, opposite Spencer Tracy in Victor Fleming's production of *Dr. Jekyll and Mr. Hyde.* Something happened on the set of *Jekyll and Hyde* that changed the dynamics of Bergman's life and career forever. What happened had something to do with her close relationship with Tracy and Fleming and her sense that these intense relationships resulted in an exceptional performance.

In her diary, Bergman is practically ecstatic about her experience on the film: "You can't get everything on a platter, you have to pay for everything. I paid with *Rage in Heaven* for *Dr. Jekyll and Mr. Hyde.* I would have paid anything for this picture." She goes on to claim that she has never been happier, that she will never get a better part, a better director, a better leading man, and a better cameraman. With these people she can give herself over entirely to her work. Then this: "For the first time I have broken out from the cage which encloses me, and opened a shutter to the outside world. I have touched things which I hoped were there but I have never dared to show. I am so happy for this picture. It is as if I were flying. I feel no chains. I can fly higher and higher because the bars of my cage are broken."[5]

The language of this passage is extravagant and conflicted to the point of mixing metaphors. Bergman feels that she has paid her dues for her success in *Jekyll and Hyde.* The implication is that she deserves her success. Still, she accepts her success as a gift, the result of working with a director and an actor to whom she could give herself completely. The results are liberating, opening up a new world, loosening chains, breaking the bars of a cage. In the throes of emotion, Bergman gropes for an appropriate metaphor and winds up simply piling them on. Lindstrom later said that Bergman needed to be in love with her costars in order to act well, but even if we discount Lindstrom's judgment, the language of this passage suggests that Bergman began to associate her emotional involvements with her performances. She had discovered that life on a movie set, her involvements with co-stars and directors, men with whom she was in daily and intimate contact, fulfilled her deepest dreams of what acting was all about. It was exhilarating, blood pounding, knee weakening. If it was not love, it was a more than an adequate substitute. And it resulted in a performance for which she would be cheered, praised, even adored.

The pattern was set and was soon to be repeated with Gary Cooper in *For Whom the Bell Tolls* and *Saratoga Trunk* and with Gregory Peck in *Spellbound*. Given her commitment to acting and the emotional rush she experienced with certain of her leading men and certain of her directors, it is hardly surprising that when Bergman and Pia joined Lindstrom in Rochester after the shooting of *Jekyll and Hyde*, Bergman began to chafe at playing the role of housewife and mother. In *My Story*, Bergman allows co-author Burgess to put this move in the starkest terms. To Bergman domestic life had become "a living death."[6]

While Bergman's career was gathering steam, Lindstrom moved to San Francisco to do his residency in the summer of 1943, and a year later he and Bergman moved into a house in Benedict Canyon in Hollywood. But things were not right. Her publicity agent Joe Steele heard rumors of marital problems on the set of *Gaslight*, and when for a magazine article he asked Bergman what quality she most admired in her husband, she at first demurred and said that she didn't want to talk about her husband. Steele covered the awkwardness of the moment by saying that he didn't mean that Bergman had to be terribly personal. She could say something vague, such as that Lindstrom was tolerant — something like that. Bergman pondered a moment and agreed that Steele could say that Lindsrom was tolerant. But early the next morning in his office, Steele got a call from Bergman: she wanted to see him on the set. Always compliant, Steele rushed to the set to discover that the only reason for the meeting was that Bergman wanted to set the record straight. She had been thinking about Lindstrom's being tolerant and she wanted to change her opinion for the record. "It is not true," she said. "Petter is not tolerant about anything." Steele promised to strike the word from his article.[7]

Between films during the Second World War, Bergman escaped from her family to go on War Bond and USO tours. Then in 1945, far from home on a USO tour of Europe, she met Robert Capa. Ironically, the affair coincided with the high point of her popularity, the year of *Saratoga Trunk*, *Spellbound*, and *The Bells of St. Mary's*, "Bergman's Year," according to *Life* magazine.

Almost all of what we know about Bergman's affair with Capa is from her autobiography. After the two anecdotes about meeting Capa in Europe, Bergman's narrative about the affair jumps to the following summer with the filming of *Arch of Triumph*, by which time, Burgess asserts, she and Capa had definitely fallen in love. She conveniently does not mention that Capa was in Los Angeles during the shooting of the film she made before *Arch of Triumph*: *Notorious*. In fact, in an apparent attempt to downplay the seriousness of the affair up until that period, Bergman suggests that Capa came to California not just to see her but to get back in touch with a number of old friends. She doesn't say who those friends were, but two of them were Irwin Shaw and Larry Adler. In addition, according to Bergman, Capa wanted to see if he could get work photographing the film community in Hollywood. Bergman says that she appealed to Lewis Milestone, the director of *Arch of Triumph*, to let Capa take pictures of the filming, and he agreed.[8]

Thus, Bergman never outright acknowledges that Capa followed her to America and was with her as early as December of 1945. We know, however, that Capa arrived in New York in October and took his time getting to Hollywood. He had taken a job with International Pictures and for a while shared an apartment in Beverly Hills with Larry Adler.

Capa continued to live life as he always had. He played tennis with Adler, bet heavily on the horses at the Santa Anita track and lost, and spent so much time lolling about the pool at Howard Hawks's house that Hawks suspected him of having an affair with his wife. He also hung around the journalists and photographers that met regularly at the English pub The Cock and Bull on Sunset Boulevard. Says Slim Aarons, one of members of the group at the Cock and Bull: "We just used to sit in the bar and fool around with girls. I also ran into him one time at a party with Howard Hughes and all of those big guys. He'd hand out playing cards with the rich boys, the big players, these producers who had a lot of money. When he didn't gamble with his life, he gambled with cards. He had to have the risk. You see, once the war was over, his charge was gone, and he needed excitement. He must have lost heavily a few times because he was always trying to borrow money from me."[9]

Capa's arrival in Hollywood was proclaimed in the Hollywood press, and he was immediately swept up with a wave of invitations to parties and requests by directors and stars to visit them on the set. They knew the publicity value of a Capa photograph placed in *Life* or *Look*. So it is not surprising that Capa had access to the shooting of *Notorious*. In a collection of Capa's photographs is a glorious low-angle shot of Bergman walking across the checkerboard tile of the foyer in Sebastian's mansion during the famous shot in which Hitchcock's camera starts high near the ceiling and zooms down to the key in her hand.[10]

Bergman was so guarded about her relationship with Capa that it is difficult to say how their romance developed or the degree to which it was based on a blossoming friendship, a meeting of minds, a physical passion. Still, there are clues. Novelist Martha Gellhorn based her novella, *Till Death Do Us Part* on Robert Capa. Her character Bara is clearly modeled on Capa: Bara is a famous war photographer who fits Capa's description. He also shares much of Capa's past: like Capa, he lost the love of his life in a war, is charming with women and has a number of women in love with him. Bergman is not a model for any of the four major women featured in the story. She may, however, share some characteristics with Helen Richards. At first Helen finds Bara colorless and a bit off-putting — Bara is both young and old, he is strange and unsafe, he speaks authoritatively but without bragging, he is confident and self-contained and very presumptuous. Gradually Bara insinuates himself into her life. Helen allows herself to be seduced and is surprised at how proud she is to be his lover. Eventually not having him near her is a kind of agony.[11]

But what Bergman does report is her sense that Capa understood her situation as an international film star, and his diagnosis of her troubles, his frankness, was part of what made him so attractive. Capa told Bergman that she was crazy for sacrificing her humanity and allowing herself to be turned into a business, for letting her husband drive her career, doing nothing but work. In her current situation she simply had "no time for living." Bergman defended herself, primarily by arguing that she was going to do more stage work, especially Joan of Arc, which was the one role she had always wanted, but deep inside, she wondered if Capa was right.[12] Later Bergman told an interviewer that Capa had made her doubt the importance of what she was doing. He warned her about doing only what was easy and what brought success, about doing things that were unfulfilling. His words "unsettled" her.[13]

Bergman also notes that even though she and Capa had fallen in love, being in love was "not easy" because she was "so moral, so prudish." Capa may have found her sense of morality difficult, but Bergman still longed to be with him. She admired his sense of adventure, love of freedom, and disregard for money.[14]

This aspect of Capa, too, is captured by Gellhorn's Bara, seen from Helen Richard's point of view, days after their affair had begun: Bara gives away lots of money to friends in need, he loses a lot of money at poker. Five days into their affair, Helen is paying for their meals, buying Bara a new suit and changing his wardrobe, making him more stylish. Bara does not seem to mind. He has no opinion about men's fashion and concedes that her taste may be better than his. But in all their time together, he does not talk about his work; and although he seems to have connections to important people in politics and the arts, indeed to important people in all walks of life, he does not talk about himself and he does not like to answer questions about himself.[15]

There is no evidence that Bergman ever spent money on Capa, but clearly Capa's carefree way with love and money was radically different from Lindstrom's demanding domesticity and tight-fistedness. Capa's love of adventure and freedom, his distain for money, was part of his charm.

Bergman may have thought of herself as prudish, but if Capa's photos of Bergman are any indication, she was not prudish when she was alone with him. There is a photograph of Bergman in the collection edited by Cornell Capa, Robert's brother, and Richard Whelan, one of Capa's biographers, and it is one of the few stills extant of Bergman that does not promote her sweetness and innocence. Bergman's face is in stark profile, her head thrown back against a stuffed chair or couch. She is staring upward, but the pinprick of light in her eye does not indicate that she is seeing anything. Her mouth is open slightly, the soft shadows on her face coalesce more darkly on her cheek and lower jawbone, her skin is not slick with sweat but seems warm, flushed; her throat is open and exposed and the light plunges from her throat down to the deep V in her black dress.[16] The photo is rawly sensuous, implying post-coital satisfaction, pensiveness, even possibly regret. This one photograph makes Bergman more sexual, more appreciative of sex, than anything else in her career other than the key scenes in *Dr. Jekyll and Mr. Hyde.*

And in fact, late in her life Bergman confessed that Capa "awakened a sexual side" in her that she "didn't know was there." And she used the kind of frank language she had never used publicly before: "Capa was lost completely when he made love, as he must have been when he took his war pictures. I learned what it was to forget everything."[17]

Capa soon became restless because Hollywood was not adventurous enough. The filming of *Notorious* ended in the winter or early spring of 1946, but Capa had left before the final wrap. The following April or May, Bergman went with Joe Steele to New York to talk with Maxwell Anderson and the producers of *Joan of Lorraine,* and we know from Steele's memoirs that Bergman met Capa in New York. In fact, Steele began to suspect that Bergman was having an affair because Bob Capa showed up in New York and Bergman became more independent and often tried to escape from Steele in his professional role as escort. And then, to Steele's amazement, Capa set up a meeting with him at the bar of 21. According to Steele, Capa expressed himself along these lines: he claimed to know Bergman better than Steele did and asserted that Bergman was "all tied up in a million knots" because ever since she was a kid, she had been bossed around by men who tried to be a father to her. She was terribly naïve and let these men treat her like a child ... even Steele treated her that way. As a result Bergman was afraid — although she wouldn't admit it to herself— to "bust out of that goddamn built-in conformity." The world was at her feet, but she only wanted to be safe and secure. She didn't have "the vaguest notion of what the world's about" and it was "a stinking shame." Bergman was "one helluva lot of woman" but the men around her had to stop treating her like a schoolgirl or a saint.[18]

We may discount the details in Steele's account because it is a recollection long after the meeting, but considering that Steele offers it without comment and only in the general context that Bergman had been secretive, it may then accurately reflect the gist of what Capa told him. Fearing the depths of character that Capa described, faced with indications that Bergman may have had a life he knew nothing about, Steele decided to deny the possibility of other Ingrids. Years later, when he was composing his memoir, Steele still could not cope with the thought that the woman he idolized had a secret life.

According to Bergman, sometime during the shooting of *Arch of Triumph*, or possibly later in New York, her affair with Capa reached a climax, a point at which decisions had to be made. Says Burgess, if Capa had asked Bergman to run away with him, she might have gone, but it was not very likely. On the other hand, if he had asked her to marry him, she may very well have said yes. But he didn't ask her.

Again, Bergman is a master of understatement. She says that Capa explicitly told her that he could not marry her. He could not tie himself down. If he had the chance to cover a story in, say, Korea in the future, if he were married and had a child, he wouldn't be able to go and he simply could not tolerate that. His job, his freedom, were everything to him. He was simply not the kind of man who married. However, Bergman realized that she could not just live with a lover. She needed to marry the man she loved, so nothing could be done. Capa left and came back, left again, came back again, and she finally understood that their relationship would never change.[19]

This has the ring of authenticity. When Gellhorn's Bara comes back to Helen Richards after a year away, she is mad with love and jealousy and makes a terrible scene:

"'But I love you,' she shouted, trying to make the lump recognize what was at stake here.

"'Good, *Schatzi*.'

"'Do you love me?' He must understand a few simple words, the way other people did.

"'Very much.'

"And the others too, she realized, with lightning jealousy. He loved women very much. In any spare moment, in any convenient place, he would take time to glimmer at the nearest attractive girl, with that brown-eyed tender charm; he would make love deliciously and leave, forgetful, grateful, loving them all and free as the air. His mind was on something else, his photographs, the state of the world, what happened to other people, not the women he slept with. She felt helpless, because she did love him and could not stop. He told no lies, he made no promises. There was no way to attach him to her."[20]

It is obvious from Bergman's autobiography that the affair with Capa sharpened her sense of alienation from her husband and her career. While making *Joan of Lorraine* and *Under Capricorn*, Bergman saw even less of her husband, and during this time she became even more alienated from Hollywood and bored with home: she felt as if she had stopped growing and was searching for something she could not articulate. She wanted to travel, but after the war there were no USO tours. She wanted to meet new people, other artists who shared her need to express herself and to "live to the utmost."

She told Bill Davidson a decade after that period: "In 1947, I had everything that a woman could expect in life. I was a big star, I had a lovely daughter and a nice husband. We didn't love each other any more, but many marriages are like this and they endure. I had a beautiful house and, of course, a swimming pool. I remember one day sitting at the pool, and suddenly the tears were streaming down my cheeks. Why was I so unhappy? I had success. I had security. But it wasn't enough. I was exploding inside."[21]

Bergman was unhappy, but in all of her recollections, she is not forthright about all of the sources of her despair. She confesses to only one affair, with Robert Capa, but we now know she had two other affairs during this period, one with Larry Adler, which also seems to have begun during the USO tour when she met Capa, and one with Victor Fleming during the preparation for and the filming of *Joan of Arc*. It is not clear where the affairs with Adler and Fleming fit into her affair with Capa. The affair with Adler may have continued in fits and starts all during the time she was involved with Capa. The affair with Fleming may or may not have begun after the affair with Capa was over.

All we know about the affair with Adler is from his point of view, what he mentions in his memoirs and what he told Bergman's biographers. Adler's version of events often seems to conflict with Bergman's. Adler, a pianist, harmonica player, comedian, and nightclub entertainer, was an amiable man who often could not stop talking about himself and sharing his opinions. Adler's recollections are fragmentary and vague about times and places. Adler remembers that he and Jack Benny and Martha Tilton were in Augsburg, Germany, for the USO sometime during June of 1945, waiting for a "name" performer, a well-known actress, to join the group. They didn't know who it would be. One night in a private home Adler was playing the piano when a woman came in and sat down to listen to him play. The woman was Bergman.[22]

Adler implies that the affair with Bergman started almost immediately and that when Capa joined the troupe in Bavaria, he and Bergman and Capa often saw the sights together. In fact, one of Adler's favorite stories was that he was with Bergman and Capa when Capa took the picture of Bergman in the bathtub in a bombed out section of Berlin. In Adler's version of the story, he and Bergman asked Capa for the pictures and Capa said that the negatives hadn't turned out, and anyway, he hated taking pictures of his friends.[23] Adler's story is a tale of three people doing Europe together, and since, according to Adler, Bergman was already his lover by the time of the bathtub incident, the story takes on a certain poignance: Adler would soon have to share Bergman with Capa in Paris.

Adler says that he and Capa accompanied Bergman to Paris, where they did the town as if they were the Three Musketeers. Then one evening the three of them were in a nightclub at Montparnasse, and Bergman asked Adler to leave. The next morning she came to his room and apologized. She admitted that she had treated him badly. After that, Adler's feelings for Bergman changed, but then Capa disappeared and he had the opportunity to stay with her in Paris. In Adler's mind, he was still Bergman's major interest.[24]

Adler asserts that his affair with Bergman continued after they returned to the states, even though he was married and had children, and that it was sufficiently intense that they considered marriage. In his memoirs, Adler says that Bergman suggested they go off together somewhere, perhaps to Honolulu, but although Adler seriously considered it, he was worried that his wife Eileen might find out and was talked out of it by his psychoanalyst. Adler often felt sorry that he hadn't married Bergman, but he "couldn't face being Mr. Ingrid Bergman" and he didn't have the courage to end his own marriage. Adler expressed similar regrets to Spoto. Adler says the affair continued "at a diminished pace," until he left for Europe in 1949.[25]

Since Bergman never acknowledged the affair with Adler, we will probably never know much more about their relationship, what she saw in him, how serious she was about him. But the affair with Adler does seriously compromise Bergman's version of her intense relationship with Capa, the love of her life, and makes it even more fascinating. Capa may have been the love of her life, but perhaps not enough of a love to keep her from having an affair with another man.

Indeed, there is a sense of Rashomon about this period in Bergman's life, a sense of conflicting chronologies, conflicting motives, conflicting stories. It is not certain how badly Bergman's marriage was deteriorating over the period. It is not certain when Bergman's affairs began and ended and whether they were simultaneous or consecutive. It is not certain why or under what particular circumstances Bergman took up with each of her lovers, whether she consciously juggled both at the same time or fled to the other man when the relationship with one of them became difficult. Conflicting stories of certain events make it difficult to establish exactly what happened, to say nothing of what those events mean.

This *Rashomon* sense of ambiguity applies especially to the Bergman-Lindstrom marriage. Bergman claims that she was so upset with her marriage that she asked Lindstrom for a divorce, perhaps in October of 1946, before she moved to New York for the opening of *Joan of Lorraine*. Because the autobiography is written in fragments of associated memories and lacks a clear chronology, Bergman presents this episode before she brings up the topic of Capa at all and describes it as the result of her relentless bickering with Lindstrom over money and Lindstrom's constant criticism of her. In Bergman's telling, she first asked Lindstrom for a divorce because she found his criticism and attempts to control her so intimidating they were frightening: "It was crazy to be married to the only person I was afraid of." To Bergman, the talk about divorce had no relation whatsoever to the fact that she was in love with another man and may have been continuing an affair with a third. Lindstrom denied that he and Bergman ever discussed divorce this early or that she had anything to be afraid of. An additional complication is that, according to Steele, Bergman never told him about this early request for a divorce until twelve years after it happened when he was writing his memoir of Bergman.[26]

Bergman says that Capa continued to write her from overseas during the run of *Joan*—she quotes from his letters—and that he came back to New York to renew their relationship during December and January. Spoto and Steele add touching details: Capa sent Bergman a white rose when the play opened on November 18, 1946; Capa attended a performance in Washington, D.C. without telling Bergman he was coming, and his presence in the front row inspired Bergman. In her performance the following night, Bergman seemed to Steele to be unfocused, just walking through the part. When he asked her in the dressing room afterwards, how she was feeling, she seemed tired and touchy. She replied that she didn't care how she had performed that night. For a reason that she would not disclose, she had given everything she had the night before.[27]

It was probably inevitable that Lindstrom would learn about Bergman's relationships with Capa and Adler. In *My Story*, Burgess adopts Bergman's understated tone about how Lindstrom learned about Capa: in 1947 Capa joined Lindstrom and Bergman on a short skiing holiday in Utah. Lindstrom saw that Ingrid and Capa laughed and drank very comfortably together and quickly inferred that they were more than friends. When Lindstrom confronted Bergman with the accusation, she did not deny it.[28]

Lindstrom accused. Bergman did not deny the accusation. That is all Bergman says about her confrontation with Lindstrom that winter. But what precipitated the confrontation and what happened between them may have been much more dramatic and a turning point of some sort. And of all the events of this tumultuous time in Bergman's life, these events are the most like Rashomon. Spoto says that there are at least eight different versions of the time and place and what occurred between Lindstrom and Capa. In Spoto's best judgment, the most probable scenario occurred at Sun Valley where Lindstrom and Capa were coincidentally on holiday. On the slopes together, Capa gave Lindstrom some unsolicited advice about how to improve his skiing, and Lindstrom refused to consider it. Ignoring Lindstrom's cold response, Capa in his blunt way continued to give advice, this time about Bergman. Not only Lindstrom needed a vacation, Capa said; Bergman did, too. When Capa had seen her New York, she seemed pale and weary.

Lindstrom quickly grasped the import of Capa's remark and called Bergman in New York that night. Bergman admitted the affair, and Lindstrom demanded a divorce. But Bergman tried to calm Lindstrom down and put off any further talk of divorce because, to Spoto, "the affair [with Capa] was history. Ingrid was also unwilling to lose both lover and husband and so every shred of emotional security — apart from the risk to her career (since Petter would certainly claim adultery as grounds for his divorce)."[29]

Leamer offers a version of the story of Capa giving Lindstrom advice on how to ski, but he places the event a year later, after the filming of *Joan of Arc*. Leamer's source is Lindstrom, who claimed that he learned about Bergman's affairs with Capa and Adler, not from an indiscreet remark by Capa but from a direct confession from both men. According to Lindstrom, Capa and Adler, who had previously only come to the house in Benedict Canyon separately, showed up together to produce an extraordinary scene. Each of the men confessed to Lindstrom separately that he was having an affair with Bergman and complained about the competition from the other lover. Both men asked Lindstrom to intercede with Bergman on their behalf. In effect, both Capa and Adler seemed to assume that Lindstrom knew about the affairs and approved of them, that Lindstrom and Bergman had "a kind of marriage where that sort of thing was acceptable." When Bergman admitted the affairs, Lindstrom says that *he* told her that he was going to get a divorce and that she should get the hell out of his house. Bergman began to cry and in Lindstrom's words "put on a show," claiming that Lindstrom was still the only man she really loved. Bergman continued the "show" for the next few weeks, so Lindstrom finally believed her and gave up thinking about a divorce.

This was Lindstrom's story from much later, in the early 1980s, when he was interviewed by Leamer. It is impossible to know how much of his story is authentic, whether it is based in truth, whether it is an unconscious creation of how it felt to be betrayed that is not literally true, or whether it is a conscious attempt to rewrite history in order to settle an old score with his former wife. To his credit, Leamer recognizes the difficulties in accepting Lindstrom's version at face value. He asked Larry Adler about Lindstrom's story, and Adler adamantly denied that he ever talked to Lindstrom about Capa, that he "would not have betrayed in any way." Adler offered as supporting evidence, as only the loquacious Adler could, that he left the country in 1949, when the blacklist was beginning, rather than betray his political friends.[30]

In *My Story*, Bergman never mentions Capa again until she learns of his death in 1954. She wrote Ruth Roberts at that time to thank her for sending newspaper and magazine clippings of Capa's obituary and stories about his death. She wrote Roberts that it felt "strange and terrible" that Capa was gone, especially when she saw in a few papers that the news about Capa's death was followed a few pages later with reports of her own appearance in *Joan at the Stake*.[31]

But she did talk to others about her emotional state in the late '40s. In a thirty-page statement, which she gave to her lawyer Monroe MacDonald to be used in her divorce and custody case with Lindstrom, she discussed her gradual separation from Lindstrom, their separate and incredibly busy lives, and her shyness with other men, which she gradually began to overcome on her USO tours. She even admitted that Lindstrom knew she appreciated being with other men but did not mind very much because he knew that these men were "fleeting enthusiasms." It was this freedom that caused Bergman some ambivalence. While she conceded that Lindstrom gave her a great deal of freedom, in her own mind she was always, in her words "free *away* from him and not *with* him."[32]

There is one other major complication to Bergman's story about Capa's being the love of her life. When Bergman made *Joan of Arc*, she renewed her earlier relationship with Victor Fleming. According to Fleming's biographer Michael Sragow, Fleming had always had a soft spot in his heart for Bergman, but they had not had an affair during the filming of *Dr. Jekyll and Mr. Hyde*. Now, thrust back into contact with Bergman over negotiations for a film version of *Joan of Lorraine*, Fleming's old passion reemerged. Back in California after the first round of negotiations in New York, Fleming wrote to Bergman, enclosing a note he had written on the train ride home. Fleming proclaimed this love for Bergman in no uncertain terms: the note was the occasion, he said, for him to tell her "boldly like a lover," to "cry across the miles," how he felt, and what he felt was total love, absolute devotion. His memories of Bergman flooded through his mind "like waves across the sand."[33]

The affair began in earnest when Fleming returned to New York to supervise work on the script with Maxwell Anderson and other aspects of production. Fleming changed hotels, from the Waldorf to Hampshire House, so that he could be in the same building with Bergman, although his room was eight floors above hers. It was at the Hampshire House that Lindstrom first got an indication of the relationship. He had flown in without telling anyone and was sitting in the lobby of the Hampshire House, when Fleming and Bergman walked in very late: they had gone to 21 after Bergman's performance. Lindstrom heard Bergman say to Fleming, "Let me come up for a little while. I don't feel a bit sleepy." The next morning Fleming woke up Joe Steele very early to angrily complain that Steele had not warned them of Lindstrom's arrival. Lindstrom had called Bergman's room, and when she had not answered, he had called Fleming's room and asked to talk to his wife. Fleming found the episode "damn embarrassing, that's what it was."[34]

On the way back to Los Angeles, again by train, Fleming called Bergman during his change of trains in Chicago and on route wrote Bergman another letter. This one he addressed to "Dear and Darling Angel," and he expresses his deep numbness, hurt, and torment at having left her. Then this: "Time stopped when I got aboard the train. It became dark and in the darkness I was lost.... Someone met me at the train. I'm very much afraid she found me crying. A hundred years old and crying over a girl. I said, 'There's no fool like an old fool.'" A month later, Fleming wrote Bergman another letter, this one ostensibly about problems with the script for the *Joan of Arc*, but Fleming couldn't help but end this way: "Angel — Angel — why didn't I get a chain three thousand miles long with a good winding device on the end. Better quit now before I start telling you I love you — telling you Angel I love you — yes — yes — it's ME."[35]

Burgess quotes the letters out of chronology but only comments that Bergman never objected to Fleming's proclamations of love. For Bergman, people falling in love was "all part of the flood of creation."[36]

When Bergman herself describes Fleming, she is studiously neutral, admitting only that she loved to watch him on the set because he was so poised, warm and outgoing, and so helpful to her as an actress. And then she allows Burgess to wrap up the tantalizing fragments of Fleming's letters with the news that Fleming died of a heart attack a few weeks after the premiere of *Joan*. Sitting in a chair at home, he suddenly slumped forward. The family rushed him to the emergency room but he was dead before they arrived.

Bergman attended Fleming's funeral. In discussing Fleming in *My Story*, she carefully distinguishes between being "in love" and "loving." She had been "in love" with Capa, and she had "loved" Fleming, much as she had loved other friends. Still, Fleming's death caused her considerable grief. She wondered if she were in some sense at least partially responsible for his death. She had known for some time that she had been "stepping out of line." After Fleming's death, she decided to reevaluate her relationship with Capa and "probably end it."[37] Of course, this seems to imply that Bergman was still involved with Capa during her fling with Fleming.

Bergman's relationship with Fleming during the filming of *Jekyll and Hyde* may have been only an infatuation; this time sex was definitely involved. Lindstrom told Spoto that he caught Bergman with Fleming a second time during the filming of *Joan of Arc* in California. Interestingly, Spoto trusts this story, even though he is often suspicious of Lindstrom's point of view. In this new version of the cuckolded husband, Bergman, as she often did, told Lindstrom that she was going to spend the night at Ruth Roberts' apartment, going over her lines for the next day's shooting. This time, Lindstrom arrived at the apartment late, looking for his wife. Roberts tried to put him off by saying Bergman was working in a locked room, but Lindstrom brushed her aside and searched the apartment. Bergman was not there. Ruth was forced to confess that Bergman had left for the night with another man. In a letter to Pia, Lindstrom also recounted that a few days after this incident, Fleming's wife Lu confronted him about the affair and cried, "You must help me! My husband has got to stop this relationship." Lu had learned about the affair when a Cartier gold necklace that Fleming had ordered for Bergman was delivered to his home by mistake. The affair so traumatized Fleming's marriage that he had a detailed separation agreement written up, indicating the amounts for alimony and distribution of property, as well as the creation of a $100,000 trust fund for Lu, if she did not marry again. The couple never signed the agreement and eventually reconciled.[38]

After discovering Bergman with Fleming a second time, Lindstrom again demanded that she give him a divorce and she again pleaded her case and promised to change her life. This time, as proof of her sincerity, Bergman suggested that they have another child as soon as *Under Capricorn* was finished in the summer of 1948. Bergman told the *New York Journal-American* that her plans for the baby included rebuilding the house so that her life would be "filled and fulfilled."[39]

Here chronology is important in determining Bergman's sincerity about her intense love of Capa, and again it is impossible to ascertain just where Bergman stood with the men in her life during her scene with Lindstrom. Leamer believes, citing no explicit evidence that Bergman met Capa for weekends in London and Paris during the shooting of *Under Capricorn* in the summer of 1948. According to Philip Whelan, Capa's biographer, Capa and Bergman parted in the winter of 1947. Adler says that his affair with Bergman continued at a diminished pace until he left for Europe in 1949.[40] Bergman's letters to Capa indicate that their affair was breaking up in the spring of 1947, but Bergman may have still been seeing Adler and Capa occasionally, when she promised to change her life and have a second child with Lindstrom.

Whatever we may conclude about Bergman's emotional state in the late '40s, it is clear that of the three lovers, Capa meant the most to her. And for complex reasons, she not only acknowledges that she was "in love with" him; she also claims that he was a major influence on her life. What made Capa Bergman's true love was that he was artistic and romantic, even reckless, in many ways similar to her father, Justus. Indeed, to several of Bergman's and Capa's biographers, Capa *looked* like Justus Bergman. Whether we see the physical resemblance or not, clearly Capa was everything Bergman was not; he did not have a family to hold him down; he could do what he wanted when he wanted to. Capa lived his life transparently, without pretense. He was who he seemed to be, and except for his affair with Bergman, he lived his life in the open for all to see. And perhaps even more appealingly, Capa was dedicated to the art of his profession and could talk about it to Bergman as an intellectual. It was Capa who created his life as if it were a work of art. Bergman could not have Capa, but under his influence she decided that she could live like him: she could live more freely and she could live for her art.

Burgess acknowledges that Capa greatly influenced Bergman and makes the connection between Capa and Rossellini. He notes that Bergman was increasingly bothered that most Hollywood movies were not true to life, and when she first saw Rossellini's films, she knew that she wanted to help recreate that kind of raw realism.[41] It may have been Capa who recommended Rossellini's *Open City* to her.

As the affair with Capa was dying, Bergman wrote to Ruth Roberts: "I know the Hungarian influence; I'll always be grateful for it." To Roberts, Bergman uses novelistic detail to suggest her grief at losing Capa. At their last meeting, she and Capa drank their last bottles of champagne together. Bergman feels as if she has torn a piece out of her life and hopes that the "operation" will be clean so that she and Capa can go on living. She ends with the exclamation, "What an Easter!"[42] In the mixed-up chronology of *My Story*, this letter is inserted as the run of *Joan of Lorraine* is winding down, so the Easter referred to may be in 1947, which suggests that the affair with Capa may have indeed been over before the affair with Fleming.

The Hungarian influence would soon show its power when Bergman took up with Rossellini. Living under the shelter of the Selznick publicity campaign and the discretion of the Hollywood media, Bergman had been as careful as possible in her previous involvements. But after her affair with Capa, she began to long for a more meaningful professional life and a simpler, more committed personal life. To accomplish all this, she was ready to risk everything.

Reflecting long afterward on her affair with Rossellini, Bergman provides a number of explanations of when the affair with Rossellini began. In response to Joe Steele's direct question about when the affair with Rossellini began, Bergman answered, as she usually did, with studious vagueness. At first she said that it was very difficult to say, then she suggested that the romance may have begun after the war, when she had no more USO trips to take her mind off her problems and her boredom with both Hollywood and her marriage.[43] The year the war was over was the year she met Capa.

In *My Story*, Bergman offers two versions of when she became attracted to Rossellini. At first she says that she fell in love with Rossellini when she saw *Open City*. From that time on, she says, she could not get him out of her mind. But much later in the memoir, she also claims that she became seriously fascinated with Rossellini during their first meeting in Paris on August 28, 1948.[44]

Bergman claims that she saw *Open City* in Hollywood in the spring of 1948 with Lindstrom, but all the evidence suggests that she really saw the film in New York in the spring of 1946 with Joe Steele.[45] Of course, this reinforces Bergman's larger narrative that there was no connection between Capa and Rossellini, that there had been a clean break with Capa and time for those emotional wounds to heal before she began her involvement with Rossellini.

Bergman saw Rossellini's next film, *Paisan*, in March of 1948. Bergman wrote her notorious letter to Rossellini the following month, telling him that she had enjoyed both *Open City* and *Paisan* very much, and offering her services if he needed a Swedish actress who could speak English and German fluently, French less well, and only two words in Italian: "*Ti amo*." According to Joe Steele, in using "ti amo," "I love you," Bergman was not flirting. These were quite literally the only two words she knew in Italian. Bergman had learned them from the dialogue in *Arch of Triumph*. They are the last two lines of the film.[46]

Irene Selznick claims that she gave Bergman the idea of writing letters not only to Rossellini but to a number of directors who might help Bergman break out of her slump. Late in 1948 Bergman's films were not doing well and Bergman was, in Selznick's words, "at loose ends, without a producer and unhappy about her work." Bergman told Selznick that she would be willing to take a considerable cut in pay in order to work with any of five great directors. She named them: William Wyler, Billy Wilder, George Stevens, Roberto Rossellini, and John Huston. Bergman wondered how to proceed. Selznick shrugged. It was simple: just write each director a letter, asking him to keep her in mind if a part right for her came along. Bergman seemed dubious, so Selznick turned persuasive: she told Bergman that she was a major star and a charming woman to boot, and any of the men she had named would be amazed, even astonished, to receive a handwritten note from Ingrid Bergman, asking for a role in one of his films. Bergman did not look convinced.

Several months later, Bergman told Selznick that she had had a marvelous letter from Rossellini. Selznick asked if Bergman had heard from any of the other directors on the list. Bergman replied, "Of course not. I only wrote to Rossellini."[47]

Perhaps the most compelling issue in understanding Bergman at this point in her life is whether she intended to leave her family for good when she flew off to Rome to join Rossellini. All her life Bergman maintained, even as she was asserting that she had fallen in love with Rossellini much earlier, that the relationship only became a grand passion after she arrived in Rome. As she put it in the autobiography, "Probably, subconsciously," she recognized that Rossellini was a way for her to escape from her marriage and from Hollywood, but she wasn't conscious of these thoughts at the time. She asserts that if she had announced to people that she was thinking of making a movie in Italy, she would have been surprised if they were taken aback. But of course this is self-serving, an assertion that she was not the wanton destroyer of her family she saw portrayed in the media.

The language Bergman uses to describe her various meetings with Rossellini suggest that she was more emotionally invested in him than she could admit, perhaps even to herself. At their first meeting in Paris at the Hotel George V, Bergman describes Rossellini as fascinating because he was so different from the smooth movie moguls in Hollywood. She didn't think that Rossellini was handsome, but he was extremely intelligent and had a very expressive face. And of course, he was a talker. The way he spoke was completely different from anyone else she had ever known.[48]

Bergman's meeting with Rossellini was successful, but what she may not have known is that from the moment he received the letter from Bergman, Rossellini had been in contact with a number of Hollywood producers, including Selznick, to see if he could leverage his contact with Bergman into backing for his next picture, whether it included Bergman or not. When Rossellini ran into difficulties, he convinced willing Italian producer Ilya Lopert to finance a film with Bergman and pay for his trip to the United States. In fact, Lopert accompanied Rossellini to America.[49]

In January of 1949, Rossellini arrived in New York to receive the New York Film Critics Award for *Open City* as the best foreign film of the previous year. Then he went to California to negotiate with Bergman about the nature of their film together and perhaps find additional financing. Rossellini kept Bergman informed of his travels. In hindsight, even their brief telegrams to each other sound like flirting. Telegraphed Rossellini in New York: "I just arrive friendly." Replied Bergman in Benedict Canyon: "Waiting for you in the Wild West."[50]

Once he was on the West coast, Rossellini stayed at first with Lopert at the posh Beverly Hills Hotel and then at the house of director Anatole Litvak, but since back in London the Lindstroms had offered to put Rossellini up in Benedict Canyon, he eventually moved into their guest house, perhaps because he had run out of money or because he had alienated Lopert, his patron and ostensible producer, by actively seeking Hollywood financing. And during his entire stay in Hollywood, Rossellini went everywhere with Bergman: on drives to the Pacific Ocean; to the mountains; to lunches at the Farmer's Market and Don the Beachcomers; to dinners, meetings, parties, and script conferences. For long periods of time, both during the day and night, they were alone together.[51]

There is one item of special significance in Bergman's diary from this period: on Tuesday, February 4, Bergman recorded that builders started the long-planned remodeling of Lindstroms' house, the project that was to add a room for the new baby the couple had negotiated two years before. Burgess adds this detail: months later, on her way to Rome, Bergman confessed to Kay Brown that when she heard a builder on the roof pounding with a hammer, it felt like the builder was pounding a nail into her skull.[52]

Other details suggest how badly Bergman was smitten by Rossellini. Lindstrom and house guest Dr. Peter Veger recall that for Rossellini's arrival at the house in Benedict Canyon, Bergman had arranged for a thirty-foot runner of red carpet to be laid at the entrance. Bergman admitted in an interview a decade later that she was "uncontrollably nervous." When Rossellini finally arrived, she had difficulty talking, and her hands shook so violently that the flame of a match she used to light a cigarette went out before the cigarette was lit.[53]

Always relying on others for money, Rossellini got "loans" from friends to shower Bergman with gifts. Actor Rossano Brazzi, who also organized a reception for Rossellini at the hotel, loaned him money so that he could buy Bergman a diamond. Screenwriter Max Colpet lent him money to buy her flowers. And Bergman herself tells the story of how Rossellini bought Pia a toy cow that Lindstrom had refused to buy her. To do so, Rossellini used the money that Lindstrom had loaned him.[54]

Still, Rossellini, with Bergman's support, succeeded in raising money for their film together. They managed to convince Howard Hughes, who had just formed a new studio, RKO, to finance the production that would eventually be called *Stromboli*. Bergman would receive the same basic salary she had earned in her last two films — $175,000 — and forty percent of the net profits. Rossellini would receive a salary and twenty percent of the profits.[55]

Because the couple were seen so often together around town, they quickly became an "item" in Hollywood. Many Hollywood insiders assumed that there was something more than friendship between Bergman and Rossellini. Hedy Lamarr remembers that as the party at Samuel Goldwyn's progressed, Bergman and Rossellini were off in a corner and she was "twisting a button on his brocade vest and looking into his eyes with a tiny, inviting smile. She was beautiful and it was clear her charm was being appreciated. When I saw Ingrid and Roberto, hand in hand, stroll over to Petter, who was still standing alone trying to look happy, I was drawn close, to hear what would be said. A dramatic moment was definitely coming."

What Lamarr heard was Bergman ask Lindstrom "very coolly" for the key to the house because, Bergman said, "Mr. Rossellini is going to take me home." Lamarr thought that Lindstrom was very embarrassed, but he silently got out his key chain, opened it, slid off a key, and without a word handed it over. Bergman took the key and walked off with Rossellini without so much as a thank you.[56]

In the closed world of movie sets, Bergman had not often disguised her intense interest in her male co-stars, but with her lovers Adler, Capa, and Fleming, she was the soul of discretion. Her behavior with Rossellini was new. She was now for the first time willing to put her reputation at risk. She did not mind being seen openly with Rossellini. Perhaps she thought that their professional relationship would provide sufficient explanation for her enthusiasm and affection.

Rossellini left for Italy on February 28, and the Lindstroms went to Aspen for a skiing holiday. "But," Burgess adds portentously, "the catalytic process had begun": Bergman's dedication to her family was "now peeling away." Bergman had known for some time that she was looking for the right man to come along and sweep her off her feet. It took only a month for Rossellini to do that. He was a commanding presence. Like Capa, he did not try to justify himself; he simply did what he wanted to do. He did not think about others, her husband or his mistress, Anna Magnani. He simply asked her to "come away" with him.

What is interesting is that Bergman did not keep her enthusiasm for Rossellini or her desire simply to be with him a secret from Lindstrom. In Aspen, she begged him to let her leave for Rome early. When he protested that the picture would not start for weeks, Bergman claimed that she needed the extra time to learn Italian and to see something of Rome. But deep inside, the real reason she wanted to go early was that she longed to sit at Rossellini's feet and listen to him talk, not only what he said but how he said it. She even told Lindstrom about the plans she and Rossellini had to tour southern Italy before the start of filming. Of course, Lindstrom said that such a trip was improper and out of the question.[57]

Bergman's letter of March 4, five days after Rossellini left California, confirms her state of mind. It is the love letter of an infatuated teenager, who is so besotted that she can only think of grand romantic cataclysmic events that will keep her from the object of her adoration. "Thank God!" she begins: Rossellini's telegram has just arrived. She had expected the telegram the day before, and she was so distraught that she had begun to browse through the newspapers looking for a story about Rossellini's having a terrible accident. She has been passing the time skiing and is especially careful because she wants to join Rossellini all in one piece. Above all, she wants to leave as soon as she can.

The Lindstroms left Aspen on March 7 and arrived back in Beverly Hills on March 9. Two days later Bergman took the train to New York. She cabled Rossellini before she left, and even Burgess admits it is ecstatic. Bergman claims that she "CAN'T HEAR, CAN'T UNDERSTAND, CAN'T SPEAK" until she arrives at the Hampshire House hotel in New York, where she can contact Rossellini again.[58]

Perhaps because Bergman had not arrived yet on March 12, Rossellini constantly called the Hampshire House. When Bergman arrived and learned about all of his phone calls, she responded with an angry and ironic letter, demanding that Rossellini be more discreet. Yes, of course, she appreciates his attention, his reveling in his freedom, but still, she says, telephoning ten times a day is stupid. The hotel has "close contact" with reporters, and where is her freedom if she has to be home by 2:00 every night to wait for his calls? Their indiscretion has already led to stories in the press about her following Rossellini to New York, about her marriage being over and about how from now on she will only be making films in Italy. She is sad she left so quickly that she did not have time to say goodbye to many friends, and Lindstrom was so silent and alone at the airport, she now realizes how selfish she is being. She can do nothing to assuage her sense of isolation but go to the theater and wait, wait for the date of her flight to Rome. When friends ask her about the gossip, she is evasive and goes back to her room to look at Rossellini's picture. She is looking at his picture as she writes the letter.[59]

It is difficult to interpret this letter. Bergman rarely resorts to irony, but the letter seems to have an ironic edge. She seems to be complaining about the very things she values Rossellini for: his attentiveness and his flouting of convention that are now actually limiting her freedom. And surely she must have been self-aware enough to realize that the rumors she is hearing could easily be inferred from her behavior. Only at the end of the letter does she become obviously sincere: she feels guilty at leaving Lindstrom at the airport and for being so selfish. But now all Bergman can do is wait: wait in her room for Rossellini's calls, wait while staring at his picture, and wait for the day of her flight.

Perhaps her ambivalence now was fueled by her sense that Rossellini's charm had a dark side. Later in their life together, Rossellini insisted that he had told Lindstrom that he was in love with Bergman. But, Bergman admits, Rossellini's English was so poor that even if he had told Lindstrom that he loved her, Lindstrom probably wouldn't have understood him. She realized later that Rossellini was confident that he could "win her over" once she was in Italy. Rossellini, she says ominously, "always got what he wanted" and "at that time he wanted me."[60]

Indeed, Rossellini had not tried to hide his intention to seduce Bergman. He told Lina Rossellini, his sister-in-law, his brother Renzo's wife, before he left for America that he would be bringing Bergman back with him. Ilya Lopert, the producer who brought Rossellini to America and felt betrayed when Rossellini abandoned him, told Lindstrom that Rossellini boasted before they arrived in California that he would have Bergman "in bed within two weeks."[61]

Perhaps the knowledge of Rossellini's motives fought with Bergman's sense that they were kindred spirits, soul mates, that Rossellini was a reflection of her true self. Bergman wrote a letter to Anna-Britta Karaste, Lindstrom's sister, which she translated orally from Swedish for Joe Steele and he "remembered" word-for-word later. In the letter Bergman asserts that despite their different backgrounds, she sees in Rossellini "a reflection of [her] true self, " the self she had been seeking for a long time.

Spoto reproduces an earlier portion of this letter that ends in a different translation of what Steele remembers: "Petter and I have grown apart. He took me as a little girl and formed me, taught me everything. But now I want to grow, and Petter doesn't want to fly where I want to fly. [par] You see, I am a migratory bird ... in [Rossellini] I found another migratory bird. He grew up like a wildcat, and is never completely satisfied with anything. What is said about his women is no exaggeration, either. But now he has met someone who he says understands him. And with him I have the world I wanted to see..."[62]

Relevant to Bergman's motives in flying off to Italy are what she took with her. Bergman says that she took hardly any luggage and three hundred dollars in traveler's checks. Art Cohn, an American writer who was with Rossellini when Bergman arrived in Rome, told the *Los Angeles Daily News* that Bergman arrived in Italy with "barely a change of clothes." She gave no indication that she had any money at the time.

But Lindstrom, filtered through Leamer's eloquence, claims something else: "Gone were two fur coats, two fur jackets, many of her dresses, and all the jewelry that she kept in the house. Gone were her clipping books, personal letters, and photo albums." But as Lindstrom also told the *Los Angeles Times*, "The last thing she did before leaving was to select the wallpaper for the new nursery. We had made plans for a second child."[63]

The evening before she left for Italy, Bergman went out with Irene Selznick. They ended the evening at Selznick's apartment, talking and drinking. Bergman talked intensely and would not stop. She was in Selznick's words "not so much exhilarated as fevered. Her spirits were higher than a couple of highballs would account for."[64] The evening dragged on, but Selznick became tired of listening. She hinted that she wanted to go to bed. Bergman did not take the hint, so Irene simply got up and went into her bedroom and changed into her nightgown. When she came out, Bergman still did not take the hint, so Selznick announced that she was going to bed and left Bergman alone.

But Bergman followed her into the bedroom and commandeered the phone to call Rossellini in Rome. Irene Selznick didn't know what to do, so she turned away on the bed and tried not to listen. Ever the mistress of discretion, Selznick never revealed how much of that conversation she overheard. When Bergman hung up, she announced that she did not want to be alone and go back to her hotel. She noted Selznick's large bed and asked if she could sleep right there. Selznick got up and found her a nightgown and a toothbrush and pointed her toward the bathroom. Bergman was so tired, fevered, and distracted that she slipped on the floor of the bedroom and cracked her head on a corner of the air conditioner. She fell heavily and did not move for a moment. Panicked, Selznick leaped to Bergman's aid, wondering if she had killed herself. But then Bergman moved and everything was all right.

The night before she left for Rome, Bergman was "not so much exhilarated as fevered." She may have thought that she was flying off to Rome just to see what would happen, but if she had been honest with herself, she would have known that, for the second time in her life, she was breaking out of a cage and flying high. This time, however, the risks were greater, the risk to her marriage and family, the risk to her career. But under the Hungarian influence she had become willing to risk everything for authenticity, for the chance to live her life for love and art. Her commitment was no longer to her husband and daughter; her commitment was to live on the edge.

Five

The Victim of Scandal

"It took exactly eighty-nine minutes, the running time of *Open City*, to start the tremors that would shatter [Bergman's] popularity and send Ingrid down that slippery slope of public adulation toward what was to become an epic scandal of the twentieth century."
— Alan Burgess, *My Story*

When Bergman arrived in Rome shortly before midnight on March 20, 1949, she was met by Rossellini and a mob of photographers and reporters, all clamoring for the one great shot or quotable phrase from the couple. Rossellini had to push and shove their way through the throng to get to his red Cisitalia sports car and sweep Bergman away to a reception at the Excelsior Hotel.[1] For the next year and a half, Bergman had virtually no peace in public.

Even though Bergman and Rossellini vehemently denied that they were lovers, Rossellini always booked them into the same hotel in adjoining rooms, often with connecting doors. It was inevitable then that their denials were not taken seriously, and the press hounded them for evidence of their affection. Their publicity man on *Stromboli* left the job and wrote stories for the British newspapers, making up dialogue and even sneaking into Bergman's bathroom to count the toothbrushes there.[2]

It did not take long for the photographers to get a damning photograph. In April, *Life* published a picture of the couple climbing up to a castle at Amalfi, their hands clasped together. This was taken as concrete evidence that the couple were having an affair. On April 13, 1949, Cholly Knickerbocker, the Hearst society columnist, broke the story of a rumored Bergman-Rossellini romance in the New York *Journal-American*, and as a result even larger numbers of reporters from around the world headed for Italy. The indiscretion was so blatant and so contradictory of Bergman's previous behavior that Steele, Bergman's former press agent, did not believe it.[3] As a result, the questioning from the press became increasingly aggressive, even hostile: reporters wanted to know when and where Bergman would be seeking a divorce from Lindstrom and Rossellini an annulment from his wife Marcella de Marchis.

Bergman claimed that she received "boatloads" of criticism about the love affair, letters expressing indignation at her behavior, cuttings from newspaper and magazine articles that portrayed her as a wanton woman, and even cartoons that lampooned her as a fallen moral exemplar. For a while she may have received as many as two hundred pieces of mail a day. Reporters and photographers interrupted the couple while they were dining out, hoping to provoke Rossellini, with his quick temper, into saying something provocative or starting a fight so that they could get an interesting picture.[4]

When it became known that Bergman was pregnant, the pressure became fanatical. With reporters and photographers camped outside her doors, Bergman suffered the equivalent of a war-like siege twenty-four hours a day, her house locked and windows shuttered. When she was finally admitted to the Villa Margherita Clinic to have the baby in February of 1950, thirty reporters and photographers representing American papers covered the event, but many of the photographers were Italian freelancers who were more interested in the pay than getting a picture. One agency that hired the freelancers may have spent a quarter of a million lira covering the birth of Bergman's son.[5]

The clinic locked all of the gates into the hospital grounds and severely controlled who could enter and exit. The steel shutters of Bergman's room were closed and locked. When the noise of the press people surrounding the entrances began to affect the patients, especially nursing mothers, the director of the clinic called the riot police. The police arrived with lights flashing and sirens screaming and beat back the reporters and photographers a few feet. Since it was bitterly cold, the news people gathered wood from a nearby park and lit small fires to keep themselves warm. The police joined them in an uneasy peace. Hoping to ingratiate himself into the sympathies of the press, the director allowed five representatives to enter the clinic reception rooms so that they could add local color to their stories. The rooms were carefully monitored but one *Life* photographer managed to get to the second floor. However, he could not get through the locked door of Suite 34, where Bergman was staying.

The siege lasted twelve days. Photographers climbed trees and walked the top of the clinic's walls, while the police tried to pull them off. One photographer did fall and break his arm. Others took rooms in apartment buildings across the street, hoping to get a shot of the soon-to-be mother. The newsmen bribed clinic staff to deliver letters to Bergman, often with emotional appeals: the reporters suggested that their jobs, their chances of promotion, even their marriages were at risk because they could not get a photograph of

Bergman. The most brazen appeal was from a photographer who said he had heard that the baby had been born a monster. If only Bergman would allow him to photograph the baby in her arms, he could prove that the rumor was "a foul lie."

After the birth of Robertino, Rossellini planned an elaborate escape from the clinic. At four o'clock in the morning, without alerting the nurses and staff, the couple suddenly left their room and raced down the stairs, baby Robertino in Bergman's arms. A number of nurses tried to stop them, yelling, "You can't go! You can't go!" but Bergman and Rossellini brushed them aside. Rossellini's car was parked at the entrance with a friend in a car behind. The couple jumped into Rossellini's car and sped off down the street, the other car trailing behind them. The assembled press, caught off guard, quickly tried to regroup, found their own transportation, and took off after the escaping vehicles. After something of a high-speed chase through the city, the friend driving behind Bergman and Rossellini suddenly spun to a stop perpendicular to the road, blocking off the on-coming newsmen. Bergman managed to get back to her own home without a single photograph being taken.[6]

All her life, Ingrid Bergman portrayed herself as a victim of the scandal with Rossellini, calling it at one point, an "almost intolerable unhappiness." Indeed, she made being a victim a major part of her life story, an essential part of who she was: a long-suffering but ultimately forgiving person whose treatment by the press during the scandal was incredibly hurtful to her personally. Of course, it must have been. The Bergman-Rossellini romance was widely covered in the press, especially the more sensational newspapers, tabloids, and fan magazines, and there is no doubt that Bergman's behavior was considered disgraceful or offensive by the defenders of the dominant morality in mid-twentieth century America. Bergman herself cites stories in *Life* magazine, the *Los Angeles Examiner*, and various European newspapers, as well as letters condemning her behavior and harassment by the press.[7]

In its February 13, 1950, issue, *Life* magazine noted that the story of Bergman's giving birth to a son not her husband's was "reported on page one by most U.S. and European newspapers." Two months later, in a more reflective and better documented piece, Janet Flanner, under the pen name Genet, in *The New Yorker* claimed that Robertino's birth was "the leading news story in the world. [Bergman] and her infant, an invisible pair, pushed even President Truman and his hydrogen bomb onto the second page of hundreds of American newspapers that evidently were more interested in love."[8]

Both of Bergman's biographers take up her cry of maltreatment and make great claims for the scandal. Leamer characterizes the affair as a "part of contemporary social history" which would help to "define an era in both the

United States and Europe." He calls Bergman a "moral bellwether," a symbol of Hollywood's social and moral betrayal during the McCarthy Era. Spoto asserts that the scandal was an indication of "the paranoia that gripped postwar America" and the smugness with which the country tried to preserve "everything 'pure' about American values and American success."[9]

Clearly, Bergman herself and her biographers have a vested interest in promoting the vehemence of the outcry against Bergman and the prominence and significance of the Bergman-Rossellini romance. Beginning a book with such a scandal is a great "hook": there is nothing like a story of true love surviving the onslaught of social condemnation to get readers to want more. But if interpreting a scandal, like the writing of biography or indeed like all of history, is the marshalling of evidence to document particular points of view, to argue for particular interpretations of events, and to negotiate their significance, there are reasons to wonder why the scandal affected Bergman so deeply and whether it can bear the weight of significance that she and her biographers attach to it.

In one sense, of course, it is easy to understand why Bergman was so upset: it cannot have been pleasant to be called a whore and a disgrace to womanhood. Bergman was emphatic that reports in the media were primarily hurtful and that the reports from America caused her particular pain. After the birth of the baby, she and Rossellini endured, she says, "everywhere — especially in America — these waves of hatred." And she told Bill Davidson in 1956, "Only one columnist — Leonard Lyons — was kind to me during my troubles. He wrote that he and Ernest Hemingway toasted me and my son, Robertino, when he was born. The others all denounced me."[10]

Much of the hurtful correspondence Bergman received during the affair came from her film producers before the news that she was pregnant. They urged her, often in personal terms, to deny the affair so that it would not affect the box office for the movie she was making with Rossellini and her three previous films. *Arch of Triumph* and *Joan of Arc* were still in theaters around the world, and *Under Capricorn* was released in the middle of the affair, the fall of 1949. Walter Wanger, the producer of *Joan of Arc*, cabled, demanding that Bergman immediately deny the affair because she was jeopardizing not only his own personal investment in the film but the future of his family. Joseph Breen, vice-president and director of the Production Code Administration of the Motion Picture Association of America, wrote to warn Bergman that the rumors of her affair might so outrage American filmgoers that her box office appeal would be ruined.[11] Clearly, Bergman was given the impression by certain people in the film community that her affair with Rossellini would be financially disastrous because it was a sign of general public condemnation.

When Bergman wrote Ruth Roberts about how awful it was to read her mail, Roberts replied with wise counsel: she told Bergman that it was not good for her to spend so much time going through letters from people she did not know. She added that fans were just like lovers: they fell in love and they fell out of love. The best way to handle the situation would be to treat her fans like characters in a play, putting herself in their place.[12] But this is just what Bergman could not do.

For complex reasons, Bergman glosses over the fact that she had an incredible amount of support from friends, fans, and others for whom sexual behavior was not a litmus test for a person's character. Moreover, much of the more inflammatory condemnations came from fairly predictable sources. Still, Bergman was hurt and angry, and she was especially hurt about criticism from America. The question is why.

It is not that Bergman did not know about much of the support she received. Major figures in the literary and film communities rallied to Bergman's side. Bergman received consoling letters from Irene Selznick and Ernest Hemingway, and a sympathetic letter from Simon Gould, director of the Film Guild. One fan, a songwriter, wrote to tell her that he and millions like him did not condemn her and that he was composing a song for her and Rossellini entitled, "My Sicilian is One in a Million. No wonder I love him so." Bergman saved the letter, but there is no record of whether she ever received the song.[13]

And certainly Bergman should have been aware that her own fan mail was overwhelmingly supportive. Although some were obscene and a few even threatened death, eighty percent of them called Bergman wonderful or courageous or mentioned Christ's warning about casting the first stone. However, she may not have known that other gauges of public opinion indicated that a majority of people were on her side. An examination by *Look* magazine in 1951 of the letters sent to Bergman and a survey conducted by *Photoplay* in 1952 indicate overwhelming support. In the *Photoplay* balloting on whether Bergman should return to the screen after her romance, four out of five said yes. One recent academic study has shown that even a significant number of American columnists and fan magazines rallied to Bergman's cause during her divorce proceedings and blamed Lindstrom for not granting her a divorce, thereby forcing her to act like a loose woman.[14]

Perhaps Bergman never read her fan mail in its entirely but relied on secretaries to give her the gist. Perhaps her friends never sent her clippings of the fan magazines that supported her. Perhaps the rush of reporters following her every move for the months she was pregnant with Robertino and then the twins made her feel beleaguered and resentful, unable to put the insults to her femininity in any kind of perspective. Perhaps the insults themselves, even though they were almost entirely from total strangers, seemed too personal, too close to the bone. Whatever the reason, for the rest of her life Bergman could not put the scandal in perspective. Despite her upbeat personality and philosophy of life, Bergman could not help coming back again and again to the hateful way she had been treated by a minority of the public and the media. And her attitude became the justification for biographers, scholars, and critics to describe the scandal as the turning point in her life — and to ponder its larger significance as defining an era and epitomizing American values after World War II.

Such an interpretation, however, overlooks a great deal about the response to the scandal. For one thing, most of those who loudly protested the scandal, especially Bergman's giving birth to a baby not conceived by her husband, represented primarily religious constituencies. The Roman Catholic Church, the Salvation Army, even the more liberal Norman Vincent Peale and the most liberal and mainstream protestant denominations, represented by the Federal Council of Churches, now the National Council of Churches, participated in the protest. Often, these religious constituencies seem to have protested not just the fact of the affair but that it received so much publicity. Their outrage is often focused on the press reports about *Stromboli* and the publicity surrounding the film that seemed to glorify adultery. As a result, much of the coverage of the scandal after the birth of Robertino is not focused on condemning Bergman per se but on the efforts to ban and boycott *Stromboli*, many of them organized by city Councils of Churches and women's clubs.[15] George Sokolsky, a columnist for the Washington *Times-Herald*, represented this point of view in a column in February of 1950. Sokolsky felt compelled "to quarrel with those who speak of facing the sinner with pity and compassion and giving the impression thereby that religion approves of sin." According to Sokolsky, the problem with the "Bergman business" is that it is public, that Bergman is brazen about her immorality. Then he begins a slide down a slippery slope: "What this means, in simple fact, is that if Ingrid can get away with such brass, why not your daughter?"[16]

Moreover, for all the newspapers and magazines that may have sensationalized the Bergman-Rossellini scandal, there were others of the mainstream press that treated the affair as a straight news story, without moral comment, and did not put the birth of Robertino on the front page. Many also provided subtle support. *The New York Times*, for example, published the story of Bergman's giving birth to her son on the day after the event, February 3, 1950, on the twenty-seventh page of the second section, under the indexed title of "Amusements," and below the fold at that. The major front page story that day was a two-column installment of Winston Churchill's memoir, *The Second World War*.[17]

However, *The Washington Post* did put the birth of Robertino on the front page. The *Post* put the United Press (UP) wire service story in the lower left, below the fold, with a picture of Bergman looking sultry. The headline across the top of the front page was "Stalin Guiltier than Hirohito — Keenan," but the headlined story was less important than the story that received a subhead: Senator Brian McMahan's proposal to outlaw the hydrogen bomb. Balanced opposite the Bergman story below the fold, also with an accompanying picture, was the story of a former football player and current army lieutenant who survived after his car drove over a 45-foot embankment.[18]

Other mainstream publications put the birth of Robertino in some kind of perspective. *Life* magazine, which had followed Bergman like a fan magazine since *For Whom the Bell Tolls*, ran a banner across the bottom of the page containing the news of the baby: "Famous People Who Were Born Out of Wedlock." Below the headline were the pictures of William the Conqueror, Cesare Borgia, Alexander Hamilton, Cosima Wagner, and Ramsay Macdonald, the first Labor prime minister of England.[19]

Newsweek covered Robertino's birth with a great deal of sarcasm about the fuss and a satirical treatment of the press coverage. The *Newsweek* story refers to "the prying press" and the blatantness of the affair as an example of "Hollywood's ever-reliable, ever-eternal triangle in Mediterranean Technicolor," in a country where "the hot sirocco wind from Africa and the fierce sun have long been renowned for melting the supposedly frigid nature of northern women."[20] In short, all indications are that the mainstream media provided a much wider range of response to the Bergman-Rossellini romance than Bergman and her biographers imply. Much of the media treated the romance for what it was: a human interest story comparable to a local football hero surviving a car crash.

In addition, despite the avid concern of Bergman's producers that the scandal would depress the box office receipts for her three previous films, both Senator Johnson and David O. Selznick, Bergman's former producer, assumed that Bergman was still popular enough to keep making pictures. Six days after his initial speech condemning Bergman and Rossellini, Johnson noted in the Congressional Record that if Bergman returned, she would " receive a reception greater than that accorded Charles Lindbergh, General Eisenhower, or the King and Queen of England" because she was such "a notorious attraction." Five months after height of the scandal, Selznick wrote a reflective memo to Jenia Reissar, his London representative, in which he talked about Bergman's career. Selznick's expert opinion was that the scandal had not destroyed Bergman's career and that she could come back if she wanted to and if she had the right vehicle. Selznick thought that in the long term the public would conclude that Bergman had been "persecuted to a ridiculous and untenable extent" and that if Lindstrom had not at first fought the divorce, the scandal would not have come about in the first place.[21] Both Johnson, a politician exploring a possible run for president, and Selznick, one of the most successful producers in Hollywood history, had their fingers on the pulse of America in the middle of the twentieth century. Neither man thought that the epic scandal surrounding Bergman meant the death of her popularity. Moreover, at the height of the scandal, having had Bergman and Rossellini reject his offer for the rights to *Stromboli*, Howard Hughes proposed that Bergman star with Cary Grant in a film version of the Broadway play *O Mistress Mine*. The play had been a hit for Lynn Fontanne and Alfred Lunt. Even though Bergman and Rossellini needed the money — Hughes offered the couple $250,000 — they turned him down. Bergman continued to get offers to do films during her marriage to Rossellini. Walter Wanger and George Cukor sent her scripts. Graham Greene thought she would be good in the film version of his novel *The End of the Affair*.[22]

In her autobiography and in later interviews Bergman also cites Johnson's speech on the floor of the Senate has being particularly hurtful. However, she could not have heard about the event on the day it occurred. She obviously learned about the speech much later and relied on press reports about what Johnson had said. Joe Steele says in his memoir that when he landed on the island of Stromboli on June 25, 1949, to help deal with the scandal, Bergman showed him a letter from Steele's daughter Olivia. Olivia's letter was accompanied by some newspaper clippings, which included mention of Johnson's speech.[23] Of course, Steele cannot be correct about the date: Johnson's speech would be given nine months later.

However, Steele's story may tell us how Bergman actually learned about what Johnson had said. Bergman's feelings about Johnson's remarks do not appear in the many reports about her stay in Italy until 1956. In that year Robert Levin published an article entitled "The Ordeal of Ingrid Bergman," in which Bergman actually quotes from Johnson's speech. Bergman acknowledged that Johnson considered her to be one of his favorite actresses, but she recited from memory the line, "Out of Ingrid Bergman's ashes, perhaps a better Hollywood will come." In a book chapter five years later, much of it based on an interview with Bergman, Bill Davidson calls the day Johnson gave his speech the worst day of Bergman's life, but that day could only have been terrible in retrospect. It may well be that the entire history of the substance and significance of the speech came from Bergman herself.[24]

In the autobiography, Burgess and Bergman selectively summarize Johnson's speech to emphasize its criticism of Bergman, but Johnson clearly criticizes Rossellini and the promoters of *Stromboli* more than Bergman. Johnson was outraged at what he called the "moral turpitude" of the offending couple, and he did say some hurtful things: he called Bergman "one of the most powerful women on this earth today — I regret to say a powerful influence for evil"; he called her abnormal, worse than "mothers among the dumb beasts" because she had "abandoned her own daughter at the very age when her daughter needed her most"; he ended with an insulting rhetorical flourish: "If out of the degradation associated with *Stromboli*, decency and common sense can be established in Hollywood, Ingrid Bergman will not have destroyed her career for naught. Out of her ashes may come a better Hollywood."[25]

Still, Johnson really did not hold Bergman responsible for the scandal, which he called "her lamentable tragedy." He labeled her abnormal because she seemed to have had a fundamental change of personality, and the person obviously responsible for that transformation was the "love-pirate" Rossellini. Johnson scorned Rossellini, who, he claimed, had "never shown any respect for marriage." Johnson accused Rossellini of bribing his former wife to agree to an annulment and of arranging for both a "Mexican mail order court" and "Swedish diplomats" to grant Bergman and Rossellini a "fake divorce."

What also incensed Johnson was the fact that the publicity for the film seemed to have been based on the real lives of the participants and that the publicity might actually pay off. Johnson claimed that RKO Studios deliberately chose February 15 as the opening day for the movie to coincide with the anticipated birth of Bergman and Rossellini's illegitimate child, and he quoted one estimate that the film would make ten to twenty-five million dollars. What made all this especially galling to Johnson was that Rossellini might have been able to escape from paying American incomes taxes on his ill-gotten gains.

Johnson also blamed the scandal on the film community in general. He blamed RKO for shamelessly promoting the scandal, particularly scheduling the opening of the film near the prospective date on which Bergman would give birth. And he blamed RKO for ignoring the recommendation from the Catholic Legion of Decency that *Stromboli* not be shown and for going to court to "thwart mayors who would restrain theaters from showing this film." Above all, he excoriated Eric Johnston, the president of the Motion Picture Association Production Code Administration, for allowing a film to be shown when it is produced by "persons who themselves are barred from setting foot on American soil on the grounds of moral turpitude."[26]

As a result, Johnson introduced Senate Bill 3237 to license actors, actresses, producers, and motion pictures in interstate commerce. The bill would give the Secretary of Commerce the power to issue licenses for a fee of $1 for actors, a fee of $100 for producers, and a fee of $10,000 per film for distributors. Such licenses would be required for work dealing with any film made "in whole or in part within the United States, its Territories, or possessions, for exhibition in interstate commerce, or after shipment in interstate commerce." No actor, actress, or producer would be eligible for a license who had been "adjudged guilty by any court of competent jurisdiction of a crime involving moral turpitude," and distributors would have to certify that each movie they handled was produced only by people with the appropriate license and that the film "cannot reasonably be expected to contribute to juvenile delinquency" and "is not reasonably calculated to encourage a contempt for law, or public or private morality." Those found guilty of working on films or distributing them without a license would be fined from $1,000 to $10,000.[27]

The response to Johnson's speech was tepid. *The New York Times* reported the speech, noting that "despite an evident intent to impose Federal censorship of film through the licensing power, Senator Johnson's speech provoked no controversy on the floor," which suggests that such censorship in the delicate period after the war was controversial enough that no senator felt compelled to join Johnson without weighing the political costs.[28]

In a brief article accompanying the report of Johnson's proposal, the *Times* gave Bergman and Rossellini's studio RKO the opportunity to respond. Said an RKO spokesman: "There already were 'plenty' of censors in the United States who have approved the film. Even the most severe censors have approved 'Stromboli.'" Only a few theaters nationwide banned the film and RKO managed to book all 300 available prints into theatres.[29]

The news of Johnson's speech was not important enough for the *Times* to mention in its "Review of the Week" the following Sunday. But in a story entitled "Censorship Threat" twelve days after Johnson's speech, the *Times* did run a story on Hollywood's response to Johnson's proposals. It was not the threat of a licensing program that bothered Hollywood moguls; they were sure that "the measure will probably get nowhere. It is regarded as unlikely that the [Senate Interstate Commerce] committee will report out the bill and even more unlikely that if it were reported the Senate would take the measure up." No, what bothered the film industry was the negative publicity, which could affect the box office. The Theatre Owners of America with more than 10,000 members and the Allied States Association, the country's second-largest group of theater owners with more than 4,000 members, had been lobbying for greater self-regulation by the motion picture industry for quite some time, and in response to Johnson's bill, they were defiantly saying, "I told you so." Apparently, no one thought that the Motion Picture Association of America, the MPAA, had the will to do the job.[30]

Time magazine ran a sarcastic report of Johnson's proposal. Entitled "The Purity Test," the article called Johnson an "ex-cowpuncher" who introduced his bill with "cattle-country oratory." After summarizing Johnson's speech, *Time* also noted with equal sarcasm how Hollywood "after one deep, horrified breath ... struck back" using the inflated political rhetoric of the period. The article quoted Motion Picture Production Code Authority head Eric Johnston as saying Johnson's proposal was an attempt to establish "a commissar of the morals of the American people," and one of Johnston's lieutenants for calling it "a police state bill." Roy Brewer, chairman of the Motion Picture Industry Council, described Johnson's bill as "the first step toward totalitarianism."[31]

Variety interpreted Johnson's speech as a purely political maneuver, a move to undercut the growing sentiment to encourage Frank H. "Rick" Ricketson, president of Intermountain Theaters, to run for governor of Colorado. Said *Variety*, Johnson's condemnation of the film industry was timed to tie Ricketson to the "big, bad people of Hollywood," just in case he did decide to run for the governorship.[32]

Oscar Davis, a columnist for the *Washington Daily News*, denounced Johnson as a bumbler and fumbler for proposing the bill and predicted that it would never come to a vote, even if it ever got a committee hearing, which Davis doubted. Davis turned out to be a prophet.

Johnson went on to denounce Rossellini several times more on the floor of the Senate while he investigated the procedures necessary to prevent him and Bergman from returning to the country. But his licensing bill went nowhere. Senator Alexander Wiley of Wisconsin denounced it several weeks later, declaring it unconstitutional and "a police-state monster." Wiley found the bill so reprehensible that he did not even want Johnson to hold a hearing. Johnson replied in an open letter to Wiley in the Appendix to the Congressional Record. Johnson briefly blustered by bringing up further instances of what he considered the ghastly advertising campaign for *Stromboli*. But at the end of his remarks he backed away from the very substance of his bill in a way that indicates Wiley's charges against him had hurt. He conceded that "Federal censorship is not the most desirable answer" and rather plaintively insinuated that he was against "regimentation" as much as anyone, that Federal censorship was obnoxious and repugnant to Americans. As a result, he argued that the great virtue of his proposal was not its substance but that it could be the occasion for a "full exploration of the legal and public interest questions involved." Although he had set the committee hearing on his bill for May 15, he acknowledged that he would not really try to defend his proposal. Rather, the primary focus of the hearing would be to give the motion picture industry "the opportunity to work out is own solution to this problem on a voluntary basis." He called on Wiley to attend and join the discussion.[33]

The next day, Johnson met with a large number of executives of the film industry, including the presidents of Paramount Pictures, Universal Pictures, RKO-Radio Pictures, Twentieth-Century–Fox Film Corporation, and Warner Brothers Pictures, as well as three representatives of the Motion Picture Association: president Eric Johnston, and vice-presidents Joseph Breen and Francis Harmon. Johnson reported that these people had managed to convince him that they shared his concerns and would consider adopting "a stringent amendment to their advertising code" which would "effectively prevent exploitation in motion picture advertising of misconduct of performers." To give the industry time to do this, Johnson postponed the hearing on his bill indefinitely.[34] Whereupon, Johnson's bill to license actors, producers, and films died, not to be resurrected again. In addition, there is no evidence that the MPAA did anything to modify its advertising code in the light of "misconduct of performers."

However, Johnson seized on the political climate of the time. In late August, he brought to the Senate floor not a licensing bill but a nonbinding resolution expressing "the sense of the Senate" that movies made by Communists, Nazis, and Fascists should be banned from interstate commerce. In support of the resolution, Johnson gave a speech that singled out Rossellini as an example of a Fascist, who was also a former mental patient addicted to narcotics. The resolution had no legal force but threatened that the Senate would pass a law banning movies made by the terrible trio if Hollywood ignored its will.[35] The resolution passed, but once again there is no evidence that any Hollywood organization responded to the threat or that the Senate did anything when its will was ignored. Johnson's bill had a political and news life of a month and a half. The ripples from Johnson's bill lasted three month longer.

Perhaps Bergman never learned about the reception given to Johnson's speech or his proposal to license members of the film community. In any case, it is surely an exaggeration to claim that the Bergman-Rossellini romance defines the postwar era or that Johnson's speech is representative of postwar American values. American culture at the time was much more complex than Bergman and her biographers imply.

In her autobiography and in countless interviews Bergman also defines the scandal entirely as a private matter, and the reaction to her behavior as a hurtful invasion of privacy, over which she had no control. This may be self-serving. Bergman was an active participant in David O. Selznick's publicity campaign promoting her as a wholesome, honest, forthright woman, for much of the time she had her own personal publicity agent, Joe Steele, and she managed to maintain her image after she left Selznick Studios and acted in a number of films financed by independent production companies: *Arch of Triumph, Joan of Arc,* and Alfred Hitchcock's *Under Capricorn.*

The question is why a person who had controlled her image so well until she flew off to Rome suddenly lost or no longer cared to exercise the ability to do so. Of course, the most obvious answer is Robert Capa. She was determined to live life as he did: doing what she wanted openly, with integrity and no apologies. And there was Rossellini. Her passion for him was complex: she admired all of the ways he was different from Lindstrom: his close attention and possessiveness, his free and easy ways, his contempt for Hollywood and the news media, his trumpeting a new kind of cinematic art, his offer of an entirely different world from the one she had known, the one which had caused her so much pain.[36]

Whatever the complex reasons, once she reached Italy, Bergman threw all discretion to the winds. Because of that indiscretion, rather ironically, in early May, Bergman received a copy of a memo from Phil Reisman, head of RKO Studios in Europe, to Ed Killy, the studio production manager on the picture, which indicates what she should have done to control the negative publicity from the start. The memo begins by stating that RKO public relations representative Michael Wilson should approve all press releases and still photographs and arrange and supervise all press interviews. It then goes on to list six ways in which Bergman and Rossellini can minimize the gossip about them. Among them are having separate living quarters, avoiding joint public appearances, avoiding being photographed together, and making no social appearances together at all.[37]

By the time they received this memo, Bergman and Rossellini had violated all six of the tenets, which made their romance obvious. The natural question for the members of the press to ask was what the couple intended to do about their affair, since Bergman was a married woman with a physician-husband, an eleven-year old daughter, and a carefully cultivated reputation for wholesomeness, honesty, and basic values. What Bergman and Rossellini chose to do was to conduct a campaign of avoidance and obfuscation; they chose to act as if their personal lives should have had no interest to the outside world. The *Los Angeles Times* reported on April 20 that Rossellini told a reporter who had asked him directly if he planned to marry Bergman, "I neither confirm nor deny. I have nothing to say as yet."[38]

Despite the pressure to deny the affair from her producers, Bergman insisted later to Steele that she wanted to tell truth, that she wanted to announce she would be divorcing Lindstrom. And in fact she wrote Lindstrom from Amalfi telling him that she was in love with Rossellini and did not want to return from Italy. But she did not explicitly ask for a divorce. Rather, she acknowledged that Lindstrom stood in the ruins of their house, their lives together, and that she did not know what to do.[39] As a result Lindstrom made arrangements to go to Italy to meet with Bergman and set in motion a series of events that would lead to the defining moment of the scandal, the best chance Bergman had to exercise control over the way the story was playing in the press: she had a chance to negotiate a divorce, announce the results of the negotiations to the press and marry Rossellini. The announcement of the divorce and marriage would not have been earthshaking news after all of the speculation and might very well have dampened the enthusiasm of the press for covering the story.

In fact, such a strategy had recently worked for Rita Hayworth and Aly Khan. At the time of their affair, a little more than a year before the Bergman-Rossellini scandal broke, Hayworth was in the process of getting a divorce from Orson Welles, and Khan too was married. As with Bergman and Rossellini, the press hounded the couple wherever they went. After Hayworth and Khan received their respective divorces and eventually married in May of 1949, the couple was still major news, still hounded by the press, but the force of the objections to the relationship was dissipated. Another result of the marriage was that the birth of daughter Yasmin seven months later caused no outcry about the baby's legitimacy.[40]

But despite Bergman's inclination to tell the truth and announce that she was getting a divorce, this obvious way of controlling the scandal was not to be, and the major reason was Rossellini. Rossellini treated the press high-handedly, as a minor irritant, until Lindstrom arrived in Messina on May 1 to talk to his wife. Then Rossellini began behaving in ways that can only charitably be characterized as jealous to the point of paranoia. Bergman herself admits that Rossellini was "determined" to never let her go back to Lindstrom, or to even talk to him alone for more than an hour. Rossellini threatened to kill himself if Bergman returned to Lindstrom. He waved a gun about; he picked out a tree to smash his car into. On the night Bergman was to meet with Lindstrom in Messina, Kay Brown, an old friend from her days with the Selznick Studio, escorted Lindstrom to Bergman's bedroom, whereupon Lindstrom locked the door so that Rossellini could not interrupt them. Rossellini went crazy. He called the police, who refused to respond to a crisis consisting of a husband talking to his own wife in a locked hotel room. And so Rossellini stationed three of his staff at each of the doors to the hotel in case Lindstrom tried to spirit Bergman away, and then jumped into his red sports car and raced around the hotel with such speed and noise that Brown, now back in her own room, could not sleep, and Bergman could not concentrate on Lindstrom's argument.[41]

Apparently, Lindstrom thought that the affair would blow over. He told a reporter the next day, "There will be no divorce. There is no reason for dissension between us."[42] And instead of returning to America himself, he went to England and entreated Bergman to meet him there.

What followed was a comedy of errors. Bergman repeatedly promised to meet with Lindstrom personally in England, and Rossellini repeatedly pre-

vented her from going. As a result of following the affair in the press and discussing a divorce by letter and through intermediaries, Bergman and Lindstrom built up a great deal of hostility and misunderstanding, and in the
process prolonged the period during which they could not give the press any
sense of their situation.

In late May or early June, Bergman learned that she was pregnant and
perhaps now out of desperation, she realized that the freedom to be herself
that she had learned from Robert Capa came with a price. She wrote to Steele,
asking him to come to Italy to help her. Three days later, Steele flew to Italy.
Steele's first advice was to repeat in effect the memo from Phil Reisman: that
Bergman and Rossellini should be more discreet; they should avoid staying
at the same hotels and being photographed together. Above all, they should
stop giving statements to the press until Bergman and Lindstrom had reached
some kind of settlement. After being on Stromboli for a month, Steele realized
that the true problem was Rossellini's refusal to allow Bergman to negotiate
a divorce directly with Lindstrom. Thus, on July 27, he wrote Bergman and
Rossellini a long letter in which he pleaded with Rossellini to let Bergman
follow her conscience and meet with Lindstrom again in order to reach some
kind of closure. Steele handed the letter to Rossellini in Bergman's presence
and asked them to read it together. The only response Steele received was "a
stretch of strained silence" from Rossellini.[43]

And so the comedy of errors continued. The couple eventually issued a
statement saying that Bergman would initiate "divorce proceedings in any
country where it could be effectuated," insuring that Lindstrom would not
cooperate, and to lessen the effect on those who were threatening to ban or
boycott Bergman's pictures, Bergman announced that she intended to retire
from the screen, even though she knew that her intention would not last very
long. The announcement that Bergman intended to retire was widely interpreted as the ruse it obviously was. To further divorce proceedings in America,
Bergman and Rossellini on the recommendation of their Italian legal counsel
hired American Monroe MacDonald to find a lawyer in Beverly Hills to negotiate for them. In order to brief MacDonald and the new lawyer he would
hire, Bergman wrote a three-thousand word combination biography, confession, and credo. MacDonald took the letter with him to American and
promptly leaked it to Cholly Knickerbocker, so that at least one headline for
a Hearst newspaper the following day read, "Now, for the first time! Ingrid's
Real Love Story!"[44] MacDonald defended himself by saying that he intended
the story to put the fear of God in Lindstrom, but instead the story only
alienated Lindstrom further and made divorce negotiations even more difficult.

When the news eventually broke that Bergman might be pregnant, there
was no strategy for dealing with the issue and so the couple did nothing but

evade reporters' questions until Bergman left for the hospital to have the baby. The most notable evasion occurred when Bergman was asked directly by Hedda Hopper in a personal interview, "What's all this about you being pregnant?" Bergman responded, "Oh, my goodness, Hedda. Do I look it?" Hopper proceeded to deny Bergman's pregnancy for her: "Ingrid declares she will bring suit against the Italian papers which said she was going to have a baby. I don't blame her; there is not a word of truth in it."[45] As a result of all this evasion and subterfuge, the press began to stalk Bergman and turned the birth of baby Robertino into the media circus that Bergman so detested.

The way the press covered the story of baby Robertino's first week in the world is a good indication of how badly Bergman and Rossellini handled the situation. The UP story carried by the *Post* and run throughout the country carried this paragraph: "Some weeks ago the rumor started circulating that Miss Bergman was going to have a baby. Only this week, when a report was published in New York that she had been rushed to the hospital in prospect of a birth, she said: 'That's crazy.'"[46] In other words, the UP story noted that Bergman had been denying for some time what many people took to be the obvious truth: she was pregnant.

The denials of the obvious, combined with the farcical attempts to legitimize the birth after the fact, explain much of the way the birth of Robertino was covered the following week, and turned the story into just what Senator Johnson had claimed it was: a soap opera involving efforts to annul Rossellini's previous marriage, get a "Mexican mail order" divorce, and cajole Swedish officials to accept the Mexican divorce.[47] The day after the birth of Robertino, the *Washington Post* carried a story in the Sports section, of all places, explaining Bergman and Rossellini's legal predicament. Since Bergman was still married to Lindstrom, Italian law demanded that the baby be named Lindstrom after his legal father, putting Rossellini in the absurd position of insisting that he was the father, a fact he had been denying up until a week or two before the birth. This report also announced the beginning of a number of melodramatic story lines which would keep the romance in the tabloids for at least a week: would Rossellini be able to get an annulment of his marriage to Marcella de Marchis, and would Bergman be able to divorce Lindstrom so that they could have a Roman Catholic wedding rather than a civil ceremony by February 12, the date by which Robertino's birth had to be registered.[48] The *Post* followed the story only for one more day, but that story is devoted mostly to a description of Rossellini's tussle with photographers. Only at the end of the story is there any more information about the forthcoming marriage and baby Robertino's legal status: Rossellini reported that he would marry Bergman in a civil ceremony and make a formal declaration that Robertino was his son, if Bergman's Mexican divorce from Lindstrom came through. So much for the "Roman Catholic wedding" story line. If Bergman's divorce did not come through, Robertino would be registered as "Roberto Ingmar, son of Ingrid Bergman, father unknown," a euphemism for "bastard," in order to prevent Lindstrom from having any legal right to the child.[49] However, the baby was eventually registered as Renato Roberto [Ranaldo Giusto Giuseppe] Rossellini.

The *Washington Times Herald*, a much more sensational paper than the *Post*, covered the birth story every day from February 3, the day after the birth, until February 12, two days after the news broke that Bergman had been granted a divorce in Mexico. The great majority of these stories focused on the melodrama of whether and under what circumstances Bergman and Rossellini would marry, given an increasing list of legal requirements: not just in the U.S. and Italy but also in Mexico, where Bergman was seeking a divorce from Lindstrom and, it turned out, in Bergman's native Sweden, which had a different set of procedures and a different timetable for registering for divorce. There was also the ongoing melodrama of whether baby Robertino would be legally declared "father unknown." Many of the stories describe Rossellini's antagonism toward the press, and in one case his attempt to prevent photographs of the baby by emphasizing the baby's "delicate condition." However, Rossellini's rationale for limiting photographs is undercut in the next paragraph by a report from the baby's doctor, who said that Robertino's health was completely normal.[50]

In other words, these stories convey the sense that Bergman and Rossellini did not know what they were doing, and that they were simply making things up as they went along, often at times for no other reason than to spin out optimistic scenarios to further their image or to frustrate the press. Clearly, many of the snippets of information given out by Rossellini to the press sound like trial balloons or wishful thinking — such as the desire for a Roman Catholic wedding — or blatantly false rationales for things he simply does not want to do — such as using the baby's weakened condition as a pretext for not allowing photographs.

It is, of course, only surmise, but it is highly likely that the Bergman-Rossellini scandal would have been much less "epic," if Rossellini had allowed Bergman to follow her instincts and meet privately with Lindstrom and negotiate a divorce settlement well before the announcement that she was pregnant. The damage to Bergman's reputation, such as it was, could have been confronted directly in two press conferences with an accompanying series of interviews: the first announcing the divorce negotiations, the second announcing the pregnancy. If the negotiations with Lindstrom had begun when Bergman first wanted them to, as early as May 1949, when she was newly pregnant, it is possible that she would have been divorced well before the birth of Robertino and all of the suspense and melodrama surrounding the birth would have been old news. There would have been no need for endless speculation on the part of the press about the couple's marital status and no need for Bergman and Rossellini to feed the press constant evasions, no need for all the melodrama of whether little Robertino would be born with a "known father," and perhaps most importantly no reason for Christian groups to promote boycotts of *Stromboli* because the film's release had been timed to coincide with the baby's birth. There would have been time to plan the divorce in four countries and Bergman would have been married, perhaps in the Roman Catholic ceremony Rossellini teased the press with a week before their son was born. There would have been time for Bergman to restore her image as an honest woman, trying to do the right thing in difficult circumstances caused by a grand passion, and reinforce her reputation as a popular star, a reputation that may not have been severely damaged in the first place. What had worked for Rita Hayworth might very well have worked for Ingrid Bergman.

Because she could not control Rossellini, Bergman had to suffer the consequences of an epic scandal of the twentieth century. And just as she could not blame herself for running off with him, neither could she blame Rossellini for making the scandal worse. Perhaps then she fell into the role of victim almost by accident, as a way of talking to reporters about what had happened. Whatever the case, in interview after interview and in the autobiography, Bergman would retell the story again and again of how she became a victim, shaping the way most people understand the scandal today. And in the telling and retelling, perhaps she had found another role that suited her, one she could play for the rest of her life.

Six

The Legend of
Stage and Screen

"[Bergman's] later career was mostly a patchwork of dignified stage work and technically proficient character roles until, in 1977, Swedish Writer-Director Ingmar Bergman cast her in *Autumn Sonata*."
— Richard Schickel, "The Price of Redemption"

In his obituary of Ingrid Bergman, Richard Schickel, one-time film critic for *Time* magazine and the author of major books on Walt Disney, Clint Eastwood, and Elia Kazan, is perceptive about her later career.[1] The plays and films that Bergman appeared in after her life with Rossellini are not, with one exception, masterpieces. Her dignified stage work included turns in Robert Anderson's *Tea and Sympathy*, Ivan Turgenev's *A Month in the Country*, Bernard Shaw's *Captain Brassbound's Conversion*, Somerset Maugham's *The Constant Wife*, and N. C. Hunter's *Waters of the Moon*. True, she had more substantial roles — the title character in Henrik Ibsen's *Hedda Gabler* and the domineering matriarch Deborah Harford in Eugene O'Neill's *More Stately Mansions*— but the critical consensus was that Bergman's natural charm prevented her from offering a definitive interpretation of these characters.

Bergman's film work during this period was popular and often critically acclaimed. Indeed, she won academy awards for her transformation from a half-mad beggar woman to a regal princess in *Anastasia* and for her quirky Swedish missionary in *Murder on the Orient Express*, discoursing in her big scene, filmed in one long take, about the care of small brown babies. But the rest of her work was hardly challenging and the suspicion lingers that she fell back on her popular persona. In the romantic comedies —*Paris Does Strange Things*, *Indiscreet*, *The Yellow Rolls Royce*, *Cactus Flower*— she needed to do little but rely on her looks, her charm, and her sense of timing. In each of the melodramas, she does not have much to do or is off key. She projects the necessary sincerity and not much else in *The Inn of the Sixth Happiness*. In

The Visit, a film she very much wanted to do, she approved script changes that turned the substantial play by Friedrich Duerrenmatt into a melodrama and miscast herself as an embodiment of wrath and vengeance. Most critics called her performance merely vindictive. In *A Walk in the Spring Rain,* her old ability to project passion failed her, possibly because of disagreements with director Guy Green and co-star Anthony Quinn. *Goodbye Again,* a melodramatic story with an existential edge about a middle-aged woman torn between her longtime complaisant lover and the attentions of a much younger man, gave Bergman the chance to recapture her trademark portrayals of devotion and anguish at divided loyalty, but the role was nothing she had not done before. In two other films, she was simply eccentric: *From the Mixed-up Files of Mrs. Basil E. Frankweiler* and *A Matter of Time.*

Ironically, some of Bergman's best work may have been on television. In *The Human Voice,* she expresses a range of emotion from joy to despair, and in *A Woman Called Golda,* she exhibits the ability to play a character part in a variety of circumstances with a heretofore hidden gift for mimicry.

Schickel interprets Bergman's later life as an opportunity to expand on the qualities she had exhibited in *Notorious*: a portrayal of a woman paying "not just the price of love but the price of redemption from some deeper despair," a portrayal that was "a highly sensual characterization, at once knowing, acceptant and brave." Schickel is implying, of course, that her career after her turn with Rossellini was a case of life imitating art, that Bergman's later life was a search for love and redemption in the eyes of the public, and that she would have preferred she demonstrate those qualities in serious work, "a growing art." But to Schickel, that was not to be: "Robbed by circumstances of the chance to play that one immortalizing part every actress aspires to, she had instead turned her whole life into such a role."

This may be just, although whether Bergman was "robbed by circumstances of the chance to play that one immortalizing part" is open to question. What is much less open to question is that "instead she turned her whole life into such a role."

The work Bergman did after her marriage to Rossellini is not the resume of a woman dedicated to making great art, to producing significant groundbreaking films or to achieving definitive performances of the major roles in the history of dramatic literature Caught between the worlds of film and stage, Bergman seems to settle for roles in minor films and inferior plays. Her work seems drifting and inconsequential. All of this is surprising considering her earlier aspirations, but perhaps not too surprising.

All her life Bergman was a romantic little girl in love with the limelight. Early in her career, the parts she relished were little girl's parts — the heroics of Joan of Arc, for example — or parts that were fun to do and technically interesting — such as Ivy in *Dr. Jekyll and Mr. Hyde* or Clio Dulaine in *Saratoga Trunk*. Even when she is brilliant in a part that she actively sought, a part that extends her range and gives her a chance to do all that she can do as an actor, we have reason to wonder if she really knew how good the script would be for her. As Paula Alquist in *Gaslight*, she is totally convincing as she gradually slips from honest confusion to bewilderment to self-questioning to madness. Still, in talking about the film in the autobiography, all Bergman talks about are the difficulties in negotiating the billing for the film — Charles Boyer wanted top billing and Bergman was willing to give it to him, but Selznick was not — and the problem of doing romantic scenes out of sequence with a new leading man. Bergman gives us no indication of why she wanted to do the film and whether she knew it would be so good for her.

Often at the height of her fame and influence, she was attracted to scripts that gave her the chance to simply play against type and have a good time. She sought the role of Cleo Dulaine in *Saratoga Trunk* because she could wear period costumes, experiment with a different accent, and perhaps renew her affair with Gary Cooper.

The nature of her ambition is not clear. Often she seems to have wanted to do pictures that were "big" and "important" and "successful" without any other measure than the box office. Thirty-five years after he worked with her, Alfred Hitchcock told François Truffaut that Bergman "only wanted to appear in masterpieces." Hitchcock counseled her that no one ever knew whether a film was going to be a masterpiece. But after *Joan of Arc* Bergman wanted to go on to bigger and better things. Hitchcock told Bergman to find a film in which she could play the part of a secretary: that film might turn out to be "a *big* picture about a *little* secretary."[2]

We may partially discount Hitchcock's analysis of Bergman's ambition because in his reminiscences with Truffaut he may have still been piqued that Bergman had not wanted to immediately do another picture with him after *Notorious* and that she actively disliked shooting *Under Capricorn*. Still, Hitchcock may have captured the paradox of Bergman's ambition: she wanted to do great films but perhaps she did not have a sufficient notion of what great films were.

What we do know is that in the late 1940s, in the depths of despair at her marriage and her career, Bergman looked to Rossellini not only for romance but to give her the opportunity to make great films. She ran off with him not only for love. On this she is emphatic.

The common thread in all the versions of the story of how Bergman came to see Rossellini's *Open City* is that she found the realism and the simplicity of the film "heart-shocking." The film is shot in gritty black and white, and all the actors are amateurs with the exception of Anna Magnani. The story is a simple one of love and betrayal in the Italian resistance during the war. Bergman recalls that no one in *Open City* looked or talked like an actor, and because of the dark cinematography she couldn't hear or even see some of the action, but she thought that such techniques gave the film a certain immediacy — they made her feel as if she were *in* the film. And besides, she goes on, life was like that. Often in life people feel that certain things are happening that are difficult to understand.[3]

Bergman raved to family and friends and colleagues about Rossellini and what a genius he was, and she talked to Capa about the film, saying that she would rather be remembered for "one great artistic film" like *Open City* than for all her other successful films combined. Joe Steele recalls how great an effect seeing Rossellini's *Paisan* two years after *Open City* had on Bergman at the nadir of her career. "Her unresolved yearnings," he says, "struggled for expression. She was a Galatea in search of a Pygmalion."[4]

But whatever hopes Bergman had for creating masterpieces with Rossellini were quickly dashed in making *Stromboli*. She had dared to hope that their work together might achieve greatness, but she soon came to detest Rossellini's methods for achieving that greatness.

Rossellini's methods *were* unconventional. Often Rossellini did not use or follow a shooting script; even when he had a script he deliberately did not let his actors see it until the last minute. He wanted to record his actors' "spontaneous" reactions to the situations he put them in, and he relied on the nature of the shot and the rhythm of editing for his effects rather than the scripted coherent development of character. All of this denied Bergman and Rossellini's other actors the ability to participate consciously in the making of the film. Instead, Rossellini used the spontaneous reactions of actors as raw material to be manipulated as he saw fit in the editing room.[5]

In addition, Rossellini was incapable of keeping to a shooting schedule. He worked on his films when he felt like it. If he impulsively got an urge to go scuba-diving, he would cancel the day's shooting at a moment's notice, throw his wet suit and air tanks into his red convertible and roar off to the beach, leaving the cast and crew with nothing to do but wait for his return. All this made it almost impossible for his actors to get a clear sense of the characters they were portraying or for them to prepare emotionally for any given scene.

As a result, Bergman's ideal of collaborating with Rossellini was not to be. Bergman told film critic Robin Wood that with other directors she had always offered her ideas about her character or how a scene should be shot, and she tried to do that with Rossellini, too. Occasionally he took her advice. But Rossellini usually knew just what he wanted to do, and Bergman wound up trying to follow his instructions as much as possible. If she did object to a particular scene, even going so far as to suggest that certain scenes were not good enough and should be cut from the film, the two would have terrible arguments. So, no, Bergman told Wood, she and Rossellini may have collaborated a little, but mostly Rossellini did things himself.[6]

Because Bergman could not appreciate Rossellini's methods of making films, she could not appreciate how good they were. As Wood puts it, Bergman's estimate of the films she made with Rossellini "seems to fall short of full appreciation of their value and full understanding of their significance — even, perhaps, of the nature of her own achievement within them." Bergman seems to appreciate Rossellini's art only in the abstract. She grants that the films have interesting ideas, but she talks about them in didactic terms: in his films with her Rossellini was trying to teach people, not give them fun.

When Wood points out particular scenes and even shots in which he finds Bergman particularly effective, she only responds that Wood remembers better than she does. About the Pompeii scene in *Voyage in Italy* in particular, she says, "I was not particularly pleased because I felt I was just walking through it like a tourist and just said, 'Yes, is that so? Oh, I see,' and the guide was showing the movie."[7]

In the autobiography, Bergman's final judgment of her work with Rossellini comes in the context of filming *Fear*, when the marriage is clearly over. "We weren't a good mix," she says there. "The world hated the Rossellini version of me, so nothing worked." She states outright that Rossellini did not know what to do with her as an international star: he did not know how to write for her; he did not know how to direct her. After some bitter initial fights, she gave in and simply did what she was told.[8] This may sound more bitter than Bergman intended, but it does indicate that her major standard for artistic achievement was popular success. And it strongly suggests that whatever Bergman thought great art was, her experience with Rossellini dampened her enthusiasm for it ... and may have caused her to wonder whether it had been worthwhile to give up her Hollywood life to make great art.

Daughter Isabella elaborates on this idea in an interview with Charlotte Chandler. Isabella thinks that her mother was disappointed in the work she did with her father, perhaps because Bergman did not understand it very well. Isabella speculates that perhaps all of the films Bergman made in Hollywood conditioned her to prefer melodrama to every other kind of film, and with the exception of one scene in *Stromboli*, Rossellini's films were definitely not melodramatic. Or perhaps, Isabella goes on, Bergman was disappointed that so few people appreciated Rossellini's work. Bergman was used to big audiences and wanted people to enjoy what she enjoyed.[9]

Whatever the reason, after her life with Rossellini, Bergman rarely talked about making great art. Entertainment was enough. In fact, in her memoir Isabella constructs an imaginary dialogue between her father and mother suggesting that Bergman's view of acting was at least partially in response to the views of Rossellini. Isabella's fantasy focuses on a discussion with her parents about luxury. Isabella quotes Coco Chanel to the effect that lipstick and bubble baths are "momentary illusions," things we can indulge because our basic needs are taken care of. Bergman agrees: "Yes, movies, too. Not yours, Roberto, we aren't talking about you! Movies in general take you out of reality and distract you for a while. It's all entertainment—film, fashion, makeup, circus, amusement park. I think it's a great gift to be an entertainer. I'm happy to have been one."[10]

Bergman's own evaluation of her professional life after Rossellini echoes her daughter's. She told Chandler that as a working actress she had always wanted to be doing something "important," but only late in life did she come to understand that "entertaining people was important and, and if you were lucky, it would be having the opportunity to entertain as many as possible."[11]

Possibly as a result of her experience with Rossellini, Bergman no longer seems to actively pursue key roles. Rather she sits at home and waits for roles to come to her. The image conveyed in the autobiography is of a woman who desperately wants to act and who has considerable box office appeal, both in films and on the stage, and therefore a certain amount of influence. It is an image of a woman who knows what she wants from a script when she reads one. But it is also the image of a woman who seems to have few resources for actively seeking out roles that might appeal to her and be appropriate for her skills.

Clearly, Bergman wanted control over the scripts of the films she appeared in. After the success of *Anastasia, Indiscreet*, and *The Inn of the Sixth Happiness*, Spyros Skouras, the head of Twentieth Century–Fox, offered Bergman a four-picture contract. The pictures would be produced approximately once a year but the time for all four could extend to five years. Bergman would receive $250,000 per picture, for a total of a million dollars, plus 25 percent of the profits; for tax and estate reasons, Skouras suggested that she spread the payments over twenty years. And on the artistic side, Bergman would be presented with a list of directors and could choose those she wanted to work with. The list included the best directors then working in America and Britain: David Lean, Alfred Hitchcock, Elia Kazan, Carol Reed, William Wyler, Mark Robison, Anatole Litvak, George Stevens, Henry King, Fred Zinnemann, Billy Wilder, Joseph Mankiewicz, Edward Dmytryk, and Nunnally Johnson.

However, Bergman took umbrage over the fact that Skouras emphasized the financial arrangements, especially the matter of deferring income for estate purposes. She was not worried about her children: let them fend for themselves in the future. She simply wanted a good part. Bergman especially bridled at one particular sentence in the Skouras contract: if she and one of the acceptable directors should disagree on a script, then Bergman would have to accept the director's judgment.[12] Bergman rejected Skouras's offer. She was willing to sacrifice financially in order to have control over the parts she would act, but it is never clear what she had in mind when she read through scripts.

With the exception of *The Visit*, she does not suggest to producers and directors plays she might like to do, novels she might like adapted to the screen, vehicles that would showcase her talent. She does not seem to read widely or have much knowledge of the classic theater repertoire. She passively waits at home for people to come to her with offers to do plays and films. Much of *My Story* is devoted to describing the circumstances in which she receives such offers and what she thinks of them. Anatole Litvak proposes *Goodbye Again*, but Bergman responds to him with three pages of complaint that the script does not adequately convey the atmosphere of Francoise Sagan's novel on which it is based. In the end, she agrees to do the picture, only to discover that after that film is released, most of the offers for more work involve spring–December romances. Kay Brown sends her a copy of Rachel Maddox's novel *A Walk in the Spring Rain*, which immediately intrigues Bergman because the romance is between mature adults; Brown sets up an interview with Stirling Silliphant, who is interested in doing a screenplay. She is offered the part of Annie Sullivan, Helen Keller's teacher, in the film version of *The Miracle Worker*, but she turns it down because she thinks that Anne Bancroft, who played the part on Broadway, should also do the film. Out of the blue, Bergman receives calls from Gustav Molander to do *The Necklace*, Michael Redgrave to do *A Month in the Country*, Mike Frankovitch to do *Cactus Flower*, Binkie Beaumont to do *Captain Brassbound's Conversion*, and Arthur Cantor to do *The Constant Wife*.[13]

True, offered the role of the Countess in *Murder on the Orient Express*, Bergman does plead to do the smaller, less glamorous role of the Swedish missionary. And she does campaign to do *The Visit* as a film, even though the adaptation from the play has script problems. But in general there is a curious passivity about her search for parts. She does not seem to know what she is looking for.

Joan of Arc seems to have exhausted her imagination. About certain classic parts, parts that many major actors would die to do, she is ambivalent. She tells Ruth Roberts that she is thinking of doing Ibsen's *The Lady from the Sea*, but she can't make up her mind because the play seems much too old-fashioned. She rejoices when Schmidt arranges for her to do the title role for a shortened version of *Hedda Gabler* for a BBC and CBS co-production on television because she wanted to "try a classic for a change." But she all can say about the part is that Hedda is "interesting" and "strange."[14]

Bergman does not like *More Stately Mansions* much either, and José Quintero has to talk her into joining that production. At the time, she is considering a French version of Tolstoy's *Anna Karenina*. Again, she gives no real reason why she chose *More Stately Mansions* over *Anna Karenina*. However, she does say that Kay Brown thinks *More Stately Mansions* is right for her because the part is "so damned dignified."[15] If this is an indication of the basis on which she chose her parts, there are good reasons her late career was patchwork and her vehicles undistinguished.

Still, no matter how undistinguished her plays and films, there was the legend to live, and the legend was real. The legend was a role she could relish without the burden and obligation of husbands and children.

The legend was forged in January of 1957, when Bergman returned triumphantly to America in order to receive the New York Film Critics' Best Actress award for her performance in *Anastasia*. Bergman was in New York for only a day and a half, but her every move, from her press conference at the airport to various stops around town — the Roxy Theater where *Anastasia* was playing, Sardi's Restaurant where she received her award, the back stage door she entered to see *My Fair Lady*— were covered rapturously by as many as sixty reporters, who described Bergman as smiling graciously and radiating happiness, her beautiful "scrubbed face" with its "peaches and cream" complexion showing no signs of bitterness or resentment for her long exile.[16]

Bergman's return came amid a flurry of press reports and interviews that she had "fled" the United States some eight years before because of the severity of her "ordeal." Indeed, the headlines of these reports and interviews convey the tantalizing image of a woman who had endured a great deal of pain and anguish but was not repentant for her presumed sins. The headline in *Redbook* was "The Ordeal of Ingrid Bergman." The headline in *Coronet* was "Ingrid Bergman, the Woman America Can't Forget." And perhaps most provocatively, the major subhead in *Collier's* under a three-quarter page picture of a defiant Bergman staring at the camera from among a mass of camera equipment, her mouth set in a straight line, not grim but deeply serious, was this: "I am not doing penance for anything."[17]

During her triumphant return, reporters accepted the story Bergman told them. She had suffered unduly because of reactionaries in the United States and a persecuting media. Italians were more sophisticated and understanding about these things. Her adultery with Rossellini was justified by romantic love, a grand passion. Her forsaking Pia was beyond her control. She had nothing to repent of and was returning simply to accept an award. Let the reporters write their stories any way they could. She was defiant and the reporters loved it. They treated her as if she were still the box office queen of 1945.

Bergman's biographers explain the phenomenal reception of Bergman's return to America by arguing that by 1957 Americans were no longer as sexually repressed as they had been at the beginning of the decade. After being displaced from work by soldiers returning from the war, women were returning to the workplace. Equality was in the air and divorce was on the rise. Because of *Playboy* magazine and the Kinsey Reports, popular culture was more sexualized than ever before. The topic of sex before and outside of marriage had become commonplace. *Peyton Place* and *Lolita* were best sellers.

But as we have seen, David Selznick, ever the pragmatist, had no sympathy for larger cultural explanations for Bergman's triumphant return. To Selznick, Bergman could always have come back to America to make films, but for her own reasons, she chose not to. Her triumphant return had nothing to do with the larger culture and everything to do with her relationship with Rossellini. Indeed, by the time of Bergman's return, Rossellini had become involved in yet another scandal, this one an affair with Sonali Das Gupta, the wife of an Indian film producer and the mother of two children.

What both the cultural and personal explanations for Bergman's return fail to take into consideration is the sheer brilliance of her performance in confronting the press about her past — and the present. In January of 1957, she swept into the country for a mere three days, but from then on, for the rest of her life, by downplaying her current life and feeding the appetite of the press for tidbits about her past, she created the legend that is now commonly accepted about her life: the legend of a woman who rose to the heights of the theatrical world, suffered an ignominious blow to her reputation because of a grand passion, and then regained the love of the public by sheer perseverance and talent.

Moreover, Bergman seemed to live the legend of a grand theatrical star. Although reporters covered her private life as best they could, she managed to keep the details of her relationship with her husbands and children a matter of speculation only. When she appeared in public to talk to the press, it was usually because she was acting in a play or film and doing interviews for publicity purposes. She was far from home, and reporters and interviewers had no way of assessing her life away from the limelight. For these occasions, she seemed to be living in grand theatrical style: out of trunks unpacked in luxury suites at the best hotels, lunches and dinners at the best restaurants, the social whirl of parties and press conferences, late rising in the morning, afternoons free to roam the city she was in at the time, to take in a matinee or tour a museum, to go on extended shopping sprees, pausing for coffee at a small cafe and to take in with deep satisfaction the glory of her worry-free life with no apparent obligations to a husband or children. She projected an image of health and vitality, honesty and integrity; an image of a woman who loved her life, loved living it to the fullest, who had few difficulties in life but if such difficulties were to arise, she could deal with them efficiently and effectively.

The legend was aided by Bergman's fans, of whom the most dedicated group was the Alvin Gang. The original Alvin Gang had numbered as many as twenty or thirty people and had formed during the run of *Joan of Lorraine* at the Alvin Theater. The group regularly attended the Saturday matinees of the play, when the doors to the theater were left open after the intermission so that people could stand in the back. The leader of the group, Warren Thomas, 12 or 13 years old at the time, saw the play between thirty or forty times. The group was composed, in Thomas's recollection, of about twelve children, a few middle-aged women, and some older fans. The group often met Bergman at the stage door after the play, and they made their presence known to such an extent that at the end of the run of the play, through Joe Steele, Bergman invited them back into the theater to thank them for their loyalty and to ask their forgiveness for her occasional annoyance at their persistence in trying to be meet her, be near her, or at least get a glimpse of her outside the theater. Once Thomas and his girlfriend had actually followed Bergman home.

Thomas wrote many letters to Bergman while she was it Italy, even though he received no replies, and distraught over the treatment of the Rossellini scandal, he even wrote to Pia in California. When Bergman returned to America in 1957, about ten of the original group met her at the airport with large placards that read "We Love You Ingrid! Welcome Home Ingrid Bergman. The Alvin Gang." In the fall of 1976, during a visit to daughter Isabella in New York, Bergman and Isabella went to Warren Thomas's apartment for a thirtieth anniversary party of the Gang. Thomas was ashamed of the way some of the Gang behaved. One member in particular kept taking Bergman's picture over and over.[18]

The legend was also aided by the love and devotion of Bergman's friends and colleagues, who did not talk about her private life to the press and who were genuinely admiring and devoted to her as a person. Cary Grant put it eloquently in a speech, accepting Bergman's Academy Award for *Anastasia*: "Dear Ingrid, if you can hear me now or will see this televised film later, I want you to know that each of the other nominees and all the people with whom you worked on *Anastasia*, and Hitch, and Leo McCarey, and indeed everyone here tonight, send you congratulations and love and admiration and every affectionate thought."[19]

Although Bergman was not in America much in the early 1960s, she was constantly in the news. The press covered her budding relationship with Lars Schmidt to such an extent that she had to resort to all sorts of tactics to meet

Schmidt without the press knowing. On one occasion, Bergman flew to Copenhagen, ostensibly to visit her Aunt Mutti, where a friend of Schmidt hid her under a blanket in the back seat of a car to get her to a rendezvous point. When she and Schmidt finally arrived at their destination, his parents' home in Dageborg, Sweden, the house was surrounded by reporters with spotlights on the roofs of their cars, and so the couple was forced to park some distance away on the far side of a graveyard, crawl through the graveyard and climb over a wall and a gate to get to the house. Bergman thought that the experience was a scene out of a movie about prisoners escaping from a concentration camp, with lights sweeping over ground and sirens sounding the alarm.[20]

The constant attention of Bergman's love life and the custody battle over the Rossellini children built up demand so that when she performed in plays in both England and the United States the public flocked to see her. Her shows were often sold out. Herman Kretzmer, theater critic for the *Daily Express* of London, was "practically assaulted" by a queue of middle-aged men and women waiting for cancellations for *Captain Brassbound's Conversion*, despite the tepid reviews. The play toured America to nothing but sold-out auditoriums, and by one estimate, of fifty-six new productions on Broadway in 1972, only *Captain Brassbound* had recouped its investment. *The Constant Wife* set a weekly box office record at the Albery Theater in London. *Waters of the Moon*, also in London, was a major hit in 1978, and the public's adulation of Bergman caused some tension between Bergman and co-star Wendy Hiller. One day before a show, Hiller went to Bergman's dressing room and told her about being stopped in the street by people who praised the play, but only really wanted to talk about Bergman's beauty. Hiller said that if she continued to be addressed that way, she would vehemently proclaim that Bergman was "a dreadful woman and terrible to play with." Hiller was joking, but acting with her must have been bittersweet for Hiller. She received much better reviews than Bergman, but Bergman was the person the great majority of theater-goers wanted to see.[21]

With all the acclaim, Bergman's public life seemed like a series of triumphs. In 1973, she was invited to be president of the jury at the Cannes Film Festival. In 1979, Bergman was the Mistress of Ceremonies at the American Film Institute's Lifetime Achievement Award ceremony for Alfred Hitchcock. Also in that year Bergman was the guest of honor at a Variety Club of America television show to raise money for an Ingrid Bergman wing for underprivileged and handicapped children at a local children's hospital. At that event, even though he had never met her, Frank Sinatra came out of retirement to sing for her.[22]

For all practical purposes, Bergman created the legend that led to all these accolades. Living the legend allowed her to replace conventional family life and focus entirely on performing. Living the legend allowed her to transcend the difficulties of her personal life. For Bergman had indeed suffered countless ordeals, but the only one she talked about to any extent was the scandal with Rossellini, the one that had happened long ago. She did not talk about her marriage to Rossellini, which, while often happy, was punctuated by intense fighting and broiling resentment. She did not talk about her custody battle over the children after the marriage to Rossellini broke up and how it caused her a great deal of anguish. She did not talk about her marriage to Lars Schmidt and how it too gradually deteriorated and how the couple managed to stay together even after Schmidt took a mistress. She did not talk about her battle with cancer, her two mastectomies, or the increasingly limited prospects for her life. Maintaining the legend was difficult, a triumph of sheer will over experience. Bergman had to downplay, put aside, and rise above a great deal of pain and sorrow.

Bergman's marriage to Rossellini was complicated and tumultuous. Although the couple often seemed to love one another, they fought constantly. They fought over Rossellini's casual attitude toward money, his luxurious lifestyle, full of vacations and fancy cars, all financed on credit; they fought over his terrible temper, his erratic and improvised way of directing films, his inability to keep a schedule or to meet appointments, his rudeness to her Hollywood friends, and his refusal to let her work with other directors. There are those who thought the relationship was doomed before the couple were even married.

For one thing, it was obvious the two had little in common. Rossellini's niece Fiorella Mariani, the daughter of his sister Marcella, recognized the differences between them. Fiorellia thought that Rossellini was too intellectual for Bergman, who was "not a cultivated woman." Rossellini simply could not talk to her about ideas or what he was reading. Bergman understood the differences between them, but did not seem to mind.[23]

Cousin Renzo Avanzo called Rossellini "an ass, impractical, a dreamer" and Bergman a "bourgeoise," which Rossellini was not. Rossellini was used to letting his imagination run rampant and staying out all night long. He could not live a regular life with meals at certain times. Bergman preferred dinner at nine o'clock and liked things neat and in their place. Renzo says that he was "bored silly" when he visited the Rossellinis. For one thing, none of Rossellini's old friends were ever there. Those friends would stop him in the street and complain that Rossellini never saw them any more. Renzo would reply, "Of course he doesn't. How the hell could he bring *you* home?"

Rossellini was more passionate and sexual than Bergman, and he found certain outlets for his sexual urges elsewhere. According to Father Antonio Lisandrini, a Franciscan friend of the family, Rossellini found Bergman "without passion" and continued to go to whorehouses.[24]

As early as 1951, director Jean Renoir visited and then reported in a letter, "Rossellini — who is charming — is not a 'spouse.' Everyone here knows that things cannot last with his attitude.... I even ask myself if he doesn't already have his eye on someone else."

A UP reporter heard rumors that the couple was separating. Sandro Franchina, who played the son in *Europa '51*, many years later recalled that Bergman hid her second pregnancy from Rossellini because she was afraid that he would be angry.[25]

In his memories of filming *Voyage in Italy*, George Sanders recalls, "It would be hard to guess whether there was any real happiness in the relationship; she was in tears a good many times." Bergman took to drinking martinis both at home and on location. Once at home, she had been drinking and Rossellini suddenly reappeared: "I leave my poor children with you," he exclaimed in righteous indignation, "and look! I've come back to take their temperatures and you're in an alcoholic stupor!" As soon as Rossellini left, according to Sanders, Bergman went back to drinking.[26]

At times their fights could turn violent. Bergman herself admits that once during a fight, she tried to calm Rossellini down by throwing her arms around him — "and bang! He threw me against the wall so hard I almost broke in pieces. I couldn't do anything. Even to get near him was to risk your life."[27]

Eventually the marriage distintegrated because the minor irritations piled up. Bergman does not describe a definite breaking point, but clearly her beginning to work for other directors ratcheted up the tension. During her work on Renoir's *Elena and Her Men* in France, Rossellini left with the children and their passports, after forcing Bergman to sign a letter agreeing to a separation. One clause in the agreement was that the children would only be allowed to live in France or Italy. Bergman wrote to her friend Gigi Girosi in Rome that she tried to talk Rossellini out of his decision, and as a result he stayed for a few days, but then finally made up his mind to go. Bergman tried to ease the tension early in the evening by offering to play a game of cards and then by offering to help him pack. He rejected her offers and lay down on the bed. Bergman joined him, snuggled close, and began crying, sniffling at first and then breaking out in fulsome tears. Finally, played out and exhausted, she rallied, found some odd sense of humor in the unhappy melodrama and began to laugh. Bergman ends the letter, expressing her honest fear of her future with Rossellini and her children, but she is self-possessed enough to ask Girosi to keep the letter, possibly as legal evidence. She was "not afraid of being alone, but of having made four children and all taken away from me."[28]

Rossellini intensely opposed Bergman's agreement to do *Anastasia* and *Tea and Sympathy*. To him, both were cheap commercial products. In response to Bergman's agreeing with Anatole Litvak to do *Anastasia* in England, Rossellini was furious. He even resorted to an old tactic of threatening to commit suicide by driving his Ferrari into a tree. By now, Bergman was inured and refused to back out of her commitment.

Rossellini was more troubled by *Tea and Sympathy*. He was uncomfortable with the idea of homosexuality, and the play is about a married woman giving herself to one of her husband's students to prove he is not gay. Rossellini did not admit his discomfort with the play. Instead, he attacked the play as silly and stupid. Bergman, however, had had enough and dug in her heels: she refused to continue to submit to her husband like a good little Italian housewife. Rossellini was certain that *Tea and Sympathy*, produced in Paris, with Bergman speaking French, would cause the audience to walk out in the middle. But the opposite happened. As Bergman took her final bow after her first performance, Rossellini was in the wings. According to Bergman, she had not experienced such an avalanche of applause since *Joan of Lorraine*. People stood on the seats and screamed and pounded their hands together. Cries of "Bravo" cascaded down on her. As she bowed, she turned and looked at Rossellini. Their eyes met, and it was then, Bergman says, that she knew: even if the two of them managed to keep living together, their marriage was finished.[29]

But the culminating event was Rossellini's affair with Sonali Das Gupta, the wife of Indian producer Hari Das Gupta. Rossellini had left Bergman in Paris to perform in *Tea and Sympathy* so that he could shoot a documentary in India. While there, he had fallen in love with Sonali. Bergman first heard of the scandal when Rossellini called in May of 1956 to warn her that she might be confronted by reporters asking about a possible affair between her husband and an Indian woman. The newspapers in India were full of the story, but Rossellini protested that it wasn't true, of course, and that Bergman had to deny it. "Not a word of it is true," Bergman recalls Rossellini saying. "Not a word." But Bergman instinctively knew that Rossellini was lying: she knew how easily Rossellini fell in love and how easily women fell in love with him. She also knew from bitter experience that his first response in dealing with the press was to deny everything.

However, this did not stop her from denying the affair to the press herself. When Rossellini returned from India, the couple staged a warm reunion in the airport — a passionate kiss and a hug — and Bergman denied to the assembled reporters that she knew anything about her husband's unfaithfulness in India. Back in the safety of Bergman's hotel room, the two tried to calmly discuss divorce. At first, Rossellini avoided the issue and insisted on repeating his contempt for *Tea and Sympathy*, but eventually he agreed that a divorce seemed to be the reasonable course of action under the circumstances. He was tired, he said, of being "Mr. Bergman." And he only had two demands: that the children never go to America and that Bergman never marry again. Apparently, Rossellini feared for his children what he had earlier feared about Bergman: that Lindstrom, now generalized to a grasping possessive America, would steal away the objects of his affection. And although he reserved the right to love Sonali and as many women as he liked, he could not face the idea that Bergman would ever love another man as much as she had loved him. Bergman laughingly rejected both demands, and perhaps sensing the weakness of his position, Rossellini did not argue for long.[30]

Bergman wrote Steele after her engagement to Schmidt what seems now like an epitaph for her marriage to Rossellini: "Many people seemed shocked that so soon after the separation [from Rossellini] I fell in love [with Schmidt]. But no one will ever know how many years I lived without any love at all."[31]

Bergman's personal life immediately after she left Rossellini in 1956 was a soap opera that included an intimate friendship with playwright Robert Anderson and the attentions of producer Lars Schmidt, even while the courts in several countries dealt with her divorce from Rossellini. Bergman married Schmidt in London in 1958, even though her divorce — or annulment or separation from Rossellini, whatever her lawyers could arrange — had not been settled in Italy. But English law considered the marriage with Rossellini illicit since it had been contracted before her divorce from Lindstrom. Hence, by the standards of English law, Bergman had been free to marry someone other than Rossellini, even while she had been married to him.

During the early years of her marriage to Schmidt, there was a bitter custody battle with Rossellini over the children until 1961, when the Italian court granted the parents equal custody of the children, each during alternate years. However, Bergman decided to let Rossellini have the children full-time, even though her lawyers thought that she could win the custody suit. After years of conflict, Bergman had had enough. She had begun to wonder how much of the custody battle had been her fault. She knew that the court fight was difficult for the children, and she realized that either she or Rossellini would have to give way if they wanted to maintain their children's happiness. And so she notified Rossellini in Italy that she would bring him the children as soon as possible.[32]

Bergman concedes that she relied on housekeepers, nannies, and governesses to raise her children. Indeed, in the autobiography, she ends a chapter with an extended paean of praise for Argenide Pascolini, who served as a housekeeper for the children for fourteen years upon their return to Italy: she watched out for the children and became a second mother to them. If something went wrong concerning a governess — and there were many during these years — and the children were worried or unhappy, Argenide would be on the phone immediately, requesting that Bergman return and settle the matter. To Bergman, Argenide was "the rock in the storm." The children worshipped her, even after they left home. Argenide was one of the witnesses at Isabella's wedding, and both Isotta and Robertino continue to visit her often.[33]

The children are brave and later in life defend their parents, claiming that all was normal. But the anxieties and sense of abandonment do break through: Isotta Ingrid accompanied her mother to America for the production of *More Stately Mansions*. She had a private teacher in the United States, but returned to Italy for the equivalent of her high school exams. When toward the end of the run of the play, the younger Ingrid had to return to Rome to take her exams, she clung to her mother, who was on the way to the theater. In Bergman's telling, Isotta would not stop clutching her. Bergman had to pull Isotta's arms from around her neck and brutally push her away. Bergman felt awful but thought that she had no choice. She had to go to the theater to put on her make-up. Just before the show, she called Ruth Roberts to ask if her daughter had calmed down. Isotta answered the phone and began to cry, "Mama, Mama, Mama." To Bergman, it was as if Isotta's tears "flood[ed] down the telephone wires." It took Bergman a while to regain her composure, and as a result she was ten minutes late for the start of the show.[34]

In all her dealings with her children, Bergman claims to have been a fussy affectionate mother intensely wrapped up in their lives, but she always leaves and her leaving always seems to cause her a great deal of anguish.

The marriage with Schmidt lasted for 17 years, but like Bergman's previous marriages, when it ended, it had been largely a matter of appearances for quite some time. Bergman and Schmidt gradually grew apart. Among other things, when they were first married, Schmidt had found shows for them to work on together. Schmidt produced Bergman's work in the Parisian production of *Hedda Gabler* and her American television appearances in *24 Hours in a Woman's Life*, *Hedda Gabler*, and *The Human Voice*. But, Bergman says, after *The Human Voice*, Schmidt stopped finding work for her, and she becomes quite eloquent in her autobiography describing his neglect. After all, Schmidt was a major European producer, a producer of plays by Arthur Miller, Tennessee Williams, Arnold Wesker, and Alan Ayckbourn; he was in constant association with playwrights and actors. Earlier in their marriage, he had called her his Golden Goose: everything she did was successful. If all this was so, why could he no longer find shows for her to do? Confronted with the charge directly — Bergman typically understates the situation, saying that the couple had their arguments — Schmidt is condescending: he told her that he did not want to exploit her or take advantage of her. It was just too easy for him to put Ingrid Bergman into a show.[35]

And so Bergman agrees to do a number of plays and films in America for prolonged periods of time, while Schmidt stays in Europe: *More Stately Mansions* in Los Angeles and New York in 1967, *Cactus Flower* at Columbia Pictures in Los Angeles early in 1969, and *A Walk in the Spring Rain* in Tennessee, New York, and Hollywood, late that year. While she is away, Schmidt falls in love with a beautiful young Swedish woman named Kristina Belfraga. In the autobiography, Bergman says that she learned about Belfraga when she returned from America at the end of *A Walk in the Spring Rain* in 1970. There Bergman admits that she did not take the news "calmly or peacefully." She was angry, but realized that she may have brought the crisis on by her absence. She talks about resisting the idea of divorce, perhaps keeping Belfraga in the background and trying to keep going, even though it hurt. She was facing "the old dilemma": whether it was more important to be entertaining people in the theater or sitting at home being bored. The answer was obvious, and when Binkie Beaumont calls to offer her the only female role in George Bernard Shaw's *Captain Brassbound's Conversion* — the rest of the cast is played by 24 men — she immediately agrees to read it, even though she has never heard of it. She is home alone, Schmidt has just called, telling her not to wait up for him because he has a rehearsal and is going to be very late. The implication of the anecdote is clear: Schmidt should tolerate her absences. She will not tolerate his.[36]

And so for the next five years Schmidt divides his time between Bergman and Belfraga, and the marriage does not recover. Bergman says that it was Schmidt's desire for a child with Belfaga that was eventually the deciding factor in their divorce: she didn't want the child to ever think that she was selfish enough to not let his father live with his mother. Bergman and Schmidt divorce quietly in 1975. Even some of their friends do not know about it, and Bergman never reports the exact date. In the autobiography, Bergman mentions that she and Schmidt decided on the divorce after the Academy Awards ceremony in which she received an Oscar for her performance in *Murder on the Orient Express*.[37] That would have been in early 1975. Presumably the divorce took place some time later that year. In August, Bergman would be sixty years old: she would be free to give herself totally to acting.

But Bergman told Chandler a different story: that when Schmidt told her that he was about to have a child with Belfraga, she hadn't even known that Schmidt had a mistress, although various people had told her not to be apart from him so much. These people had warned her that she was running the risk of losing Schmidt. So when Schmidt broke the news, Bergman says that she was shocked and at sea.

> I should not have been surprised, as shocked as I was. I tried to keep at least the appearance of composure, though I didn't feel composed. I didn't want Lars to feel guilty. I didn't feel he was guilty. I was.

One is supposed to be an adult about those things, but though I tried to be civilized, very adult, I didn't feel that way. It made me feel like a lonely little girl, and I didn't know how to cope.[38]

But Belfraga became pregnant in 1976, and Bergman learned about the birth of Schmidt and Belfraga's son in June of 1977, two years after her divorce from Schmidt. The emotions are raw in both versions of her story, but Bergman's response is different. In the first version, she is not calm and peaceful but is angry. In the second, later version, she is shocked but attempts to keep her composure in order to save Schmidt from feeling guilty. The second version is more dramatic and makes Bergman seem more noble and long-suffering.

Interestingly, Bergman learns about the birth of her former husband's son, days after she learns about the death of Rossellini. In *My Story*, she is philosophical: after death, there is life. And she is happy that Schmidt finally has the son he had wanted for so long.[39]

After her divorce from Schmidt, Bergman lived alone. Earlier, in 1971 on the set of *Captain Brassbound's Conversion*, she had become good friends with Griffin James, the stage manager, and after her divorce James became a fixture in her life. After the American run of *The Constant Wife* in 1975, Bergman hired Margaret Johnstone as a masseuse. They become close and soon Johnstone was cooking and running errands. Johnstone accompanied Bergman to Israel for the filming of *A Woman Called Golda*.

Schmidt's relationship with Belfraga gradually deteriorated and eventually they separated. In any case, even after the divorce he was the person Bergman relied on to help her through the everyday ordinary troubles of life. It was Schmidt who diagnosed that Bergman would need extra care after her second mastectomy and so, at the end of filming *A Woman Called Golda*, he hired Johnstone to be her full-time companion and nurse.

Despite all this pain and suffering, Bergman endured, seldom spoke in public about the difficulties of her life, and if she did, she only gave brief glimpses of what she had suffered, always in the context of how she had come out of the experience a happier, wiser woman. She refused to be tragic and lived up to the romantic image of what it means to be a star.

In 1945, Bergman gave Larry Adler a copy of Marcia Davenport's *Of Lena Geyer*, which had been published in 1936. She told him that the heroine, Lena Geyer, was a portrait of her, both good and bad, and one day she would like to star in a film version of the book. She kept the book all her life — it was in her apartment when she died — and, according to Spoto, a major disappointment of her life was that she never managed to star in a film of the book.[40]

The jacket blurb gives an indication of the style of the book: "From a poverty stricken home in Bohemia to the dizzy height of grand opera was a long road and a hard one. Beautiful and indomitable, Lena Geyer trod it, although she met defeat, tragedy and abnegation before her ultimate triumph. Her story is the magnificent and moving narrative of a great woman who held her genius sacred. Her vital and passionate personality unfolds against the glamorous background of the operatic stage in Paris, Salzburg, Berlin and New York of the great days...."[41]

It is fascinating to speculate what Bergman saw of herself in Lena Geyer, the opera singer. Spoto notes a number of parallels. Like Geyer, Bergman was tall and strong and a glutton for work. Like Geyer, she could rehearse all day and still have enough energy left to give spirited performances in the evening. Both women, the one fictional, the other real, did not like cooking, enjoyed travel, were fluent in a number of European languages — Geyer knew four, Bergman knew five — and had no head for money. Most of all, both were disciplined when it came to work and absolutely dedicated to their art. Lena tells her lover that she will try to be his and still live for her art. But if she cannot do both, she hopes he will understand what her ultimate choice will be. The narrator comments approvingly on the greatness of Lena's "psychological dependence" upon singing before audiences. Lena says elsewhere that her art is her life, "the one thing I've given up everything on earth for."[42] Bergman said much the same thing many times.

But there are other parallels that Spoto chooses to ignore.

Geyer tells her biographer, David Freeman, that she refuses to write her memoirs and that she wants him to wait until she is dead until he publishes his book. When he presses her as to why, Geyer says, "Because I would not tell the truth."[43] However, she does make the truth available, introducing Freeman to her colleagues, friends, and closest associates. Bergman, too, had difficulty telling the truth about her life, but allowed the co-author of the autobiography Alan Burgess, to have limited access to her diaries and letters and the people who knew her.

Geyer is dependent on a series of mentors, conductor Giulio Pizzeti, singer Lilli Lehmann, conductor Guido Vestri, Maestro Mahler. Bergman broke out of her artistic "cage" with the support of Spencer Tracy and Victor Fleming.

Geyer gives herself to Louis, the Duc de Chartres, after he woos her ardently for months. The affair is passionate but more so on Louis's part, and it is discreet but awkward for Geyer's career. Eventually, Geyer gives up the Duc because she must work harder than he wishes, she must travel where he cannot accompany her, and finally, she gives herself up to an American fan, deHaven, who accompanies her to America to sing for Mahler. The symbolism is blatant: Geyer gives up a man and physical love for the love of her fans, represented by a woman, Elsie deHaven. This, too, Bergman did but in an ironic twist, the love of her life, Robert Capa, would not give up his career for her.

Geyer spends the rest of her life in hotels, except for late in life when she marries husband Harry Loeffler — read, Lars Schmidt — who provides her with a series of rich homes.

She is supported by a faithful maid, Dora: read, Griffin James and Margaret Johnstone.

Geyer has her rude, petulant, dismissive side that she artfully keeps from the press, for which she has contempt. Bergman was never overtly dismissive of the press, but she was suspicious of them and kept them at arm's length. As a result her clippings and reviews do not come close to capturing her private life.

The novel is organized by a central narrator, Freeman, who needs to rely on others for information. Most of the central section of the book is from the memoirs of the Duc de Chartres. At the end of the novel, Freeman interviews Loeffler and George Phillips, Geyer's manager, and asks if Geyer had any faults. Phillips mentions only what we already know, the minor sins of rudeness and petulance. One reason the book is sentimental is that its structure, a series of flashbacks from different points of view, much like *Citizen Kane*, produces not a complex multifaceted portrait of conflicting visions but a single unified point of view. Except for Phillips's brief recitation of her unfavorable traits, all of Geyer's colleagues and friends, everyone who knew her, agree on who she was and the extent of her greatness. This is the universal judgment and acclaim that Bergman worked so hard to achieve.

The ironies are too numerous to elaborate fully, but three stand out. Bergman achieved Geyer's fame but at a much greater personal cost: she had more husbands, lovers, and intimate friends; she had to some extent sacrifice her children to the demands of her art. Unlike Geyer, Bergman did not recognize her own best work. Geyer also knew when to quit. Bergman never did.

After her marriage to Rossellini, Ingrid Bergman had a script for her life. She was acting the legendary part of Lena Geyer.

Seven

The Mistress of the Media

"After I hung up the phone, having said no to writing my memoirs as I had for the last twenty years, my son Roberto gave me a look of great concern. 'Mother,' he said, 'do you realize that when you are dead many people will throw themselves on your life story taking information from gossip columns, rumors, and interviews. We, your children, can never defend you because we don't know the truth. I wish you'd put it down.'

"That gave me a lot to think about. Therefore, my dear children — Pia, Roberto, Isabella, and Ingrid — here is the truth."
— Ingrid Bergman in an Author's Note to *My Story*

"Everyone has the right as well as the instinct to restructure his own past. The contemplation of the past might otherwise be unbearable."
— Victoria Glendinning, "Lies and Silences"

"I am direct and simple and outspoken — it's just that people aren't used to it — they're used to sham and artifice and pretense, and they think I'm putting on an act." — Ingrid Bergman to A. E. Hotchner

In the classic theory of the genre, autobiography reveals more about the autobiographer herself during the present (the time of the telling), than about the past (the time being told about). In an influential essay, Georges Gusdorf defines the essence of autobiography as self-creation and self-discovery. "Confession of the past realizes itself as a work in the present: it effects a true creation of self by the self. Under guise of presenting myself as I was, I exercise a sort of right to recover possession of my existence now and later. 'To create and in creating to be created,' the fine formula of Lequier, ought to be the motto of autobiography."[1]

Autobiographers write under the pressure of current circumstances, the demands of those still present in their lives, to say nothing of their feelings about their past behavior, feelings that can range from bravado to shame. Given these current pressures and emotions, and the human memory, which is inherently selective and notoriously unreliable, given how they feel now about a past that may be unbearable, it is not surprising that autobiographers restructure the past, that they discover and create out of the stuff of memory a version of themselves that they can live with.

Like many people telling stories about their past, autobiographers lie, not necessarily out of cynical motives — to protect their own reputations, for example — but for the best of motives — to tell good stories, to avoid slander, to protect the people they love, to be the selves they want to be, the selves they need to be.

Creating, discovering, or lying in autobiography may even be principled. We are not necessarily entitled to know every squalid detail of a public figure's private life, especially details concerning the nature of her sex life, her fantasy life, or kinky habits that have no direct bearing on her public persona. If all of us do indeed have a core self, an essential self, buried deep beneath layers of carefully trained and cultivated social behavior, why is it anyone's business but our own?

The only convincing justification for tell-all confessional autobiographies, despite their current vogue, is that the private lives of public people should be relevant to their public personas, their public performances. No autobiographer has a moral obligation to treat her readers as if they were psychoanalysts, to divulge her childhood longings and fixations, her adolescent fantasies, her initiation to sex, or her deepest dreams and disappointments.

This may be especially true for movie stars like Bergman. Unlike the work of politicians, government workers, and diplomats, the work of actors has no direct consequences for society as a whole. Nowadays we may enjoy pondering the social and moral implications of Bergman's role as a spy in Hitchcock's *Notorious*: What does it say about our government that it countenances sex traps as a legitimate technique for ferreting out enemies of the republic? What does it say about Bergman's character, Alicia Huberman, that she would have sex with and then marry a man only to learn about his dealings with his Nazi friends, even if it is for the good of the country? But Bergman's convincing portrayal of Huberman says nothing about her own personality and history, and nothing in Bergman's life can necessarily account for the quality of her performance. Even if Bergman had been a Method actor, which she was not, and focused on her own memories and feelings in order to express Huberman's anguish at being abandoned by Cary Grant's Devlin, those memories and feelings would be at best metaphoric approximations of the motivation driving Bergman's portrayal of Huberman. We, the members of the audience who revel in Bergman's performance and are driven to watch it again and again, may instinctively want to know whether her own life is reflected in some aspect of her portrayal of Huberman, but the answer to the question, *Is there something in Bergman's life that can necessarily account for the depth and truth of her performance?* is obvious and one we do not want to hear. The answer is no. That is why we call it acting.

This is not to say that when we view Bergman's performance in *Notorious,* we cannot enjoy speculating about the connections between Bergman's public performance and her private life. As we shall see, there is a minor industry dedicated to interpreting *Notorious* as an expression of Hitchcock's voyeuristic fascination with Bergman as a person, his helplessness and frustration over her love affair with Robert Capa, which was painfully obvious on the set. And it is certainly possible that Bergman was aware that her portrayal of Huberman had echoes in her own life: even though she was passionately involved with Capa, she was still going home to her husband, and she must have known that Hitchcock was infatuated with her. Huberman's double life is the reverse of Bergman's. Bergman was betraying her husband and keeping Hitchcock at a distance. Huberman betrays her lover because he will not declare his love and marries out of resentment and patriotism. Noticing such connections between art and life is the stuff of criticism, but much of criticism is grist for the mind-mill, pure speculation, the relishing of possibilities for their own sake. No autobiographer has any obligation to fuel the interpretive speculation of scholars and critics. If an autobiographer has any moral obligation at all, it is to herself. The autobiographer needs to come to terms with her own life.

In creating her own autobiography, *My Story,* Bergman finally articulated to herself who she was and revealed that self-discovery to the rest of the world: she was a performer, not just on stage and screen but in everyday life. Even when she was not on stage or in front of a camera, she created a public persona, the persona of an open, forthright, and honest person, a person larger than life, full of vitality, good humor and charm, who could tell detailed anecdotes with a dramatic flair that build to a climax, punch line, or moral. Over time, the anecdotes Bergman told became part of her personality. She composed a script for her life, an extension of the official biography publicized by Selznick Studios, honed by her admiration for Lena Geyer. She offered the first version of this script in the mid- to late-fifties, as she was preparing to leave Rossellini. She would perform this script over and over for the rest of her life, improvising variations, providing riffs and grace notes, until the account gradually solidified into the "truth" of her published memoir.

Bergman composed her life, then, in two major forms: the interviews she granted to the press over the years, and her own memoir, *My Story,* which was composed in the late 1970s and finally published in 1980, two years before she died. The major interviews in which she is most revealing and reflective about her past occurred over a period of twenty-six years, but in a sense they tell us about her "eternal present." The interviews stretch from 1956, when her marriage to Rossellini was ending and she was promoting the release of *Anastasia*, to 1982, the year of her death. Although the interviews cover a wide range of topics, they return again and again to what has come to be considered the defining period of her life: her affair with Rossellini. Her account of that affair is a key indication of how she composed her life.

What makes the interviews so autobiographical is that despite the twenty-six year span, they seem so artful, so consistent, so composed and created. Despite all the turmoil of her double life, the covert relationships with husbands and lovers, the constant threat that she would reveal more than she wanted to, Bergman's accounts are remarkably consistent. Taken as a whole, the interviews with Bergman comprise a new genre in itself: call it the celebrity biographical interview, a running dialogue on what constituted the major events in Bergman's life and what those events meant to her.

Her memoir, written late in life, is for all practical purposes a continuation of the celebrity interview, a collection of audiotaped recollections with her collaborator Alan Burgess. The book is an extension and elaboration of the earlier interviews, and a good example of what Bergman had learned about controlling the press and presenting her image to the world. The interviews and memoir give us a good look at a few fundamental aspects of Bergman's character: the deliberate and self-conscious sins of omission to protect her private life and control her image, her natural tendency to romanticize her past and look on the positive side of life. As a result, it is almost impossible to learn whether the image she created, what David O. Selznick called her "inherent dignity," was a façade or an indication of what lay behind it.

Celebrity interviews are a genre all their own, and some day linguists and discourse theorists should study them to determine whether there are deep-structure rules for the ways reporters approach celebrities, the conditions under which the interviews are conducted, and the ways celebrities respond to both the reporter and the immediate circumstances of the interview. Stars of stage and screen grant reporters interviews for only one reason: to publicize their current projects. No matter what their higher goals and journalistic intentions, interviewers are an extension of the publicity machines of entertainment production companies or the stars' agents. Reporters interview stars in order to file stories and meet deadlines about the up-coming or current play or film the star is appearing in. Most interviewers do little background checking and rely on the official press releases of the stars' publicity departments for their story lines. During the interviews, reporters are totally at the mercy of the stars, and if they are aggressive in their questioning or ask hard questions or demand that the stars elaborate on evasive answers — if they antagonize the stars — they may find themselves no longer able to conduct interviews with the stars they have offended or any other personality connected with the stars' agent or producers.

Not all celebrity interviews are puff pieces — many of the Bergman interviews reveal aspects of her character we would not have learned anywhere else — but celebrity interviews are not a vehicle for significant reporting, either. One reason that Bergman's interviews are so consistent is that she was allowed to give her version of events with no significant questioning or contradiction. And when she was pushed to talk about topics not on her agenda, she simply and politely refused. She elicited such sympathy from interviewers that they quickly changed the subject.

Bergman developed her methods of dealing with the press over time. Selznick severely limited Bergman's access to reporters. It is not clear whether this was a deliberate promotional strategy on Selznick's part or a response to Bergman's wishes. Bergman was perfectly fluent and capable of holding her own with reporters, and often seemed to enjoy interviews, although early in her career she had a reputation for being shy and uncomfortable talking about her personal life. One reason for that discomfort may have been pressure from Lindstrom. In *My Story*, Bergman eloquently details Lindstrom's excessive desire for privacy. Often, Lindstrom told her that during her interviews, she never said the right thing and talked too much. He told her that she should follow the example of Greta Garbo, who never gave anything away. Bergman protested that she enjoyed being interviewed: she wanted people to understand her. "But," she concluded, "of course experience taught me that was silly."[2]

According to Bergman, Lindstrom gave her a set of rules for interviews: never mention his name, never give interviews at home; never allow photographs of their home, or of daughter Pia. Once the two had a terrible fight over the fact that Bergman had allowed herself to be photographed at home in a big chair. The photo was only a head shot, so Bergman thought that no one would be able to recognize where the photo had been taken; she does not elaborate on the circumstances of the photo shoot, but she implies that she simply wanted to avoid having to go to a studio or hotel room. In any case, Lindstrom saw the published photograph, recognized the chair, and was furious. Bergman conceded that she had made a mistake but argued that everyone makes mistakes. In his rage, Lindstrom insisted that he did not. Bergman asked incredulously, you don't make mistakes? No, Lindstrom replied vehemently; he thought carefully before doing anything, looking at all sides, pondering consequences. Only then did he decide.[3]

It was then, Bergman recollects, that she first began to think seriously about divorcing Lindstrom and actually suggested the idea to him. Bergman concedes that Lindstrom denies the truth of her story. Indeed, Lindstrom denied to Leamer that he and Bergman ever discussed divorce until he learned about her affairs with Adler, Capa, and Fleming.

Whatever the truth of Bergman's anecdote, clearly in her mind, Lindstrom enforced a rigid code for dealing with the press and that may have been the source for much of her initial reluctance to talk to reporters. In a letter to Selznick in 1943, she says that she is ashamed of two interviews she gave for the fan magazines *Silver Screen* and *Movies* during the publicity campaign for *For Whom the Bell Tolls*: "In one interview I discuss the part of Maria and good and bad women in general. I am not the inventor of that part of the article (though I ok'ed it) but of course I have spoken too much of Pia and my famely [sic]." In her interviews, Bergman usually only corroborated the broad outline of her life put out by the Selznick publicity machine. She wanted to avoid giving too much detail about her husband and child. But this letter hints that reporters could ingratiate themselves with Bergman. They could make her feel comfortable or safe, and then she would let her guard down and talk more freely about her personal life or she would offer opinions she would later regret making public.

Still, Bergman was well aware of the image that Selznick was promoting — that she should at all times appear dignified — and she was in total agreement with that image. When she chatted openly about her family or conveyed the latest news from the set, or even expressed opinions about the issues of the day, she ran the risk of seeming like a gossip or, worse yet, a publicity-hungry starlet trying to win over the press. In the letter in which she apologizes for her conduct during two interviews, she goes on: "I know you dislike it as much as I do and to prevent the same to occur I wonder if I could use your publicity men to check also the interviews I give at other studios and do some cutting for me. The different studios publicity departments don't know me and I hate to go around pounding my ideas about interviews." Bergman was particularly afraid of a "life story" coming out in *Photoplay*.[4]

Three days later, Selznick followed up Bergman's letter with a long memo to Joe Steele, her personal press agent. Selznick suggests that Bergman henceforth grant no interviews at all and that Steele should handle the photographers. If Steele has any reservations about the photos, Selznick recommends that he should send them directly on to him: "I don't want to do this with all our players, but I am most anxious to do it in connection with Miss Bergman." To Selznick, Bergman's publicity in general could always be supplemented by articles written under Steele's direction. Bergman's primary publicity should come out of her work, and Selznick again mentions Bergman's dignity. Then he addresses Bergman's concerns directly: the magazine article in which she discusses "good and bad women" he labels absurd. It reflects on the publicity people at whatever studio arranged it: "This is just old-fashioned 'space for space's sake,' and is undignified, as I am sure you agree, and is the very type of thing that we should scrupulously avoid, and should protect Miss Bergman from." He goes on: "I don't think Miss Bergman should worry about talking about her child, Pia, or her family. This is perfectly all right. She has a very fine family life and the position of her husband, the simple life that Miss Bergman leads, her enchanting child, and everything connected with her personal life is completely consistent with the position that she is entitled to have with the public, and that I have tried to build and preserve. There is no need to stress her marriage or her child; there is no need to avoid it; we should be guided in these matters *completely* by whatever Miss Bergman's wishes are in the matter. There is nothing whatever to hide...."[5]

"The position that she is entitled to have with the public": the phrase is rich in ambiguity. Selznick may be simply asserting that Bergman has a right to a certain amount of privacy, or he may be implying that Bergman, with her dignified persona, fine family, and simple life, is entitled to something more, an image that only Selznick can build and preserve.

"There is nothing whatever to hide...." But, of course, by this time there was. By 1943 Bergman had, in her words, broken out of her cage during the shooting of *Dr. Jekyll and Mr. Hyde*, and had been seen to be very close to Spencer Tracy and Victor Fleming on the set of the film. And she would become passionately attached to Gary Cooper on the set of *For Whom the Bell Tolls*.

Bergman gradually became less concerned about interviews. Having her own personal press agent helped. Joe Steele went with her everywhere, and with Steele carefully crafting her public statements and coaching her on how to say things, Bergman became more comfortable with the press, perhaps even confident. All of which may have been another reason why Bergman was willing to follow Robert Capa's example and risk everything for Rossellini. She had had such success with the press, her private life had been so well shielded from the public, that she may have thought that she was impervious to scandal.

When Bergman found out that she was wrong, when she learned that she and Rossellini could not control the scandal over their romance, Bergman called in Steele to help them limit the damage to their careers. But after she broke up with Rossellini, Bergman confronted the press on her own. She had learned her lessons well from Selznick and Steele, and she had suffered the consequences of not following their advice.

Dealing with the press during her marriage to Rossellini, she had honed her public persona to a fine point. She was engaging and personable. She looked interviewers in the eye. She pondered questions thoughtfully. When she had gathered her thoughts, she was fluent and straightforward and did not hem and haw. She was self-deprecating and often funny. She charmed interviewers with her seeming candor and good humor, and as a result, interviewers took her at her word and allowed her to set the agenda for an interpretation of her life.

Bergman's ability to promote her legend — her apparent happiness, her positive philosophy, her love of performing — is never more apparent than when she appeared at a National Press Club luncheon in Washington, D.C., in April of 1972. She was in town, performing in *Captain Brassbound's Conversion* before record-setting crowds at the 2,400-seat Kennedy Center Opera House. She did not give a formal speech or do dramatic readings. She simply answered questions for forty-five minutes. Although the National Press Association includes many more people than theater and entertainment critics — people such as reporters and columnists who cover politics and culture — the assembled group acted like star-struck fans. For the first time in club history, there was a waiting list of 150 for reservations. And when the question-and-answer period began, it was clear that the best reporters in the business had not done their homework and would not be grilling Bergman the way they would a political figure. They would ask no difficult questions about Bergman's life and career.

Club president Warren Rogers started the proceedings with this question: "How do you stay so brilliantly beautiful?"

To which Bergman replied that she had always been taken to be younger than she was, even when she was 18: "I suppose it was my parents, maybe good air, the fact that I'm happy and working, don't overeat." Following are other sample questions and answers.

"What are your favorite stage and screen roles?"

"Joan of Arc, which I played in Maxwell Anderson's *Joan of Lorraine*, not the Shaw *Joan*, which, I once told him, was too masculine and war-loving for my tastes. My favorite screen role always is the last one I played in, *A Walk in the Spring Rain*. But it didn't go over very well."

On acting: "I don't take a part unless I can understand and feel it."

Perhaps the question that delved the deepest was this one: "If you could live your life over, what changes would you make?"

But Bergman had the perfect non-answer: "If I had the memory to profit by the experiences I've had, of course I would do some things very differently, but without the memory stored up, of course, being me, I'd wind up doing the very same things." And later: " [I handle] life's most difficult problems with a laugh and try to look at myself as though I was critically viewing a role on the screen — sometimes not good, sometimes ridiculous."

Still, she did deal, at least obliquely, with some major topics. On politics: "I would be an idiot to give an opinion. I'm an entertainer. Humanity, prisoners of war and orphans of war are my only political concern." On race: She says that "[s]he is glad to be playing to racially integrated audiences, which wasn't the case when she last appeared here in the '40s and upset me so I told the press I'd never come back."

In response to the question, "Is Hollywood's Golden Age gone?" she says, "Time marches on. Of course there's a loss but other things happen. There came a time for me, when Hollywood's glamour wore false. There was another world, a world of reality, which a picture called *Open City* revealed to me as an actress for the first time." This was the only reference to the Rossellini scandal during the entire session.[6]

As in her appearance before the National Press Association, Bergman stays rigorously "on message" in her public interviews, ringing changes on her basic story line and refusing to discuss other topics. That story line is one of hollow triumph, exile, and return. Her early fame is accompanied by an increasing alienation from Hollywood and her husband. She comes to think of her work in Hollywood films as insufficiently artistic. She wants to move on. Her difficulties with Lindstrom have to do with his attempt to dominate her and their constant bickering. She does not acknowledge that her constantly being away from home and the other men in her life may have contributed to the failure of her first marriage.

About the scandal, Bergman constantly reiterates the pain and suffering she endured. She does not acknowledge that she received significant support from friends and fans. She does not acknowledge how badly she and Rossellini handled the press, how they avoided advice from professionals about how to lessen the effect of the scandal. Above all, she talks about her love for Rossellini in the broadest terms and carefully finesses any sense of how the affair developed or her own responsibility in leaving her family. She expresses her agony about being separated from Pia but does not account for how she could have stayed away from her daughter for six years.

When the press pick up this story line and begin to trumpet her return to America as a triumph, she tacitly concurs with this judgment and then encourages it.

Bergman first unveiled this scenario for her life in 1956. As part of the publicity for *Anastasia*, Bergman gave an interview to Robert Levin for *Red-book* magazine. Here, Bergman establishes the major themes she will return to again and again. One major theme is her sense of alienation during the height of her success, but she is studiously vague about the source of that dissatisfaction. She does not know when or why her alienation began — "Who knows," she says, "where anything *really* begins?" — but she was restless in Hollywood for a long time and tired of making the same old films. When she went to Italy, she was not running away. She loved Broadway, but Broadway simply did not have enough plays for her. It is all too difficult for her to understand, but "something had been dead inside" her for quite some time. Everything was wrong, but not wrong enough for her to do anything about it ... until Rossellini came along

About her affair with Rossellini, she is equally vague. She confesses that she probably loved him the first time she saw his films. Love did not suddenly come over her. She just felt as if she had known Rossellini for a great many years and he seemed so "alive" that he made her come alive.

Based on what Bergman tells him, Levin reiterates the basic story, noting that the marriage had been strained and that Bergman's love for Rossellini only blossomed after she went to Italy. Only at the airport in Rome, their third meeting, did the couple become aware of any possible romantic attachment, and even then to call it love would have been "an exaggeration."

When Levin asserts that Bergman and Rossellini met each other for the third time in Rome, he is stretching a point. Bergman's arrival in Rome was technically her third time together with Rossellini, but Levin's language glosses over the fact that the second "meeting" with Rossellini in Hollywood lasted for six weeks, while he was arranging financing for *Stromboli*. During this period Rossellini actively courted Bergman and their association, as we have seen, caused a minor sensation among Hollywood insiders.

Still, prompted by Bergman, Levin states baldly that the two lovers only recognized their love on Stromboli, where they refused to hide their love from the press and were caught in the famous *Life* photograph, holding hands. But Bergman is coy. She only admits that her love for Rossellini required a decision on her part: it was only in Italy that she was forced to decide about her love for Rossellini. So to Bergman, she had been in love in some abstract sense with Rossellini before she went to Italy, but a decision based on that love was only necessary after she had arrived in that country. This carefully finesses any sense of her own responsibility in leaving her family or when the affair with Rossellini was consummated.

Bergman vividly expresses her agony at leaving Pia — she says that she was "sick" over leaving her and claims that nothing before or since has made her feel "half so rotten" — and concedes that she was selfish, that she put her own happiness ahead of her daughter's. But she is adamant that she never dreamed that things would turn out the way they did. Bergman understandably emphasizes her own suffering and the pain she caused Pia, but by constantly focusing on her own feelings, she manages to avoid the issue of just what kept the two apart, even after she was divorced from Lindstrom and Pia was old enough to understand the pressures on her mother.

Another major theme is introduced in Bergman's interview with Levin: her suffering at the hands of the press. Levin summarizes the case that Senator

Johnson made on the floor of the Senate, that both Bergman and Rossellini were condemned in the American media. Then Levin quotes Bergman quoting Johnson: "Out of Ingrid Bergman's ashes, perhaps a better Hollywood will come. " Well, Bergman tells Levin, she hopes so. But now it does not matter. She has learned from her experience, and she hopes that Hollywood is now a nicer place than it was eight years before.

It is only a surmise, but it seems reasonable to infer that Bergman told Levin about what Johnson had said. There is no mention that Bergman's fan mail was running four to one in her favor; there is no mention of the support she received from friends and colleagues in the film industry.

Given what we now know about Bergman's love life, it is a rich irony that Levin prominently features the statement by Jean Renoir that Bergman is "the most completely honest woman" he has ever met. Other Hollywood starlets, says Renoir, may have had lovers and kept it from the newspapers, but Bergman is incapable of that kind of hypocrisy: "If she loves someone, she would no more try to hide it than she would try to keep the sun from coming up."[7]

In 1968, twelve years after the interview with Levin, Bergman talked with friend and journalist Oriana Fallaci on the occasion of her appearance in José Quintero's production of *More Stately Mansions*. By then Bergman has developed her story line to such a degree that she is comfortable offering a more broadly philosophical view of her rise and fall. At ease with Fallaci, whom she considers a friend, Bergman is talkative and boldly assertive. She feels no need to explain or justify. She continues to blur the details of her affair with Rossellini, focusing instead on her successful career in America before the scandal, her image as the girl next door, a woman who appealed to men because she reminded them of their mothers, sisters, and wives, and who appealed to other women because she seemed like them, not like "European prima donnas" who throw tantrums and wear outlandish clothes. Bergman thinks that Americans even thought of her as a kind of nun, but "a nun does not fall in love with an Italian. My falling in love with Roberto was too much of a betrayal for them."

Fallaci asserts that there is still in 1968 "a sort of unconfessed uneasiness" when Americans talk about Bergman, to which Bergman has a ready answer: Americans do not understand that she did not "flee" from their country just because of Rossellini. Rossellini was only "the instrument of my flight, the consequence of a deeply matured tiredness." For years, Bergman had dreamed of escaping from her life in America. Rossellini gave her that chance.

Bergman subtly shifts to how she also loved escaping to New York, but Fallaci, to her credit as an interviewer, reminds her that she didn't ultimately escape to New York; she went to Rome. Bergman agrees without missing a beat, relating the story of how she saw a Rossellini movie and found it "so unbelievably beautiful" that she fell in love with Rossellini without knowing him at all. When the two finally met, Bergman "had the confirmation of being in love with him. And I knew I had found my road."

This is a grand story, but once again, it obscures the messy details of how Bergman came to fall in love with Rossellini and what was not a fairy tale romance.[8]

In 1971–72, four years after talking with Fallaci, Bergman gave an interview to John Kobal, during the London run of *Captain Brassbound's Conversion*. In this interview, Bergman still has the attitudes she expressed with Fallaci, but now the emphasis is even less on Rossellini and more on the professional, even existential, reasons she left the United States: to be a serious actress and get at the "truth." Here, Bergman reiterates that she was happy in America until the last few years, when she just became "tired" of being in Hollywood because "it didn't seem to belong to the world." She wanted to be among real people and make movies that were more realistic. Something inside of her was "just straining for a challenge and the *truth*." She claims that being a star in Hollywood did not interest her very much, and thus: "Why would I have gone to Italy if I'd wanted to be a star and on top of everything? I hadn't fallen down at that time — I still got the best scripts. But I didn't *want* it. I wanted to become a serious actress — and I went to Italy to work with Rossellini."[9]

Finally, shortly before her death, Bergman granted an interview to A. E. Hotchner as part of the publicity campaign for the 1982 TV movie *A Woman Called Golda*. Her memory perhaps refreshed by work on her autobiography, Bergman is now somewhat more detailed. She blames Lindstrom for their failed marriage and focuses on Rossellini as the instrument of her escape: it was leaving that mattered, not the romance. It was Rossellini, not Capa, who taught her to be brave and take risks. On being prompted by Hotchner that Lindstrom had been a father figure for her, Bergman first expresses puzzlement but eventually warms to the idea. She relates how she used to come home after a hard day on the set and try to tell Lindstrom about what she had gone through, but he would barely listen and instead nag her about her image, telling her not to wrinkle her forehead, to sit up straight, to stop playing with her fingers, and above all, to avoid eating so much. He seemed pathological about her not putting on weight. He treated her as if she were not his wife, but his daughter, to the point that she became afraid of him. Still, Bergman lacked the courage to try to escape her marriage, until Rossellini gave it to her. Rossellini was the opposite of Lindstrom: he was spontaneous and free and he took risks. And when Bergman whispered to him that she was terribly frightened at being pregnant, Rossellini would say, "Frightened of what? What is there to be frightened about? We have each other, and we have talent, and who can take any of that away from us?" Bergman endured the scandal with Rossellini only because he was such a bulwark against the storm.[10]

Once again like a good storyteller, Bergman provides convincing details about her state of mind before and during the scandal, but she provides no evidence of just what went on between her and Rossellini before the scandal broke or her actual intentions in leaving for Rome. There is a remarkable consistency in Bergman's story line. Perhaps in her mind her public statements became the truth. But those statements ignore, hide, aggrandize just as much as they reveal.

One obvious justification of Bergman's story line is that it protects her privacy: it reveals aspects of her life she wants revealed; it hides aspects of her life she wants to hide. One other part of her life Bergman insisted on hiding was the state of her marriages. She does not acknowledge any difficulties in her current circumstances, only those in the past. She talks openly about her marriage to Lindstrom because so much of it is on the public record. But about her current relationships, Bergman gives away nothing. The Levin interview in 1956 is accompanied by a picture of the Rossellini family, Bergman bending over Rossellini as he holds the twins in his arms and leans his head into Robertino's chest. Robertino has his hand on Rossellini's head. Levin notes that the interview occurred during the year in which the Rossellinis celebrated their sixth wedding anniversary. Bergman conveys the impression that her marriage is happy, unified, and "closely-knit," that its unity "springs from two sources — Ingrid's determination not to let her profession separate her from those she loves, as had happened in America, and Roberto's strong sense of family solidarity."[11] Now of course we know that when the interview occurred, the marriage had been on the rocks for years, that Bergman was negotiating to leave her family to do *Tea and Sympathy* in Paris, and that by the time the magazine containing the article hit the newsstands, Bergman had left Rossellini.

Until the autobiography in 1980, Bergman never acknowledged that she had become estranged from third husband Lars Schmidt, even after she learned that he had taken a mistress. Interviewed in her dressing room during the run of *The Constant Wife* in 1973, Bergman was asked about the rumors that her marriage to Schmidt was in trouble. She replied, ""We'll sort it out. I don't want to say anymore."[12] She kept up the appearance of a healthy marriage for five long years after Schmidt's announcement that he had a lover.

Bergman's apparent openness and frankness about the narrow range of topics she allowed was occasionally tested. In the introduction to his interview with Bergman, John Kobal captures the anxiety Bergman experienced when she became too casual in talking about her personal life. The occasion was a public question-and-answer session before a large and adoring audience at the National Film Theatre in London after a screening of *Casablanca*. Kobal was the MC, Bergman the Celebrity Lecturer, who had expressed a preference to answer questions from the audience rather than give a formal talk. Kobal had planned to begin with a few easy questions and then open things up to the audience, but when he and Bergman exchanged a few remarks and Kobal turned to the room full of adoring fans, there were no hands in the air and a prolonged silence. It was as if Bergman's mere presence has struck the audience speechless. Rattled, Kobal began to ask a few simple questions about what Bergman thought about her directors and costars — Fleming, Rossellini, Cooper, Tracy — and his language implied intimacy, gossip. One question was simply whether Bergman had been close to Cary Grant. Bergman replied, "Well, not that close," and sweat appeared on her forehead and she began to noticeably redden. She stared at Kobal, as if signaling that she wanted the interview to move on and avoid topics she found embarrassing.[13] Kobal managed to salvage the afternoon. The session lasted two hours, and Bergman did not blame Kobal for her discomfort. But the anecdote conveys Bergman's physical response to revealing more about her life than she wanted to.

Normally, on her own, Bergman would have announced that there were certain topics she did not talk about. As Kobal stumbled on, asking her to talk about her feelings for the men she worked with, she prompted him in a whisper to see if there were now any questions from the audience. In other contexts, she could be more blunt. Asked her views on religion at a National Press Club luncheon in 1972, she replied, "I do not discuss religion. I was born in the Protestant faith and that is as much as I ever say about religion."[14]

Bergman's public performance in celebrity interviews may not have been as polished and freewheeling as they seemed. They may have come at a price. Fiorella Mariani is eloquent in describing how in public Bergman always seemed to hold herself back, to keep some aspect of herself in reserve. Mariani could never tell what Bergman really felt: to Mariani, Bergman could be "bursting with laughter and holding a tragedy within." And Mariani sensed that Bergman was afraid of many things: she was afraid of suffering, evil, violence, and things she could not even articulate.[15]

If Bergman's interviews were performances designed to finesse the truth, to hide her true motives and actual behavior, her autobiography is an artifact of her performance art. The book began as an authorized biography to be written by Alan Burgess, but because of a host of circumstances, it became an autobiography. Begun in 1976, the writing of the book quickly spiraled out of control.

Alan Burgess was a BBC correspondent who had written the novel, *The*

Small Woman, on which the screenplay for *The Inn of the Sixth Happiness* was based. Bergman had met him in conjunction with that film and found him congenial. Although she had previously resisted the admonitions of Kay Brown and others that she really should write a memoir, she finally succumbed to the idea of Burgess doing an authorized biography if she had complete control over the final draft. Why she settled on Burgess is not clear, but he was a writer and she knew and trusted him. Unfortunately, Burgess had no experience in writing a biography.

Once she had decided upon the biography, Bergman set to work gathering together, sorting through, and organizing her diaries, letters, clippings, and other memorabilia. She withdrew to Choisel to do this work, but after two months, she became bored and frustrated. "I can't look at it anymore," she told Pavo Turtiainen, a young Finnish man who was helping her. Turtiainen had done occasional work for Bergman and Schmidt for years, he was careful and thorough and Bergman trusted him, so she allowed him to continue organizing the files on his own.[16]

Because Bergman found working on the biography so tedious, Burgess gave her a tape recorder and told her to speak into it whenever she had the opportunity. Bergman laughingly replied, "What, Alan, without an audience?" And so Burgess and Bergman began to spend long days together while Bergman reminisced for Burgess's tape recorder.

Eventually, Bergman went back to the stage, and Burgess worked on his own, taping Bergman when he could, incorporating her primary sources into a working draft, interviewing the people in her life, including Lindstrom, who was cooperative because Burgess insisted that he was writing an objective biography and would be fair to both Bergman and Lindstrom. Burgess even managed to arrange several meetings between Lindstrom and Bergman to discuss certain areas of disagreement in their recollections. Lindstrom was insistent in particular that the biography include his version of his first meeting with Bergman at Messina during the Rossellini scandal and certain details about the custody battle over Pia. These meetings were polite and formal, and only occasionally broke out into hostilities. They also occasioned a flurry of letters about details, Lindstrom insisting dogmatically on the accuracy of certain points, Bergman ignoring or dismissing Lindstrom's concerns.

But despite all this attention to detail, Burgess missed several deadlines for completing the book set by the publisher, Delacorte Press. By 1979, he seemed incapable of ever finishing the book. The draft he had produced thus far was loose and anecdotal, a stitching together of the taped interviews with Bergman that lacked the factual detail and clear chronology most people associate with biographies. Spoto claims Burgess was "incapacitated" by drinking. Be that as it may, by this time, Bergman was upset enough to tell Spoto that she was terribly worried about the book because it was too long and disorganized. She feared that it would be a total failure.[17]

Given that Burgess's draft was such a mess, the editors at Delacorte recommended that Bergman should provide additional interviews and turn the book into an autobiography. She agreed. But when Lindstrom found out that he had been contributing not to an objective biography but to Bergman's personal memoirs, he became outraged. He contacted Harriet Pilpel, a New York attorney, about revoking his permission to quote from the interviews he had granted and the letters he had handed over to Burgess. Burgess countered with accusations of slander and threats of legal action of his own, whereupon Lindstrom wrote Burgess a stern letter that began by addressing Burgess as someone Lindstrom thought he knew. Lindstrom complained that he had difficulty admitting that he may have trusted Burgess when he should not have. In response to Burgess's threat to countersue for libel, Lindstrom hinted darkly that Bergman and Burgess would not look good in court when they were under cross-examination. Jeanne Bernkopf, the editor of the book, acknowledged to Leamer that the publisher was swamped with legal problems. Burgess and Bergman were frantically writing parts of the book even after a draft had appeared in galleys, and finally, Bernkopf told Bergman and Burgess to paraphrase Lindstrom's letters and simply eliminate everything in the book that came from Lindstrom or that made Lindstrom look good.[18]

When the book was finally published in 1980, Bergman was suffering from a second bout with cancer. Nevertheless, she managed to supervise the final manuscript, especially the Swedish translation, and go on an extensive five-country book tour, involving exhausting television interviews and book signings in England, America, Sweden, France, and Italy.[19] Bergman knew what was in the book, stood by it as "the truth," and freely promoted it to the world at large.

My Story was a huge success. It was on the *New York Times* non-fiction best-seller list for eleven weeks, rising as high as number four. The reviews were universally laudatory, although reviewers were more appreciative of Bergman as a person than of the book itself. In an interview, *Times* reporter Judy Klemesrud noted the classic Bergman dignity: "Unlike many recent movie star autobiographies, Miss Bergman's skips explicit sexual details and avoids naming lovers she did not marry.... 'I'm a tasteful person,' Miss Bergman said."[20]

Because of the chaos of its creation, *My Story* became, in effect, an extended version of a celebrity interview. Burgess could not manage to incorporate his interviews with Bergman into a larger, more traditional biographical form and corroborate much of what Bergman said from other sources, either from documents or from interviews with family, friends, and co-workers.

Consequently, the book is overwhelmingly a record of Bergman speaking into a tape recorder and responding to Burgess's promptings. Like a celebrity interview, *My Story* is a record of Bergman speaking to a friendly audience under carefully controlled conditions. In these circumstances she is free to stay on message and express herself without fear of contradiction or confrontation; she can avoid any topics she finds distasteful.

Interspersed among the as-told-to oral taped recollections in Bergman's first-person voice, transcribed, edited, and briefly elaborated on by Burgess, is Burgess's third-person narration. That narration is often in a voice similar to Bergman's own. It often transcribes, without commentary, brief snatches of conversation Burgess had with people who knew Bergman or quotes from letters to and from Bergman. More commonly, though, Burgess quotes from the glowing reviews of Bergman's performances. It is as if Burgess could not find his own voice: that he became so dumbstruck working with Bergman, all he could do is transcribe or quote the words of others, and when he was forced to speak for himself, he had become a dummy to Bergman's ventriloquist. Burgess told Leamer that the form of the book gave Bergman the opportunity "to say what she wanted to say in the first person and have me, the narrator, say what she didn't want to say or couldn't really say."[21]

The non-chronological associative structure of the memoir helps Bergman evade the issues she wants to evade — the trouble in her marriages, the suppression of her love life — and most of what Bergman did not want to say, Burgess says in so veiled a fashion that Bergman might as well have said it herself. *My Story* cuts from Bergman's discussion of her love affair with Robert Capa to an extended anecdote about her meeting with George Bernard Shaw. Intentional or not, the leap of thought becomes a trope for how the autobiography functions as a whole. Whenever Bergman becomes too detailed about what she considers a dangerous subject, she always finds a way to change the subject.

Nevertheless, despite the mixed narration and the elimination of Lindstrom's material, *My Story* says a great deal about Ingrid Bergman.

In deciding what to say on the spur of the moment with the microphone nearby, in carefully doling out the diary entries and letters she finds appropriate, free from having to deal with anyone's contrary recollections, Bergman repeats and refines the stories she had been telling for years, coming to terms with what her life means to her in the late 1970s after forty years on stage and screen. Not surprisingly, the autobiography is an apotheosis of the previous interviews. Bergman justifies her life as a performer, entitled to create her own scenes, dramatize herself, create her own personal legends because, after all, that is what performers do.

In a sense, the autobiography becomes another way for Bergman to escape the control of the dominating men in her life and to recapture the joy of the passionate artistic life. In Alan Burgess she had found a compliant man she could control, and in the process of retelling the stories from her past, she could continue to elaborate on her legend. She could dramatize her life; she could recreate her life and control the public's understanding of it.

The dual narrators in *My Story* pretend to offer both subjective and objective reporting, but the book is all Bergman. Burgess's third-person narrative allows Bergman to include material that would otherwise be embarrassingly immodest in a personal narrative. For example, Burgess often sums up and evaluates Bergman's character in ways that can only be called pure adoration. In relating Bergman's triumphant performance in *Captain Brassbound's Conversion* in Washington, D.C., in 1972, and her appearance before the National Press Association, Burgess notes that her popularity refuted Senator Johnson's claim in his Senate speech in 1950 that "out of the degradation associated with *Stromboli*.... Out of [the] ashes [of Bergman's career] may come a better Hollywood." Says Burgess, assuming Bergman's point of view that in the first-person would be very immodest: Johnson's charge hurt Bergman very deeply. She had been brought up to be a decent, upright person, someone who spoke truthfully and lived with integrity, someone who tried to live better than the Golden Rule: to treat others *better* than they treated you.

And, Burgess goes on, answering questions before the National Press Association was also a way for Bergman to settle scores. Bergman wanted very much to respond to Johnson's charges, even though they were 22 years old, and had prepared a statement if she had the chance. Her reply would be that if by 1972, if anything lay in ashes, it was not her but Hollywood itself. The movies had been supplanted by television, while Bergman had risen from the ashes like a phoenix to become an international star. Late in the interview Bergman gets her chance. She is asked whether it is a good thing or a loss that the golden age of Hollywood is past. Bergman replies that she thought Hollywood was wonderful, but she understood that the star system could not last. Increasingly pictures became glossy and unrealistic, so she left to make pictures with Rossellini. Here was the natural place to get in a dig at Johnson, and so Bergman recalls that a noted senator some time ago gave a speech, which ended with the words "out of Hollywood's ashes will grow a better Hollywood." The audience looks on blankly. They haven't caught the irony. Only later back in Paris when she hears a tape of the interview does Bergman realize that she had said "Hollywood's ashes," not "the ashes of my career." She had flubbed her chance to criticize Johnson. But Burgess, like the fan he is, scores the point for her.[22] As a result, Burgess makes Bergman look personable and charming, not out to retaliate against a perceived insult over twenty years old. When Bergman hears the tape, she can only laugh at her mistake. In the end, with Burgess's help, Bergman can be winningly inept and still have the last word against Johnson.

Burgess is shameless in offering good opinions about Bergman's performances. His coverage of Bergman's work in *The Constant Wife* is adulatory and ignores obvious problems with her work. His primary source for Bergman's participation in that show is Griffin James, the stage manager, and later caregiver, who worshipped Bergman. James thinks everything Bergman does is "an occasion," from arriving on stage to entering a person's life, as she had entered his. James cites a number of situations in which Bergman fluffs lines, breaks character, and invents blocking, actions which could be interpreted as unprofessional if the actor's primary responsibility is to the play, but James thinks Bergman's mistakes fascinating, charming, hilarious. Clearly, for James the play is not the point; the play is just an opportunity for him to watch Ingrid Bergman.

To do him credit, Burgess does note that the critics of *The Constant Wife* were "lukewarm and condescending," and he cites Clive Barnes in *The New York Times* to the effect that Bergman, while glowingly beautiful, is playing a part written for someone twenty years younger. Still, Burgess gives Bergman a rebuttal and the last word: to Bergman the style of the play may be antiquated, but the theme is timeless. And women today, Bergman argues, have romantic lives well past the age of thirty-six. Her character, Constance Middleton, for instance, could very well be any age from fifty to seventy.[23] Here, Bergman seems to be arguing that women well into late middle-age may have intense romantic lives. She also seems to imply that she herself has had such a life. This is just the kind of opening for a perceptive and engaged interviewer to ask follow-up questions, but Burgess lets the point go, unexplored.

Indeed, much of *My Story* can be understood as an argument and rebuttal to what Bergman considers misconceptions about her in the popular media at the time *My Story* was being assembled. The numerous examples that she was difficult to work with are rebutted with cheerful rationales that everything eventually turned out all right. Over the course of the autobiography we could get the impression that Bergman never changed, never learned, never adapted; in short, that she was always combative in rehearsal or on the set. But after each confession that she confronted and contradicted directors, refused their counsel, and made their lives miserable, she cheerfully announces that the results were worth it, or Burgess quotes members of the cast or reviewers of the play or film to the effect that Bergman's performance justified the pain and misery. Quintero may have been right about her entrance downstage center in *More Stately Mansions*, making her objections unnecessary and distracting, but the end result was dramatic and Quintero managed to assuage her insecurities so her objections were justified. On the set of *Cactus Flower*, she badgers director Gene Saks with her "usual" advice, and he seems grateful, but screenwriter I.A.L. Diamond does not appreciate her many suggestions to cut his jokes. She simply does not find them funny. Still, she persists, even though during the first read-through the rest of the cast was laughing uproariously. It seems as if her taste in humor should trump everyone else's.

During the filming of *A Walk in the Spring Rain*, she again indulges in what she calls her "great difficulty in being diplomatic": after an elaborate scene preparation that in the end had to be done quickly — the sun was moving out of position — director Guy Green organized a quick run-through with Anthony Quinn. Aware of the time constraints, Bergman lashed out at Quinn, questioning his interpretation of the scene. Quinn became furious, questioning who was really directing the film, Bergman or Green, and eventually decided to quit the picture. Quinn went so far as to suggest a replacement. He knew that Burt Lancaster was available and was sure Lancaster would be happy to take his place. Says Bergman of the episode: Quinn could not tolerate her "interfering" with Quinn's character. Burgess follows this scene with a letter from Bergman to Schmidt, saying that she has calmed down considerably since the scene took place. Now she understands that the people on the set may have found her "tiresome." Still, she excuses herself: she was suffering from fatigue, and she has lived alone too much and has gotten into the habit of making decisions by herself. But both Quinn and director Green have helped her see that she often doesn't listen to other people and she changes the subject in the middle of a conversation. Surely Schmidt knows how often she does these things. And addressing Schmidt as "my little old man," Bergman promises him that she is much kinder now: he will see that when she gets home. This apology would have more force if it seemed to prompt a change of behavior. There is no evidence that it did. And if we are to believe Quinn's leering memoir, he had reignited his previous affair with Bergman on the set of *Spring Rain*. If we trust Quinn, Bergman's need for the man's forgiveness is not just professional; it is part of a lover's quarrel, and her promise to her husband that she is kinder now has all sorts of implications.[24]

The free-floating structure of the memoir also gives Bergman the chance to give her version of a story floated by Anthony Perkins that she tried to seduce him on the set of *Goodbye Again*. Over twenty years after the film, Perkins told reporter Brad Darrach from *People* magazine that Bergman "would have welcomed an affair. Every day she invited me to her dressing room to practice a love scene. I insisted on standing near the door, which I kept open." Perkins later denied the story to Leamer, but Darrach stands by the quotation. In *My Story*, Bergman does not refute the story directly in a discussion of the filming of *Goodbye Again*. She mentions Perkins in passing while she is talking about *Gaslight* and how difficult it was to begin the shooting of the film with a love scene with Charles Boyer, whom she barely knew. And so the Perkins story becomes an anecdote about how to help her male leads deal with love scenes. Bergman says that she invited Perkins into her dressing room in order to practice kissing. Because she may have asked Perkins to kiss her rather bluntly, Perkins was taken aback and asked, What for? Bergman told him that the two of them had to kiss later, and she was shy and often blushed, so she thought it would be better to have their first rehearsals in the privacy of her dressing room rather than in front of all the technicians on the set. Perkins smiled and said he understood. At the time, Bergman thought that Perkins was sweet, and their rehearsal helped her overcome her shyness.

One major discrepancy between the two stories is the number of times Bergman invited Perkins to her dressing room. Bergman says that she only asked Perkins once. Perkins says that she invited him to her dressing room every day. Spoto is hard on Perkins, a gay man, and in defending Bergman's honor he accuses Perkins of being dangerously promiscuous in pursuing gay sex and very awkward and self-conscious in sex scenes with women. To Spoto, Bergman sensed Perkins's awkwardness with women and was simply trying to make their work together easier. But in the autobiography, Bergman does not say that she was worried about Perkins; she says that she was worried about herself. And we have to judge from her other relationships with co-stars whether her shyness is believable and her story rings true. The tone of Bergman's version of the story is casual and off-hand, but the details are vivid and the dialogue sharp. It sounds composed and seems, once again, carefully crafted to promote her image.[25]

Indeed, the tone of *My Story* as a whole is self-effacing, generous, and forgiving, but it is also self-serving, subtly argumentative and suspiciously gracious. What Bergman gives with one hand, she takes away with another. About her husbands, Bergman can be maddeningly ambivalent. She is especially hard on Lindstrom for being so domineering that for the rest of her life she would be "helpless without a man to tell me what to do." But then she turns around and acknowledges that it was not entirely Lindstrom's fault: "I was the one who asked him for advice and help in those early days."[26]

Bergman is discreet about her life with Rossellini. She focuses on stories about the birth of the children or about the films they did together. She only hints that the marriage was not a success but her resentment keeps breaking through, and we are left to wonder why she keeps up such a happy front. She is especially clear about Rossellini's domination of her. Bergman reflects that she should have gone back to America to talk Lindstrom into a divorce and to see Pia. She is blunt about "the force and the fury" of Rossellini's will and her own inability to stand up to it. She did not go because of what would have happened when she returned: "Riots would have broken out." She also notes the fact that Rossellini would not let her work with other directors: "In Roberto's terms, I was his property." By the time they made *Fear* together, Bergman admits that the silences between them were getting longer, and if she did say something Rossellini would pounce on what she said and make a scene: "He liked to fight."[27]

Bergman tries to give Rossellini his due, but the catalogue of her grievances is constantly breaking through: Rossellini's being late to their wedding, his inability to handle money, his rudeness to her guests, his refusal to let her work with other directors, the silences and the fights. There was also the competition for the attention and affection of the children.[28]

Bergman is also alternately self-effacing and critical of Rossellini in talking about the films they made together. On the one hand, through Burgess's third-person voice, she takes the blame for the fact that the films were not critical successes. Burgess says that to many people Rossellini almost ruined Bergman's career, but to Bergman the truth was that she almost ruined Rossellini's career. But then she suggests that the fault is Rossellini's for not recognizing that she was not appropriate for his production methods, that he tried to integrate a Hollywood star into his documentary realism, which "simply did not work." Two pages earlier, in her own voice, Bergman hints at a deeper bitterness: that in courting her as a Hollywood star, Rossellini did not know what he was doing; he had only worked effectively with actresses like Anna Magnani, perhaps because they were both Italian and fit together. To Bergman, she and Rossellini were not "a good mix."[29] As a re-creation of her feelings at the time, this may be accurate. But as a reflection twenty-five years later and stated as an authoritative judgment about their collaboration, without the qualifications that time and experience can provide, it is spectacularly wrong. Because she did not enjoy making the films with Rossellini and because she did not understand them, Bergman seems to want to take some of the blame — Rossellini was stuck with her and she ruined him — and yet she cannot help herself: her unhappiness with the films is Rossellini's fault. It was he who seduced her into working with him; it was he who did not see that she was not the right actress for his style of filmmaking. The ultimate irony, of course, is that she *was* appropriate for his style of filmmaking; she just did not know it.

About her marriage to Schmidt, Bergman admits that their being apart so much put the marriage in danger. Liana Ferri, a friend of Rossellini and his translator, told her bluntly that by being away for so long, she was straining her marriage to the breaking point. Bergman could only reply that she had to work, that acting was her life. Bergman details the difficulties she had getting together with Schmidt when she was working in the theater, and she grants that he had a right to feel abandoned. Schmidt wrote her heartbreaking letters, confessing his loneliness and intense desire that she return to him. Bergman says that she knew she had been warned but that somehow she thought Schmidt would understand her own intense need to work. Ultimately, Bergman does not take responsibility for the marriage breaking up. It is also Schmidt's fault. He was not at home either: he went on trips to Germany and Sweden and Denmark to supervise his business interests. Schmidt himself never stayed home more than a week before he went off again on some business trip. So Bergman, too, trapped on their country estate in France, felt lonely and abandoned.

Bergman was treated by Schmidt the same way she treated him, but the irony escapes her. And so she consciously decides to put the marriage at risk by continuing to perform in plays that could keep her away for months at a time. She says that she "thought it out very carefully" and deliberately chose to leave the estate regardless of when Schmidt would be there.[30]

There is also the resentment that Schmidt stopped looking for shows for them to do together. Bergman says that it took her some time to get over feeling hurt about Schmidt's unwillingness to dedicate more of his work to her career. And of course, Schmidt eventually took a mistress. Bergman repeatedly says she feels guilty and sorry for letting the marriage deteriorate. But she simply cannot deny herself her only joy: performing. Throughout her recollections of her marriage to Schmidt, Bergman on the one hand takes full responsibility for neglecting her husband, but faced with making some larger judgment about the failed relationship, she clearly blames Schmidt for not being able to maintain the uneasy status quo of their constant separations.

Bergman controlled her image until her death. Six months before she died, Larry Adler called to invite her to a party. Ingrid declined because of her cancer, but she told him that if he had called three months earlier, she would have hit him over the head with "the hardest object I could find." The reason: a story attributed to Adler in a Swedish newspaper headlined "I WAS INGRID'S LOVER." Adler defended himself by admitting that he had talked to the journalist but that he had considered him "a sober, serious man," "more like an accountant than a journalist." Whereupon Bergman replied, "Well, *you* thought he was sober and serious. Larry, how could you be such a child? He wanted something sensational to write about *me* and he was just using you as an excuse.... But, Larry, really — to say *anything* to a journalist about me!" Then: "You know who talked me out of wanting to kill you? It was Lars. Lars said, 'Come on, Ingrid, you know Larry. And you know the Swedish press, what they're like.' He was right, I realized that. But, Larry, please don't ever do such a silly thing again." Adler promised he wouldn't and wondered how "such a respectable sort of man would write a hack story like that."[31]

Even in her dying, Bergman had no desire to set the record straight, and she had the power to keep her old friends and lovers from contradicting her legends. Poor Larry Adler was proud of his affair with Bergman, but she would not permit him to do anything but hint at their relationship in public. To do so would, according to Bergman, be doing something silly, and Adler grants Bergman her premise: talking to reporters about sex is silly, the basis for hack stories no respectable journalist would report.

Despite her apparent interest in maintaining a certain image, Bergman herself never acknowledged any responsibility for that image and often talked as if it were a kind of accident, as if her image had nothing to do with her. In a letter to Spoto, dated May 8, 1975, she argued that during the Rossellini scandal, "Nobody could have lived up to that unreal image people created of me." Elsewhere in the letter, she states, "A movie star is a ridiculous commercial product. People said that once I was a perfect model of a wife and mother. They saw me in *Joan of Arc* and thought I was a saint. I'm not. I'm just a human being."[32] But Bergman actively participated in the creation of her unreal image, and all her life she steadfastly promoted variations of that image, which had little to do with the life she actually led. When she claimed to be direct and simple and outspoken, avoiding all sham and artifice and pretense, Bergman was indeed performing once again. Her directness, simplicity, and outspokenness were part of her sham and artifice and pretense. She was giving her audience what they wanted from her. And she was realizing her deepest sense of herself, that her life was her own greatest role, which was beyond criticism. We may never know whether or in what sense the role Ingrid Bergman created for her life was true. And we may never know whether in creating that role, Ingrid Bergman was fooling even herself.

Eight

Actor and Star

"This is the movies' way of creating individuals: they create *individualities*. For what makes someone a type is not his similarity with other members of that type but his striking separateness from other people."
— Stanley Cavell

"[With *Autumn Sonata* and *A Woman Called Golda*, Bergman] had become, just too late, a really good actress, if not perhaps a great one."
— Sheridan Morely

In 1943, the year *Gaslight* was filmed, Ingrid Bergman was already a star. She had performed in *Intermezzo*, *Dr. Jekyll and Mr. Hyde*, *Casablanca,* and *For Whom the Bell Tolls*, and Selznick Studios had sold the American public on her wholesome star image. Nevertheless, Bergman longed to break out of the straightjacket of her star persona and expand her range. While in New York, she had seen the play on which *Gaslight* is based, Patrick Hamilton's *Angel Street*. Metro-Goldwyn-Meyer had bought the film rights, so Bergman was delighted when Selznick began negotiating with MGM to loan her out for the picture. Her co-star would be Charles Boyer, an established leading man, and her director would be George Cukor, who was famous for his work with actresses. When Selznick, always conscious of the status of his players, called to say that he was breaking off negotiations because Boyer demanded top billing, Bergman protested. She didn't care if she received top billing or not; she wanted the part. Selznick adamantly refused to give in. He did not want the star whose career he had so carefully built up to now get second billing. Bergman claims that she had to cry, sob, and plead before Selznick very reluctantly gave in.[1]

The opening fifteen minutes of *Gaslight* promise yet another typical Bergman romance. The story line is quickly established: this will be a film about a woman in love whose devotion will be tested. Paula Alquist, a young woman orphaned and living with her aunt, a famous singer, is ushered out of her London townhouse by the police. Her aunt has been brutally murdered.

145

Jump forward several years: now in Europe on her own, Paula tells her singing coach that she intends to gives up a promising career because she is in love, but she will not name her lover. This is not a matter of building suspense. In the very next shot, Paula meets her lover, the pianist who quietly left her lesson in the previous scene. His name is Gregory Anton, played by Boyer. But Paula still has reservations about running off with Gregory, so she travels to the Hotel Del Lago at Lake Como to decide her future. Gregory follows her, she falls into his arms, and the romance is culminated in one of those ambiguous Production Code scenes in which the lovers meet in their bathrobes on a terrace outside a lavish hotel bedroom. According to the PCA, we are not to necessarily infer that they have slept together because, after all, they are not yet married.

These scenes and the way Cukor shoots them repeat many of the clichés that Selznick had promoted and Bergman's first American directors had slav- ishly followed since *Intermezzo*. Clearly this movie, too, is about a beautiful young woman deeply in love, and we are shown just how noble and spiritual the young woman is. Cukor resorts to the standard Selznick glamour shot: on the terrace steps outside the bedroom the camera looks over Boyer's right shoulder as Bergman gazes up at him adoringly. We see the left side of her face, the good side, shot from above, the light is again soft with misty high- lights, especially on her hair, and Bergman's eyes are moist in the intensity of her love. Several shots later, Cukor films Bergman the same way, but this time she and Boyer are sitting on the stairs and she has her head on his chest.

However, the triumph of *Gaslight*, and the reason Bergman fought for the role of Paula, is that the film turns out to be not a romance but a suspense film that, despite its generic qualities, does require its heroine to express a range of emotions different from those expressed by a typical romantic heroine. Upon returning to live, at Gregory's insistence, in her aunt's old row house, the place where the aunt was murdered, Paula becomes increasingly forgetful and confused, and Gregory constantly points out her lapses. To prevent her from embarrassing herself socially, Gregory insists that Paula stay at home and avoid meeting people, even as he goes off alone in the evening to his "pri- vate studio" in order to work as a composer. While he is gone, Paula is ter- rorized by sounds in the attic and the flickering gaslight of the house. It soon becomes obvious that Gregory is "arranging" events so that Paula cannot remember them accurately. He is trying to drive her mad so that he can have her institutionalized and thus have complete access to the house, which con- tains some famous jewels given to the aunt by an old lover.

Gregory's scheme to drive Paula insane gives Bergman the chance to por- tray increasing consternation and fear, doubt and confusion, a confusion so profound that toward the end of the film Paula often becomes hysterical to the point of genuine madness. Bergman portrays all these emotions in a bravura performance, especially in Paula's final confrontation with Gregory in the attic of their town home. In that scene, Paula has been granted permission to talk to Gregory, now captured by the police and bound to a chair. Cukor shoots most of the scene in a mid-range version of the Selznick glamour shot. The camera is at Gregory's level; Gregory is low and to the left, looking up at Paula, who bends over him, filling the frame on the right, hovering like an avenging angel. The key light comes from off-camera, high and to the left behind Gregory, and in another context, we might be marveling at Paula's beautiful face, which is illuminated brightly with only a small shadow on her left cheek.

Gregory asks Paula to get a knife and glances toward the skylight. Paula looks up and recognizes what Gregory has in mind. "Yes," she says, "I'll get it for you." She goes to the chest of drawers behind her and after some fussing with the drawers, announces that she cannot find the knife, as she slowly turns, revealing that she has the knife in her hand. "It isn't here," she proclaims, walking toward Gregory. "You must have dreamed you put it there." Gregory protests that he put it there the previous evening. Paula shows Gregory the knife, and says slowly, with a kind of mild surprise, "Are you suggesting that this is a knife I hold in my hand? Have you gone mad, my husband?" She bends over Gregory — now the two are in close-up, the knife blade between them — and Paula whispers, "Or is it I who am mad? Yes, of course, it is I who am mad." And there is a vacancy in Paula's eyes as she talks about her penchant for losing things. Paula drops the knife, and her vacant eyes shift to wide-eyed anger and then to a narrow-lidded glare of deep suspicion. She backs toward the chest of drawers, all the while keeping her gaze on Gregory, saying, "That was a knife, and I have lost it. I must look for it," and her voice lowers to a huskier tone — and whether Paula is insane or whether she is performing madness to frighten Gregory and pay him back for his abuse, Gregory cannot know, just as we cannot know whom we are watching: Bergman the star, Bergman the actor, or Paula Alquist, a fictional character totally embodied and portrayed in such as way that whichever Bergman we had just been watching has dropped away, and we are experiencing something that only great acting can give us — the perception of character laid bare, grand emotion, real and immediate, seemingly unmediated by acting at all.

At the end of *Gaslight*, Bergman does much more than fulfill the requirements of her star image. Even as she is being filmed in a manner that draws attention to her glamorous image, Bergman creates a character and expresses a range of emotion quite beyond that persona. Paula Alquist is Bergman's greatest performance as an actor during her early career.

More than most famous films stars, Bergman complicates the categories of what makes us appreciate her as both a star and an actor Even at the height of her career, she was expanding the boundaries of the star image created for her by Selznick Studios, and later in her career, responding to the demands of very different directors, she managed to create a body of work that truly transcends that image. The question remains, however, of just how good an actor she was; there are certain roles she could not do well, a certain range of emotion she could not portray convincingly. The question is whether Sheridan Morely's ambivalent opinion is just: that in Bergman's last two films she became, "just too late, a really good actress, if not perhaps a great one."

Stardom

Actors become stars for complex reasons, many of them outside the actor's control. Scholar Richard Dyer has enumerated them: promotion, publicity, the right films as vehicles, the support and praise of critics and commentators. Much of this involves the extension of celebrity into stardom, either intentionally or accidentally: the right studio publicity, the politics of critical acceptance, or sheer chance — having the right qualities and abilities at the

Bergman as Paula Alquist demonstrates a range of emotions from fear and doubt to hysteria and madness, when she confronts Charles Boyer as her husband Gregory Anton in the climactic scene of George Cukor's *Gaslight* (M-G-M, 1944).

right time. In contrast to the deliberate glamour of such early '40s stars such as Joan Fontaine and Hedy Lamarr, Bergman was marketed as natural: a breath of fresh air, the girl next door, wholesome, honest, dignified; a faithful and loving wife and mother, not the subject of salacious gossip, and in interviews and public appearances, dignified and discrete. In her major films she expressed a form of love and devotion that could be interpreted as spiritual. And so by the time she got the roles of Sister Benedict in *The Bells of St. Mary's* and Joan of Arc, it seemed as if she were "made" to play these characters. Audiences readily transferred the image of love and devotion in romantic love that Bergman had portrayed in *Intermezzo, Casablanca,* and *For Whom the Bell Tolls* to her portrayal of spiritual devotion in *The Bells of St. Mary's* and *Joan of Arc.*

But Bergman's difference from other stars at the time doesn't begin to explain the basis for her appeal. Whatever the vagaries of becoming a star, an actor must possess some qualities that have "star potential," a possible fit between her personality and performance skills and the roles she plays.[2]

One theory is that all film actors, but especially stars, are essentially types. But unlike journeymen film actors who may be examples of social types that border on stereotypes — the authoritarian father, the doting mother, the rebellious son, the ingénue, the faithful servant, the gruff blue-collar worker — the essence of a star-type is an abstraction of a particular performer's personality and performance skills. Over time we come to appreciate the way certain performers consistently look and behave in a number of films. Philosopher Stanley Cavell calls film stars "individualities" because they are distinctive and original. They do not represent a class of people; they represent themselves. Stars become embodied in a concrete image of how they are different from other people.[3] After the American version of *Intermezzo, Dr. Jekyll and Mr. Hyde, Casablanca* and *For Whom the Bell Tolls,* "Ingrid Bergman" became a "presence" that would not exist if those films did not exist, and "Ingrid Bergman" became a name for a certain image, a certain persona, a certain way of being in those films.

Critic Robin Wood has offered the most comprehensive theory of how Bergman's star image was constituted and how or in what sense that image was composed of "a certain kind of professionalism" linked to certain kinds of roles and genres and certain performance skills. Wood suggests that Bergman's star persona had four components — nature and health, niceness, the lady, and the actress — which were in some sense contradictory. Wood develops these contradictions: the "nice" woman who is also sexual; the "natural" woman who is also a "lady." Bergman's naturalness and health were indicated by her appearance: "the radiance of the smile [that] betokened an openness and generosity" and that seemed to deprive her of any sense of mystery. Bergman's naturalness and health, Wood goes on, was also associated with "normality" and being a lady, which in our patriarchal society forces women to repress their sexuality; however, as a "natural woman," Bergman's sexuality was constantly threatening to break out of the constraints put on normal, nice ladies.

But Bergman's image, according to Wood, was also comprised of her abilities as an actor. She was identified with major parts, versatility, and emotional authenticity, in roles as various as Maria in *For Whom the Bell Tolls*, Alicia Huberman in *Notorious,* and of course Joan of Arc. Bergman's contradictory images, Wood argues, were exploited by Hollywood, which never cast her as a "bad" woman, only as "an essentially nice woman in a morally ambiguous position."[4] Bergman's persona was associated with roles in which she was caught up in circumstances beyond her control — swept away by love or history — and these roles emphasized certain performance skills: the ability to project vulnerability, pathos, longing, and devotion. The typical Selznick glamour shot was crucial in defining and reinforcing this image.

Bergman's star image, then, is complicated both by the roles we associate with her image and what we know about her off-screen life, filtered through her studio's publicity and the public media. But, of course, there is also a match between Bergman's image and her acting ability. In one simple taxonomy, actors can *personify* a character or they can *impersonate* one. Personification occurs when actors are placed in roles "by virtue of a physical presence (and off-stage life narrative) which conforms to the 'type' of that role." In the 1940s, the public may have thought of Bergman as the personification of, say, Ilsa Lund in *Casablanca*, not just because Bergman's on-screen image seemed to embody Ilsa's appearance and behavior but because her off-screen image promoted by Selznick Studios seemed to confirm that "individuality." Given Bergman's image, it seemed natural for Ilsa to sacrifice the love of her life for a greater good.

Impersonation involves "creat[ing] a role from the range of skill and imagination [actors] possess."[5] Clearly, Bergman "impersonates" a character like Ilsa in the ways she responds to situations consistent with Ilsa's character. In fact, her impersonation may be so subtle we do not notice it at all. In the scene in which Rick drunkenly insults Ilsa for not meeting him at the train in Paris, Ilsa conveys a range of emotions: hurt, pity, and then anger. At that moment, we may not associate Bergman's star image, her on- or off-screen personality, with Ilsa's character; rather, we may be so caught up in the intense emotions of the scene that Bergman the star drops away and we see only Ilsa Lund. In this case, we might say that in portraying Ilsa's response to Rick, Bergman's performance is all impersonation, entirely a matter of performance skills, her ability to project hurt, pity, and anger consistent with Ilsa's character.

In any case, stardom depends on a consistent image, usually linked to certain roles or certain genres, so that audiences can count on "the pleasures of stability and repetition and the guarantee of consistency" when they choose movies to attend.[6] During her career, "Ingrid Bergman" the star gave audiences reason to expect a certain image when they flocked to her films, most of which were variations on that Hollywood staple, the romantic melodrama.

Thus, we might say that in her early films, Bergman is not yet a star (say, in her Swedish films before *Intermezzo*), although we may recognize her potential star quality. She has not yet been "packaged" as a certain kind of actor by a studio or the media; she has yet to be associated with specific aspects of her acting abilities or with certain parts in certain kinds of films. In some of her later films she is less "Ingrid Bergman" the star than she is an accomplished actor, such as in the films she made with Roberto Rossellini or in the TV movie *A Woman Called Golda*. After she became a star, a presence, Ingrid Bergman could act in a film and be either "Ingrid Bergman" the star or Ingrid Bergman the actor playing a part, or some complex combination of the two.

We have seen the difficulty in sorting out just what we appreciate about Bergman's acting in the final scene in *Gaslight*. We might say that in *Gaslight*, Ingrid Bergman, the actor-impersonator, is struggling to break through or go beyond the image of "Ingrid Bergman," the star, who personifies wholesomeness, naturalness, and devotion in love. Now, knowing her as a star and as an actor in a range of films from her forty-year career, when we watch Ingrid Bergman, just who are we watching? Of course, that depends on what we know about Ingrid Bergman as both star and actor, on the degree of our fascination with her image, and what we are looking forward to when we sit down to view one of her films. And of course, it also depends on the kind of acting we appreciate.

Acting

Acting is an odd business. For one thing, we often make a great deal out of professional acting, when acting is something all of us do a great deal of. We are acting when for the sake of marital harmony, we tell our spouses that we love their latest purchase when we really detest it. We are acting when we put on a "good face" at the office, pretending to be healthy and happy when we are really in fact miserable. But this kind of acting seems too easy, too natural, too intimately connected to our everyday lives to recognize as an artistic achievement. It seems like simple behavior.

And so we tend to call what we do acting when it is deliberately done as a performance in front of an audience, what James Naramore calls "being held up for show."[7] We may behave very differently in front of a personal video camera, knowing we are being filmed and knowing that what we say has the potential to be viewed again and again. We may become more self-conscious, more deliberate, and not act as spontaneously as we would when we intuitively behave contrary to what we honestly think, believe, or feel. Still, once again we may not like to think of the choices we make in front of a home video camera as "real acting," even though in a sense we are performing. In this case we may think we lack the skills and training to be really acting.

After all, professional actors have mastered the art of expression. They have been trained to use their faces and bodies as instruments for *being* expressive, the conventions of which seem to be true for almost all times and cultures. These conventions — the standard rhetoric of face, gesture, and body movement — were codified in late-nineteenth-century and early-twentieth-century textbooks on elocution and rhetoric by François Delsarte and Henry Siddon, in handbooks on pantomime and acting by Charles Aubert and Edmund Shaftesbury: the furrowed brow, clenched eyes, and downturned mouth of physical pain, for example, or the raised eyebrows, wide eyes, and open mouth of terror, the leaning forward of aggression, the folded arms of stubbornness and refusal, and the leaning backward of doubt, indecision, and anxiety.[8]

Acting in films is very different from acting on stage, and not just because of the obvious physical differences between the two media. Actors on stage are always seen in long shot, framed by the proscenium arch or the auditorium on the other side of the thrust stage or the "round." Actors on stage are usually seen in sequential long scenes, each scene in "real" time, so that actors can develop characters continuously in front of our eyes. As a result, actors on stage must be trained to project emotion beyond the front rows of the auditorium, to talk much more loudly than normal, even when seeming to whisper and engage in intimate conversation. Whatever their circumstances, the facial expressions and gestures of stage actors must be bigger than life.

Acting for the screen is much more intimate and requires underplaying, compared to acting for the stage. The camera is close and can record the most subtle shifts in facial expression and gesture. A broad expression of surprise on stage can be conveyed in a film with a slight lift of an eyebrow. On the other hand, developing a consistent character for the camera is much more demanding than on the stage. Because of production costs, film directors usually do not shoot scenes in the order in which they will appear in the movie and they do not often allow a great deal of time for rehearsal. Film actors must know their characters well enough to do scenes in any order and with only the slightest rehearsal just before the shot. Moreover, it is rare that films are shot in extended scenes; rather they are shot in fragments, bits and pieces of scenes that may last only a few seconds. Film actors must be able to conjure emotions on the spur of the moment, and they have little time to develop those emotions over the course of the shot.

And during the shot, the crew with their camera and lighting equipment hover nearby, at times only a few feet away. Often the equipment moves during the scene, which can be very distracting. Film actors have to not only just act, but hit their "marks"; they must move about the area set up for the shot, always knowing their relationship to the camera, to the lighting setup, and to the depth-of-field of the shot. At certain moments they must be exactly at a specific "mark"; otherwise, they will deliver a line or convey an emotion that is off camera, unexposed, or out of focus, or they may simply destroy the composition of the shot.

Now we may be only vaguely aware, if we are aware at all, of the many technical difficulties actors deal with while performing in film. However, a much more important difference between the stage and film is crucial to our ability to appreciate film acting. That difference involves the way the camera focuses our attention on actors and how the various shots of actors are edited together. On stage we see actors in long shot and in continuous time, and we must infer their character and their emotions from what we might call "fully-body acting" in continuous time. In films, we often see the actors in long shots, but more often we see bits and pieces of them in medium shots and close-ups, interspersed with bits and pieces of other actors and the surrounding context. The editing of these shots together takes an actor's performance out of the context in which the actor was filmed, the scene in its entirety, analogous to the stage set, and inserts various clips, various shots of the actor, into a new context, the sequence of the edited clips. In this new context, aspects of the actor's performance may take on a whole new significance. In a sense, the range of the actor's performance is narrowed and focused by this new context, making it possible for directors and editors to highlight aspects of perform- ances that actors themselves did not intend. That context usually includes the editing of a particular clip or a particular scene, but it may encompass the entire film. The role of actors and their characters as agents in the structured narrative of the film may influence the way we perceive them in an individual scene.[9]

The most famous example of this phenomenon at the level of basic edit- ing is somewhat legendary. The Kuleshov Effect is named after Lev Kuleshov, a Russian filmmaker, who possibly with a partner named Vselovod Pudovkin, conducted an experiment, showing an audience the same shot of popular actor Ivan Mozhukhin juxtaposed with various other shots: a plate of soup, a girl, a child's coffin. According to Kuleshov and Pudovkin, the audience interpreted the same expression on Mozhukhin's face as hunger when juxtaposed with the soup, desire when juxtaposed with the girl, and grief when juxtaposed with the coffin. The difficulty is that Kuleshov's and Pudovkin's accounts of the experiment differ; they are vague about how they assessed the audience's responses, and the actual footage of the experiment has not survived. Still the Kuleshov Effect has become shorthand for what is generally accepted about film editing: the same shot of an actor can express different things depending on its context. Alfred Hitchcock refers to just this effect in explaining how he filmed many of Jimmy Stewart's reaction shots in *Rear Window*— not on the set but in another studio. In splicing these shots into the film, Hitchcock caused the audience to associate the expression on Stewart's face with the images before and after the shot.[10]

As a result, there is what Naramore calls a "polysemous" quality to film acting, the sense that an actor's performance can be manipulated by editing to suggest a great deal more or a great deal less than what she thought she was accomplishing in her original performance; film acting is "capable of multiple signification; its meaning in a film is usually narrowed and held in place by a controlling narrative, a context that can rule out some meanings and highlight others."[11] There are a host of stories about veteran screen actors telling Broadway actors newly arrived in Hollywood not to overplay their parts, to let the camera and the editors do their work. Watch Cary Grant listen to Bergman's drunken rambling at the party near the beginning of *Notorious*, and you may be impressed with the range of emotion he expresses: clearly he is attracted to her but he is also disdainful, perhaps even contemptuous, about her drinking and morals. Study the clip more closely and you will realize that Grant barely changes his expression at all. You have been doing all the work.

This ability of directors and editors to manipulate images for certain effects complicates our ability to assess the performance skills of film actors. For one thing, all of us are to some degree inherently expressive, those of us who do a certain amount of acting in the normal course of our lives as well as professional actors. And indeed, many filmmakers use non-actors in their films in order to capture a certain sense of reality: in Italian neo-realism, for instance, or the realistic film makers associated with the Danish Dogme 95 Manifesto. For another, many well-known film actors have had exceptional careers with very little formal training; Gregory Peck comes to mind. And so when we revel in the emotional impact of a particular actor in a particular scene, it is not always easy to locate the source of our involvement.

This is true even though film allows us to return to these images again and again, to freeze them before our eyes and savor them the way we would savor an oil painting in a museum, leaning forward to study the brushwork, stepping back to see how the dabs and strokes of paint catch the light and produce an effect that does not seem to be literally "there" in the painting itself. Because film allows us the luxury of studying actors up close to this degree, returning to the same scenes in the same film again and again, rewinding the videotape or fast-forwarding the DVD to view the softening of a performer's eyes, the quiver of a lip, the throb of a vein in the neck — all this allows us to "see" what we might not otherwise have seen, to treasure the subtleties of acting, and to make a fetish of certain aspects of our favorite actor's performances.

When we appreciate Bergman's acting, we may be responding not only to her star persona and her performance skills, but also to the way she has been captured on film, the way her performance has been edited, and the way her portrayal, the images conveyed, the emotions portrayed, seems to fit into the larger purposes and themes of the film.

Bergman as an Actor

Bergman's versatility and authenticity allowed her to succeed on both stage and screen. On stage, she could develop her character in front of the audience and project her voice, convey her emotions, to the back of the auditorium. Still, as we have seen, some classically-trained British actors who played with her in *Captain Brassbound's Conversion* and *The Constant Wife* privately complained about her lack of stage technique: her inability to maintain her blocking, her inability to develop her period characters in ways consistent with the period. In treatment for cancer during the run of *The Constant Wife* she muffed line readings and missed entrances, but did not try to cover them up. Instead, she drew attention to them by talking directly to the audience, explaining what had happened, providing a kind of meta-commentary in the style of Theater of the Absurd. Late in her life, Bergman occasionally allowed her status as a star to trump her creation of a character on stage.

We can study Bergman's performance skills in film much more closely. If we study a range of films scene by scene, shot by shot, even frame by frame, we can see that her versatility and authenticity manifested itself in a number of distinctive performance skills: her ability to display adoration and devotion (the skills we associate with her stardom) but also her ability to project hidden emotions in quick facial shifts, her emotional range revealed in scenes of breakdown and emotional release, and her ability to sustain that range through long takes, something that many film actors cannot do. But Bergman's greatest successes as a film actor also owe a great deal to the nature of film. Her greatest performances were framed by directors who knew how to manipulate her star image in provocative ways, who knew how to use her performances skills in ways she was barely aware of. They showcased her performance skills in ways that resonated with the major themes and emotional arc of the film.

Bergman's ability to display adoration and devotion can be seen in all of the romantic melodramas she made during the 1940s, captured in the Selznick glamour shot. Perhaps the most well-known is when Ilsa confronts Rick in his room near the end of *Casablanca* and confesses that she has never stopped loving him.

Bergman's ability to project hidden and often conflicting emotions in quick facial shifts is not commonly mentioned in analyses of her acting, but she displays this ability surprisingly often. In fact, it is a key element in her first film role in 1934, the part of Elsa, a maid in a hotel, in *The Count of Old Town*, also called *The Count of Monk's Bridge*. Elsa is alternatingly attracted to and suspicious of Ake, a new arrival to the hotel and to the Old Town district. The reason for her suspicion is that Old Town has been suffering a series of burglaries, most notoriously of a local jewelry shop, and the town newspaper has been full of headlines about a diamond thief. Ake arrives under suspicious circumstances, followed by two plainclothes policemen. Elsa's complex attitude toward Ake gives Bergman the opportunity to reveal what will become one of her signature performance skills.

In her very first scene in this, her first motion picture, Bergman, dressed in a nightgown, pops her head out the door to call for Larsson, the desk clerk, and asks to see a copy of the morning paper. Her face is round, almost plump, her smile broad and cherubic, her delight in the day palpable. Ake, trying to escape the policemen, on a signal from Larsson, slips into Elsa's room. By now Else is in a slip, and seeing Ake, she screams and tries to hide her semi-nakedness behind the dress she is holding. Ake runs to her and tries to cover her mouth with his hand. After Larsson convinces the policemen that Elsa's calls for help were really from another woman upstairs, the two men leave. Cut to Ake, who checks the door to make sure the men have gone, and then saunters over to Elsa, who is trying to get into her dress. Ake admits cockily that he owes Elsa an explanation. Yes, and an apology, too, Elsa replies heatedly. Ake nods. "Yes," he says, "I have —[He has not.]— If you'll accept it, I'd be happy if you did." Whereupon Elsa's anger melts away, her eyes light up, and a sly smile crosses her face. She is obviously intrigued and attracted by the arrogance of this man and feels confident that she can deal with it. When Ake identifies his followers as police officers, Elsa is surprised, but when he suggests in an insinuating manner that he might stay in the hotel "if you have room for me," the sexual innuendo is clear and Elsa is up to it. Another quick confident smile slips across her face, and she watches Ake leave the room with a sense of fascination.

In less than a minute, Bergman has run the gamut of sexual game-playing, from distress and fear to anger and then to attraction and on to something close to flirtation. She accomplishes all of this with a quicksilver mouth and expressive eyes that register subtle shades of feeling.

You can see similar subtle shifts of emotion in her first scene in *Casablanca*, when she responds to Sam's warning, "Leave him alone, Miss Ilsa. You're bad luck to him." Ilsa's smile fades to a quick haunted look of surprise and then acceptance, before she recovers the bright smile and asks Sam to play "As Time Goes By." Or the scene in the MG sports car with Anthony Perkins after their first meeting in *Goodbye Again*. When Bergman chastises Perkins for belittling his mother, he responds, "I am not a child," and Bergman asks how old he is. "Twenty-five," he replies. "How old are you?" Bergman's polite smile again slips away, replaced this time by a look of evasion and doubt as she wrestles with just how to respond. "Forty," she manages to say. Perkins responds with a wolf whistle, and Bergman looks panicky. She makes a stammering, shuddering attempt at a smile, and in the context of the larger film, the story of an "older" woman whose longtime lover, played by Ives Montand, will not marry her, this is poignant. Bergman can also shift emotions much more broadly and more overtly, as when she goes from hysterical laughter to sobbing at the end of the first interrogation scene in *Anastasia*.

Bergman's emotional range and versatility are revealed in scenes of breakdown and emotional release, the final confrontation with Anton in *Gaslight*, for example. In these scenes, Bergman often relies on a conventional range of pantomimic gestures, and at times she seems to rely on them too much. In the bedroom scene in *Stromboli*, when Karin and Antonio wake from their first night on the island, Bergman runs a gamut of emotions. Responding to Antonio's insensitivity and her sense of being trapped, Karin moves from the window toward the bed and then hearing a child crying goes back to the window. In response to the crying, Karin turns away sobbing and with a very histrionic gesture puts both hands on top of her head. Going to the bed, she drapes herself over the bedstead, once again sobbing in contemplation of being trapped. When the child begins crying again, Karin straightens up and puts hand to mouth before picking up her coat to smooth it out — a nice metaphor for her attempt to get control of herself. She folds the coat over the bedstead, then wipes away tears and throws herself on the bed in despair. Rising up and realizing that she is lying on the money that Antonio has thrown on the bed, she stuffs the money in her purse and puts it under a pillow before exiting out the bedroom door, where we see her in long shot through the open door go down the stairs and out another door. In this scene, Bergman's hands on her head and her throwing herself down on the bed seem clichéd. She is relying too much on stereotypical ways of expressing certain emotions.

And there is one physical attribute that she could not do anything about, despite her versatility: her straight-backed posture. No matter what the emotional intensity or the violence of a scene in which Bergman has to walk or run, she moves as if she is balancing a book on her head. She can act with her face. She can act with her arms. She cannot act with her torso. She cannot act with her total body. In *The Bells of St. Mary's*, her stiff body is hidden in a nun's robe, and besides, Sister Benedict is not really supposed to be a fighter. Her knowledge of boxing is entirely from books. Her stiffness is appropriate to her character. In *Joan of Arc*, Bergman is encased in armor, which accounts for her physical awkwardness in the battle scenes. But when Bergman runs with the children in *Inn of the Sixth Happiness*, nothing can hide the fact that she does not lean forward or pump her arms. She runs straight up, a flagpole without a flag borne vertically through the countryside. It is impossible to imagine her writhing in pain or even hunched over like a witch or a crone.

Even more indicative of her skills is Bergman's ability to sustain emotional consistency through long takes, which was honed in the theater and finetuned in working with Hitchcock. Hitchcock delighted in playing with film as a medium and solving certain technical difficulties. He appreciated long takes. Indeed, he made one film — *Rope* — as if the entire film were shot in one long take. The only editing in the film resulted from the camera running out of film. With Bergman, there is the famous long nuzzle in *Notorious* and the eight-minute take in *Under Capricorn*.

But perhaps more typical of Bergman's career is the fight scene in *The Bells of St. Mary's* between Sister Benedict and Eddie. That scene takes about five minutes but only involves five shots. The opening long shot lasts a minute-and-a-half and sets up the scene. Benedict teaches Eddie the basic boxing stance and the various punches. The shot is not very demanding. Bergman has to simply stay to the left in the shot and move toward and away from the camera to consult a book on boxing on a table in the foreground. But as she introduces Eddie to the basic boxing stance and the various punches, Bergman adds some nice touches. She lifts her skirts to show off her fancy footwork and she shakes her fist slightly before delivering a mock "payoff" punch, a right uppercut. She conveys a bouncy girlish delight in the sheer technique of boxing.

But it is the second-to-last shot in the scene that shows what Bergman can do. This shot, too, lasts a minute-and-a-half, but it is much more technically difficult. Bergman must spar with Eddie, dancing around him, stop to hug him for his efforts, then decide whether to continue with an additional lesson in footwork. Deciding to forgo the extra lesson, she must then continue sparing but finish away from the camera and to the right with Eddie in front of her, so that when Eddie delivers the "payoff," his swing looks as if it lands on Benedict's jaw and she can stagger to the left toward the chair, where she will be in closeup for the last shot. During the sparring, Bergman expresses a range of emotions from bubbly enthusiasm to surprise and quiet reflection when Eddie remarks that learning to box is better than turning the other cheek. Upon being hit, Bergman's enthusiasm is transformed into stiff-jawed pain and muffled speech. Her pain seems just as real as her joy, and when in the last shot of the scene, as she sits in the chair nursing her sore jaw, her painful laugh and ironic recognition that Eddie was able to hit her because she did not follow her own advice is a complex mixture of humor, pain, and self-awareness.

Bergman did not have to be histrionic to be convincing. Her portrayal of the Swedish missionary Greta Ohlsson in *Murder on the Orient Express* is a triumph of underplaying and subtle film acting. Bergman's big scene occurs in one long four minute and forty second take when Greta is interrogated by Hercule Poirot, played by Albert Finney. For once, her stiff posture is an expression of character and as the camera follows her down the train car, slightly hunched, hands folded together in front of her, she is the embodiment of a repressed frightened spinster. After Bergman sits, the camera moves into close-up and for four long minutes it moves only once, to dolly slightly to the right, so that Poirot/Finney can move from confronting her face-to-face, to above and to her right, where his face hovers over hers like a bad conscience. Throughout the interrogation, Bergman maintains a straight, grim, slightly downturned mouth, as she explains Ohlsson's trip to America to raise money for her missionary work. The high angle of the camera makes her eyes seem like a basset hound's, worn and mournful. Referring to "Jesus, in the sky," her lord and savior and the judge of her parents, she glances upward and makes a small gesture, a finger pointing upward, and having to confess that her parents had no respect for God, her voice catches, her eyes well up, and she sobs haltingly at the idea of their punishment at God's hands. All the while, she stares at Poirot with simple trust, conveyed primarily in her eyes, but as the inquest proceeds and she must talk about her movements on the night of the murder, Bergman's eyes turn furtive and we sense that she is lying. Her nays seem exaggerated and her modesty suspect. She has to whisper the words "bed gown," she is so modest, and this comic touch makes her artful performance seem excessively artful—a pose, a ruse. Poirot lets Ohlsson go without a major confrontation, but Bergman's consistent portrayal of character, sad, moving, comic, has hinted that Ohlsson cannot be trusted. It is the kind of performance that would have made Bergman a grand character actor, if she had played more roles that allowed her to express such a range of emotion in such intimate circumstances.

As we have seen, working with Rossellini broke Bergman's desire to make "big" films and great art. She also seems to have stopped looking for great parts that would extend her range and test her abilities. It is possible that with Rossellini she realized that she loved making films and wanted to enjoy her work more than she wanted to be a great actor. She always most appreciated the films which she had the best time making. And she may not have had the imagination or the intellectual resources to deal with complex roles. She could not step back critically and distinguish her own emotional involvement from what she had accomplished

One reason for this is that she lacked training. Bergman left the Swedish Royal Dramatic Training Academy after a year to become a film actor and did not sufficiently develop her skills, her analytic ability, her knowledge of the repertoire. The Swedish Royal Academy in the 1930s was a rigorous training ground for actors. Only eight students — four men and four women — were accepted every year from over a hundred who auditioned. Students took three years of classes and were gradually, after the first year, allowed to appear in more and more minor roles in the Academy's productions. First-year students attended lectures on world literary and theater history, with special attention on those historical figures who appear in the classical repertoire that they might wind up playing. There were also small-group and individual classes in acting technique. Over the next two years, students continued to take two kinds of courses along the lines of the first-year curriculum: courses in what we might call literature and culture — Shakespeare, world art and music, and the manners, customs, and psychology of other countries — and acting technique — what was called "body culture, how to stand, how to sit, how walk out of a room, how to move up a flight of stairs"; Swedish diction, poetry reading, and makeup.[12]

By leaving the Academy early, Bergman denied herself the chance to further hone her knowledge of the classical repertoire and the larger world, to receive guided practice in how to prepare for roles, especially challenging roles outside her own limited background and experience. As a result, she had little training in analyzing character and chose roles primarily because they suited her personality and her limited range of sympathy; she chose roles in which she could rely on her ability to personify rather than her ability to impersonate. She chose roles because she intuitively identified with the character. In *My Story*, she says that when she is on stage or in front of a camera, no one can give her any advice except the director because she always knows with unerring instinct what she must do.

Bergman confessed to Donald Spoto that she had never really read much about acting and did not know much about it. During her one year at the Swedish Royal Academy, she may have learned some things about using her voice and body and listening carefully to other people. But once again, she claims that instinct is her primary guide, that and "simplicity and honesty," because only those qualities touch people.[13]

Bergman's attitude toward formal training in acting borders on contempt.

In an interview with Richard Dyer in 1975, she says that acting schools can only teach basic techniques, such as "how to walk, move, sit," and "how to use your voice." Actors need these techniques, Bergman goes on, to get and hold the audience's attention, and if actors can keep their audience's attention, they will have long careers. Good looks, youthfulness, cuteness — all those qualities fade away. Bergman admits that even after forty years as an actor, she is still working on her technique and her ability to concentrate.

She was also skeptical of method acting, claiming that she never understood the graduates of the Actors Studio. To Bergman, method actors make acting entirely too difficult, trying to express all those feelings trapped deeply inside. She confessed that she had never had any problems "releasing any kind of emotion." Bergman did not "inhabit" the characters she portrayed, as she made clear in a discussion about acting with Giulietta Masina, Fiorella, and Father Lisandrini. Masina, who had just finished doing Fellini's *La Strada*, said that she felt she was a part of her character. Bergman admitted that in playing Joan of Arc she was like "a shoemaker doing his shoe."[14]

In response to a question during a presentation at the National Press Association in 1972, Bergman reiterated that she used no techniques associated with method acting, or even any kind of formal analysis in thinking about her roles. Instead, she simply tries to understand the characters she portrays and looks for physical ways of indicating their personality and emotions. This involves, she says, constantly observing the people around her while she is walking about town or taking the bus and remembering the way a person is dressed or a particular gesture, a way of sitting. She can use such details later as clues to a character's particular personality. She insists, rather oddly, that she interprets her characters "from life more than from [her] brain."[15]

Because of her reliance on feeling, on intuition, on external appearance, Bergman did not often have profound or even insightful things to say about characters that were outside her range of sympathy. She had only a fleeting sense of the heroine of *The Visit*, whom she recognized as being "obsessed by a great vendetta" and "the death of the man who had ruined her." Even though she herself could not be "compelled like that," she could understand the emotions behind that character's behavior.[16] Ingmar Bergman had to carefully explain to her the character she portrayed in *Autumn Sonata*, despite the obvious connections between the role and Bergman's own life. Bergman simply could not see herself in Charlotte, the pianist who neglects her children for the sake of her career.

And perhaps because she left the Swedish Royal Dramatic Academy early, she had little sense of the potential for her in the great tradition of theater. Early in her career, she told Joe Steele, "In Shakespeare, Ibsen, Strindberg, men have all the good parts — the best parts. But in history there were great women I want to portray, such as Queen Christina and Charlotte Corday and, most of all Joan of Arc. I was sure I looked like Joan, who was a big peasant type. From the very first time I discovered her, when I was a little girl, I wanted to play her trial."[17] Here, Bergman is, to put it mildly, misguided, or perhaps ignorant. Bergman seems to mean that only heroic characters in the romantic tradition — women who changed the course of history — are truly the good parts. Even granting the inherent sexism of the male tradition in playwriting, to deny that Shakespeare, Ibsen, and Strindberg wrote great parts for women, to deny that Juliet, Beatrice, Rosalind, Portia, Gertrude, Lady Macbeth, Nora Helmer, Hedda Gabler, Miss Julie or wife Alice in Strindberg's *Dance of Death*, are not great parts, is to have a blinkered view of an entire tradition and may expose Bergman's most damning limitation: her ignorance of that tradition or her inability to appreciate it. At her best, Bergman may be articulating her own sense of her limitations, that given her skills she was perhaps incapable of doing the intellectual work, the imaginative exploration, the self-examination necessary to take on the great roles in dramatic history.

Bergman's one major role in a play from the classic repertoire is disastrous. As Hedda Gabler, she is — there is no other way to put it — awful. The essence of Hedda's character eludes her. She portrays nothing of Hedda's sense of self-importance and superiority as General Gabler's daughter, nothing of her condescension to lesser beings, no sense of Hedda's ability to cunningly manipulate men, nothing of her frigidity, her desire to revel in power but not succumb to sex. Instead, Bergman is, as critic Jack Gould put it in a review in the *New York Times*, "too much the suffering heroine of the cinema."[18]

All this is obvious in Hedda's entrance, which Ibsen has carefully prepared. All the talk between her husband George Tesman and his aunt Julia has invoked the classic Hedda, but when Bergman enters, she is preoccupied, distantly pleasant, and dismissive of both her husband and Aunt Julia. She roams the room, clearly snubbing Julia, and before she settles into the chair between Julia and Tesman, she surveys the room as if she were considering buying it. This is not the Hedda of cold disdain. It would have been better if Bergman had staked out Hedda's territory and glared unmoving at poor Aunt Julia. When Hedda complains of Aunt Julia's hat in another chair, it is as if she is an overwrought housewife complaining of messy guests, not as if she were deliberately snubbing Julia, whose hat it is. And her protest at Julia's comment that she is "filled out," an allusion to her possible pregnancy, is not with a sense of fear or an attempt to control her revulsion at the idea but mere exasperation. At Julie's leaving, Hedda bows her head and clenches her fists in frustration. This is melodrama.

Bergman shows the same inability to convey Hedda's complex feelings about sex in the famous scene at the beginning of Act Two, when Judge Brack enters through the garden. Hedda shoots at Brack with her father's pistols and again Bergman portrays a Hedda who is frustrated and bored. This time, however, Bergman has added a touch of hysteria. She conveys no sense of calculation, no joy at the sheer exercise of power and control. And when Hedda and Brack sit down to negotiate their relationship, she does not revel in the battle of wits and the equality she demands. Rather, the conversation is calm and pleasant, as if the two were planning a tea party. Bergman expresses no fear at Brack's sexual references and the loss of power that it implies. In fact, she leans over the sofa and exposes her cleavage, as if the sexual game, not power itself, is what she enjoys. When Brack obliquely refers to his preference for "triangular relationships," she shows no signs of anything but pleasant acceptance of Brack's friendship, as if she did not grasp the implication that Brack is blackmailing her into becoming his mistress. Later in Act Two, Hedda picks up on Brack's stated goal to become the "cock of the block" in the Tesman household, but she repeats the phrase "cock of the block" as if it were amusing and not the threat it is. She utters the phrase with no irony and no sense that she is afraid of Brack's ability to impose on her sexually or to determine the course of her life.

Because she does not grasp or cannot *act* Hedda's burning sense of entitlement, her sublimation of sex for power, her fear of loss of control, Bergman conveys no sense of the demonic when she sends her old lover Lovborg off to a beautiful death and no sense of the maniacal when she throws Lovborg's manuscript into the fire claiming that the book is his child. And at the end of the play, when Hedda finally faces the fact that she would be in Brack's control and not free, Bergman is weepy. We see nothing of Hedda's steely resolve and the strength she has to commit suicide. Indeed, Bergman's Hedda Gabler does not die a good death, a tragic death, the death of a woman trapped by the choices she had made and for whom suicide is the only way to shape the kind of life she wants to live. The death of Bergman's Hedda is not tragic at all. It is the death of a poor, bored, frustrated woman who simply gives up in despair because she never had the courage to fight for the life she wanted in the first place. Bergman's Hedda is not Ibsen's.

Five years after the production of *Hedda Gabler*, José Quintero convinced Bergman to take the part of Deborah Harford, the matriarch in Eugene O'Neill's *More Stately Mansions*. *More Stately Mansions* is not in the same league as *Hedda Gabler*; it is not even major O'Neill. But the role of Deborah Harford was well outside Bergman's usual range. Deborah Harford is a difficult woman who has great ambitions for her son Arthur. She believes that Arthur's wife Sarah is beneath him socially and may prevent him from fulfilling his promise. The central conflict of the play is, as Leamer puts is, "the relationship between mother and daughter-in-law, between the refined, cold, brutally realistic, conniving Deborah and earthy, lusty, ambitious, greedy Sarah, and their struggle over the heart and soul of Arthur."[19]

There is no filmed record of *More Stately Mansions* as there is of *Hedda Gabler*, so we have to rely on the opinion of reviewers to get a sense of whether Bergman did justice to the part of Deborah Harford. The reviews of *More Stately Mansions* tend to confirm what Bergman revealed in portraying Hedda: that she found it difficult to portray complex characters with attitudes and feelings outside her experience. John Chapman in the *New York Daily News*: "Miss Bergman returns to the stage after a long absence, and being an assured and beautiful actress, her presence is welcome. But I still can't fancy her as the greedy grandmother of Hill's and Miss Dewhurst's children." Richard Watts, Jr., in the *New York Post*: "Miss Bergman, looking more beautiful than ever, seemed too young and in command of herself to be realistic as the loving and hating mother, but she plays with skill and her characteristic charm." Clive Barnes in *The New York Times*: "Ingrid Bergman, returning to the Broadway stage, is a woman so beautiful that she is herself a work of art. But as an actress she is less perfect, and cast as one of O'Neill's archetypal mother figures, she seemed strangely gauche. She trades heavily on her natural charm and, in a sense, her very real inner goodliness ... but makes less of the strangely disparate character of Deborah Harford than you might have hoped."[20] It is clear here that the reviewers were in awe of Bergman's star quality, but as an actor she did not impress them with her ability to capture the "greedy," "hating," "strangely disparate" side of Deborah's character.

Which may be a clue to Bergman's limited range: she could not convincingly portray power, hate, lust, distain, condescension, or simple evil. It is impossible to imagine her as Lady Macbeth or even *Hamlet*'s Gertrude. Perhaps it was the limit of her emotional sympathy or perhaps it was her lack of technique, but she is not a great actor in the tradition of great classically trained British stage actors who have made the transition to film, actors such as Judi Dench or Emma Thompson, both of whom have a much greater emotional range and can convey the complexities of a much wider range of characters than Bergman was capable of. Bergman was, first and foremost, a star, a film actor whose primary claim to fame is her ability to personify the "individuality" of her image: being natural, healthy, nice, longing for an end to conflict and devoted to love.

Occasionally, Bergman could break out of that image, as we have seen in *Gaslight* and *Murder on the Orient Express*. But she was, perhaps, only a great actor in three films: Hitchcock's *Notorious*, Rossellini's *Voyage in Italy* and Ingmar Bergman's *Autumn Sonata*. Interestingly, each of these directors exploited her performance skills in very different ways, which demonstrates the breadth of her range.

Many film scholars and critics scale the heights of eloquence describing the pleasure they get from watching their favorite stars run through their paces, the sheer joy they experience at watching these stars simply embody their "individualities": Cary Grant's cool insouciance, Katharine Hepburn's regal command, John Wayne's good-humored toughness. Bergman is at her best as a star-actor in this sense in *Notorious*. In that film, she personifies the character of Alicia Huberman consistent with her star image, but is able to develop Alicia's character and exhibit a much wider range of emotion than in her usual star vehicle.

But being a great star, embodying an "individuality," is not always synonymous with being a great actor. Great actors can also produce great performances by developing complex characters consistently over the course of a film, without resorting to the standard repertoire of mannerisms and emotions we associate with their stardom. Great actors can produce great performances not by embodying their star qualities but by transcending them. Bergman does this in *Voyage in Italy* and *Autumn Sonata*, even though Rossellini and Ingmar Bergman had very different philosophies and styles of directing and demanded very different things from her. Rossellini demanded that she respond intuitively to his immediate suggestions for character, movement, even dialogue. For Rossellini, Bergman had to improvise. Ingmar Bergman demanded that Ingrid plumb the depths of her soul and express the complex emotions of a character she found incomprehensible. For Ingmar, Bergman had to approximate the kind of acting she disliked — the Method — finding the resources locked away in her memory to portray deep grief and guilt. Her performance in *Autumn Sonata* comes close to psychotherapy. For each of these directors, Bergman was able to respond to their demands magnificently.

And perhaps most important, for film actors to achieve a great performance, they may simply need to rely on chance: they must portray the right character in the right film, expressing the right emotions in ways that make us want to go back and watch their performance again and again, always to discover new things we had not seen before, one reason being that the performance is framed in such a way, both in individual shots and scenes and by the narrative of the film as a whole, that the performance resonates with the subject matter and themes of the film. In *Notorious*, Bergman's deft manipulation of her image resonates with what the film is about: seeing and being seen, the voyeurism of frustrated love, acting as spying, sex without love for a higher cause. In *Voyage in Italy*, Bergman's eloquent nonverbal responses to the sights of Naples and Pompeii resonate with what that film is about: the effect of culture and history on the present. In *Autumn Sonata*, Bergman's baring her soul makes concrete what that film is about: the pervasiveness of guilt.

Notorious

In *Notorious*, Bergman is a star, and Hitchcock photographs her as a star in the Selznick tradition: in the close-ups of her drunken conversation with Devlin, in the opening shots of her in bed with a hangover, and at the end of the film in the misty close-up of her in bed, poisoned, whispering her love to Devlin. In all these shots, she is the romantic heroine, beautiful even in distress.

Hitchcock tended to let his actors interpret their characters as they wished as long as they filled the frame according to his preconception of how the shot ought to look. So, too, with Bergman. What we see in *Notorious* is Bergman on her own, developing the character of Alicia, providing grace notes to the character and exhibiting considerable range. She begins as a playgirl vamp, tipsy, fatigued, leaning provocatively into Devlin, encouraging a pass with

Bergman as Alisha Huberman flirts with Cary Grant's Devlin in Alfred Hitchcock's *Notorious*, trying to convince him that she is a new person. When Devlin rejects her, Bergman beautifully captures Huberman's insecurity and pain (RKO, 1946).

drooping lids, at one moment primly covering her mouth to cover a burp or a rush of stomach upset at all the booze. She progresses to a love-struck ingénue, glowing radiantly at Devlin's attention. Offered the job of sleeping with and then marrying a Nazi enemy, Sebastian, she looks to Devlin for help, begging for his love and then making fun of his detachment. When Devlin seemingly abandons her, she plays the tough gangster moll and dismisses him with a sneer. Once she becomes Sebastian's lover and then wife, she alternates between matrimonial devotion and furtive spying. The film reaches a climax when Sebastian discovers that Alisha is a spy, and he and his mother start to systematically poison her. This gives Bergman the chance to play a damsel in distress. At first she becomes worn and withdrawn, then when she discovers the plot against her, she becomes horrified and hysterical. At the grand finale of the film, Devlin dramatically rescues Alisha, sneaking into her bedroom, and helping her down the staircase as he faces off against Sebastian and his mother. Here, Bergman is almost entirely passive, but she conveys a complex mixture of fear, gratitude, and love. The sheer range of emotion during the entire film is remarkable.

Perhaps this range is best captured in the café scene when Alisha confesses that she is going straight, attempting to stop being, in her words, a crook and a tramp. Devlin, however, resists her flirting. And so Alisha treats Devlin sarcastically, commenting on her attempt to achieve daisies and buttercups, having been on the wagon for eight days and having had no new sexual conquests. Devlin replies, "Nice daydream." Alisha's face falls, and she wrestles to produce a shaky smile. Her reply is not quite pleading: "Why won't you believe in me, Dev, just a little?"

In *Notorious*, Bergman fulfills the requirements of her standard star image and goes well beyond it, but perhaps the reason she achieves greatness is that the very nature of her performance, the things she does so well, the quick shift of emotion, the ability to do long takes, are framed by the narrative with its themes of seeing and being seen, voyeurism, and acting as spying. On her first date with Sebastian, Alisha denies that she is attracted to Devlin with a coy smile and gladly agrees to another dinner at Sebastian's house. Only at the end of the scene does Alisha show us her dismay and anxiety. Similar facial shifts happen throughout the film, as when Alisha shows her dismay when Devlin walks out on the meeting about whether she should marry Sebastian, and when she realizes that she is being poisoned. And as for the long takes, the long nuzzle between Alisha and Devlin is one of the most famous shots in film history.

In the film, Bergman's trademark image of longing and devotion is turned inward and needs to be hidden. She has to show us that when Alisha expresses her disgust at Devlin, she really loves him, that when she expresses her devotion to Sebastian, it is at a terrible cost. This Bergman does with one of her signature strengths. Her strengths as an actor reinforce the themes of the film. The complexity of the romantic feelings that Bergman portrays so well illustrates the conflict between public love and devotion and a hidden, private mental life. We can appreciate Bergman's performance in itself and for the way it gives us a great deal to ponder.

Voyage in Italy

When she first began working with Rossellini, as we have seen, Bergman did not know quite how to respond to his demands for improvisation. Forced to respond quickly to suggestions for motivation, action, and dialogue, she may have relied too much on her repertoire of pantomimic gestures. In *Voyage in Italy*, Rossellini biographer Tag Gallagher argues that Rossellini carried his improvisatory technique to the extreme: he worked hard to "inspire maximum embarrassment between [George] Sanders and Bergman."[21] Says Laura Mulvey, Rossellini "dispatched" both stars "facing crises in their real-life marriages, into unknown professional territory," where they had to in effect re-enact the crises in their lives, "to undergo and then endure a loss of power, a decentralizing of the traditional unity of star and story."[22]

Rossellini does this, according to Mulvey, by confusing and troubling the actors, neither of whom was a natural improviser. In forcing them to work without a script, Rossellini was after a kind of spontaneity, "the action image," over which he had little control himself, but it was just such a lack of control that he was after: what Gallagher calls the logical extension of Italian neo-realism, putting being/existence over essence, positing certain character types and then letting these characters play themselves out over the course of the film.[23] In an interview, Rossellini confessed that for *Voyage in Italy* he deliberately treated Bergman and Sanders, especially Sanders, badly. He wanted to unsettle Sanders and make him edgy and irritable: "To be frank ... you have to make [actors] work for you.... Don't you think [Sanders] was obvious for the part? It was his own bad moods rather than his own personality that suited the character in the film."[24] For all practical purposes, the same could be said of the way Rossellini treated Bergman.

But, of course, Rossellini required his actors to improvise in situations in which the shots were planned ahead of time and the shots and the situations were designed to fit into his larger ideas about where the film was going and what it was doing. Sometimes the results are remarkable. Most of *Voyage in Italy* was improvised from notes. Rossellini and his crew did not know that the Pompeii sequence in which Katherine and Alex view an archeological excavation would result in the unearthing of a buried couple and thus provide a climax to the film "until after it happened."[25]

Eventually Rossellini's demands forced Bergman to rely on the essentials of her craft, the fundamental basis of her image. The result is a Bergman without all the Hollywood tricks for making actors look good and hiding their limitations. Rossellini forced Bergman to rely on the core of her abilities, and despite Bergman's denials and ambivalence, she succeeds magnificently, especially in her eloquent nonverbal responses to the sights of Naples and Pompeii.

Earlier, in *Stromboli* in the scene in the village garden maze, Bergman begins to respond to Rossellini's improvisatory methods by creating a brilliant visual metaphor of her situation. In one long tracking shot, the camera follows Karin as she walks along the far side of a low stone wall, contemplating her situation, having just been repelled by a young boy from the village with whom she tried to establish contact. The boy refused to even tell her his name. The camera follows Karin as she walks along sadly, taking in this new version of her prison, the narrow lane in the garden maze, which allows her only two directions, forward or backward. She stops and rests her head on her arm on top of the wall, picks out a plant and sensuously strokes her face with the leaves, and nibbles the edges, eyes closed, in a moment of quiet longing. The moment is broken by the sound of cleaning men in her apartment, so she climbs the wall to go back home, ironically breaking the bounds of the maze, only to return to her old prison, the apartment. In this shot, Bergman's stroking her face with the plant becomes a powerful image of how her sexuality is being contained, and the image resonates with the themes of the larger narrative.

By the time she does *Voyage in Italy* for Rossellini, Bergman has become more comfortable with his improvisatory methods: she relies much less on her repertoire of pantomimic gestures. She becomes more cinematic, underplaying the part of Katherine Joyce and relying on the camera and the context to do some of the work. Most of what she contributes are her responses to what is going on around her, to what she sees. We understand Katherine because of what we see in Bergman's face, especially in her eyes. In the National Archeological Museum in Naples, Rossellini's fluid camera glides in sweeping dolly and crane shots over and around the statues and then pans to Bergman's face looking up at them. Bergman responds minimally — indeed she uses no gestures at all — but her eyes express a complex attitude: blankness at first, resistance to the frozen life in the statues around her, but as she continues to look and see, her wonder increases and she becomes fascinated, and we see her struggling not to acknowledge these feelings. When her guide shows her a torso of Venus and notes how much he appreciates the statue because it is "not as young as the others. She is more mature. Don't you think so, Lady?" Katherine, repressed and shocked out of her reverie, is dismissive: "I wouldn't know," she says curtly and turns away. But toward the end of Katherine's tour of the museum, Rossellini's camera puts her responses in context. In a crane shot that swoops around the head of the ten-foot Farnese Hercules high on a stone pedestal and then backs off, the statue of Hercules filling the left side of the shot, Katherine and her guide become small insignificant figures in the lower right, lost in the echoing space of the museum, and by implication in history itself. Katherine breathes the words, "Oh, it's wonderful."

All Bergman has done in this scene is react, but in the context of the film, her performance is rich in detail; it resonates with implication: the overwhelming and humbling sense of the past. This is, in effect, what the film is about: Katherine Joyce's gradual realization of her position in time and space. As she visits the major tourist sites of Naples — besides the Naples Archeological Museum, she also sees the fortress and caves at Cumae, the Catacombs, and Pompei — she is constantly reminded of the rich fecund life around her, the sweep of history, and the emotional poverty and insignificance of her own life.

Katherine comes to realize that her relationship with her husband is the only thing that gives her life meaning in the grand sweep of history, and this insight becomes the motivation for her attempt to reconcile with her husband at the end of the film. Said Rossellini in an interview, "I consider *Voyage* to be very important in my work. It was a film which rested on something very subtle, the variations in a couple's relationship under the influence of a third person: the exterior world surrounding them."[26] Rossellini frames Bergman in individual shots to show us her response to where she is and what she sees, and the film as a whole frames Bergman's performance in such a way that we come to understand that Bergman's responses *are* what the film is about. The narrative of the film gives Bergman's performance extraordinary power.

Autumn Sonata

In working with Ingmar Bergman, Ingrid confronted a director whose methods were diametrically opposed to Rossellini's. Ingmar demanded that his actors self-consciously analyze their characters and meticulously detail their emotional lives. And he expected his actors to express the complex feelings of their characters in a hothouse atmosphere in which he was in ultimate control. Ingmar was willing to negotiate with his actors about the fine points of their characters, but he made it very clear that it was his vision of the character that would wind up on the screen. To get the performances he wanted, Ingmar would encourage, cajole, demand, and browbeat his actors into clawing their way deeper and deeper inside themselves to find the truth of their characters. Ingrid instinctively resisted this kind of overpowering direction, and she had little initial understanding or sympathy for her character in *Autumn Sonata*, Charlotte Andergast, a concert pianist who has abandoned her family for her career. But Ingmar tolerated no resistance and was willing to battle Ingrid for as long as it took to get her to do what he wanted. Ultimately, she put aside her reservations about the part of Charlotte and did the emotional work that Ingmar demanded. In *Autumn Sonata*, Bergman's obviously theatrical gestures disappear, and often as in *Voyage in Italy* she does not have a great deal of dialogue. What we see instead is naked emotion. We see Charlotte's frightening psychological dominance over her daughter Eva and then we see her break down as Eva fights back, accusing, berating, beating Charlotte into submission, at least for one evening.

On the surface, the situation of *Autumn Sonata* is commonplace: a mother, Charlotte, visiting the home of her daughter Eva and her son-in-law Victor. But unbeknownst to Charlotte, Eva and Victor have taken Helena, Charlotte's handicapped daughter and Eva's sister, out of the institution in which Charlotte had placed her and brought her home to live with them. We quickly learn then that Charlotte is not a typical mother: she is a world-renowned concert pianist, who is so caught up in her career and her own love affairs that she has difficulty finding the time to visit her family. For two years now, Eva, burdened with her handicapped sister and still mourning a son who died young, has been begging Charlotte to visit. Charlotte may have given in to Eva's request this time because she too is in mourning: her lover and companion of thirteen years, Leonardo, has recently died.

Soon after her arrival, Charlotte insists on hearing Eva play the piano. Clearly Eva is nervous and fearful of what her mother will think of her, but her husband Victor gives her no choice. He tells Charlotte of Eva's desire to play for her mother. Eva proceeds to play Chopin's "Prelude no. 2 in A-minor" in a solidly competent manner. Eva is not a professional, but she plays well with only a few awkward moments. While she plays, Charlotte sits quietly on the arm of a nearby chair, listening with rapt attention. Bergman here does a masterful job of conveying a succession of feelings without uttering a word. A small, affectionate smile plays on her face: she seems proud of her daughter. She closes her eyes to listen more carefully; her lips move, as if she were softly singing the lyrics to the piece or talking herself through her own performance. Coming out of her reverie, she glances again at Eva, but ever so slightly her demeanor changes. Her smile slides away; she hints at a frown: something is not right. The critic has taken over.

Ingmar films this sequence cutting back and forth between Charlotte and Eva. Charlotte is shot full front, Eva in three-quarter at the piano, as if from Charlotte's point of view.

When Eva finishes, she is desperate for her mother's judgment but worried. Her fingers play at her lips. "Eva, my dearest," Charlotte says severely, without a smile. Eva immediately asks Charlotte to give her an honest assessment of her playing, perhaps because she knows that Charlotte will ultimately tell her anyway. But Charlotte will only say that she was "moved." Asked by Eva if she liked her playing, Charlotte says, "I like *you*." Eva turns away, hurt and angry, saying only that she doesn't know what Charlotte means.[27]

But Charlotte will not say what she means and wants to hear Eva play more. Eva now knows that her mother is being falsely gracious. She demands to know what she did wrong. When Charlotte insists that Eva did nothing wrong, that everyone is entitled to her interpretation, Eva becomes overtly angry. She insists on knowing what Charlotte's interpretation of the prelude is: "I'm upset because you evidently don't think it worth the trouble to tell me *your* idea of this prelude."

This is the cue Charlotte has been waiting for. She crosses behind Eva to the piano and sits, forcing Eva to slide away. She begins to talk, as if giving a lesson to a new graduate student, and quickly implies that Eva's playing is beneath contempt. Her criticism is all the more devastating by being so impersonal, indirect, and offhand. She dismisses Eva's technique "which wasn't at all bad," but she strongly hints that Eva's interpretation is sentimental — Chopin is "very emotional but not mawkish" — and that she cannot endure. Chopin, she says, was "proud, sarcastic, passionate, tormented, furious, and very manly," but not "a mawkish old woman." And so Eva should have played the piece not so ingratiatingly but to make it sound "almost *ugly*." "Like this!" Charlotte says, and begins to play the prelude herself.

During her speech and her turn at the piano, Bergman is involved, intense, focused on her inner vision of the prelude, lost behind her eyes. Eva is no longer there. Charlotte is in her own world, the world she has mastered, the only world she is comfortable in, a world in which she is in absolute control. Her concentration is total. This is an Ingrid we have never seen before, intensely understated and focused inward, and the intensity of her performance is heightened by the way Ingmar shoots the scene. First, each of the women is trapped in her own close-up world, and the scene proceeds, crosscutting between the two. At the piano, the scene expands to medium twoshots, first of Eva and Charlotte seated at the piano and viewed from in front of the piano, and then of Eva watching Charlotte play, as if the camera were a third person on the piano seat, Charlotte in profile, Eva partially eclipsed behind her. This last shot is one of the high points of the film. Eva alternately looks down, as if not daring a glimpse of the sun, then up, staring at her mother in awe, envy, disappointment, self-pity, and anger. Charlotte is oblivious to all that Eva is going through, and the shot captures her complete absorption, as Eva looks hopelessly on.

The final Walpurgisnacht between the two women is shot in the same way. Away from the rest of the family after a day together, Eva proceeds with the determination of a committed prosecutor to list Charlotte's sins: her abandonment of her family (both Eva and Helena); her career as a professional pianist, leaving Eva with the dilemma of caring for her sister herself or leaving her in an institution; on her last visit, years before, running off to another concert date and leaving her lover Leonardo behind as a kind of surrogate parent, which caused Helena's final disintegration. Ingmar films the scene only in close-ups. The close-ups emphasize Charlotte's ravaged, wrinkled face, her eyes worn and red-rimmed, her cheek streaked with tears, and as Eva elaborates her indictment, Charlotte can only respond fitfully, mostly with her eyes that are full of pain and anguish and just once seem to flare up in defiance. The close-ups cut off any gestures, and the image is of Charlotte's face filling the frame, not moving, suffering the brutal attack of her daughter with only one slight shake of the head. She accepts the attack with sorrow and resignation and perhaps hopelessness.

At the end of Eva's indictment, Charlotte asks if Eva is accusing her of deliberately making Helena ill. No, Eva admits. Then Charlotte breaks in, "Then you can't blame me." But Eva is relentless: she accuses Charlotte of always expecting to be treated as an exception, that she believes the normal decencies of life do not apply to her, that she needs to realize just how guilty she is. Charlotte recoils: "Guilty of what?" But Eva won't say; she may not even know. She simply knows that Charlotte is guilty of something terrible. Charlotte is overwhelmed and pours out her anguish, crying out, "Won't you come here to me? Won't you put your arms around me? I'm so horribly afraid. Darling, won't you forgive me for all the wrong I've done? I'll try to mend my ways. You must teach me.... Your hatred is so terrible. I haven't understood. I have been selfish and childish and anxious. At least touch me! Strike me if you like! Eva dear, help me!"

But Eva does not move to her mother. Then suddenly Helena calls out from her room, "Momma! Help me! Come!" And we see a close-up of Helena through the posts of a stairway, on the floor, as if in prison, her head twisted, unable to get up. Cut to a close-up of Charlotte, who looks down, then up, her jaw quivering as she asks for help, for forgiveness, for some sheer physical contact. Cut to a close-up of Eva, who is relentless and will not bend. And the scene ends with alternating close-ups of Eva, Charlotte, and Helena, each locked in her own separate world. Neither Eva nor Charlotte moves to help Helena.

Once again Bergman is working with a director who knows how to frame her performance is ways that resonate with the larger narrative and the themes of the film. The piano scene is shot in simple close-ups and two-fers. The final fight with Eva is filmed in suffocating close-ups. Both scenes are shot to capture the very nature of Bergman's and Liv Ulmann's performances. In the piano scene, the two women sitting together emphasizes the contrast between them. What at first appears to be a happy family ritual, a mother listening to her daughter perform, quickly degenerates into a ghastly form of oneupsmanship. We see Charlotte take control, we see Eva shrink away in the same shot. And in the final unmasking, the cross-cutting of extreme close-ups dramatizes for us the separate worlds of Charlotte, Eve, and Helena, how the three women are locked apart in separate realities. The framing of these two key scenes becomes a metaphor for the entire film, and undercuts whatever optimism we may feel that Eva has finally mustered the nerve to confront her mother, that things might be different in the future. An early scene of what alienates the two women is shot to show us their relationship. The dramatic finale, the daughter desperately standing up to her mother, is shot to show that they are still far apart, each isolated in her own frame, alone.

Bergman's successful career is, of course, due to the star qualities that inspired filmmakers to want to work with her, to find parts appropriate for her. Her success is due to the honed skills and acumen she possessed as a professional actor. But her success is also due, to some degree, by sheer good luck. For complicated reasons of fate and free choice, Bergman managed to appear in three films that exploited her strengths. Two of these films exploited strengths she did not know she had. And all three films provided a narrative, a style, a frame for showcasing what only she could do. In at least three films, Ingrid Bergman is not just a star; she is a great actor.

Nine

The Actor as Auteur

"There are no good and bad movies, only good and bad directors."
— François Truffaut

"The auteur theory can be revised and reproposed with actors in mind:
under certain circumstances, an actor may influence a film as much
as a writer, director, or producer...."   — Patrick McGilligan

Ingrid Bergman's bravura performances in Alfred Hitchcock's *Notorious*, Roberto Rossellini's *Voyage to Italy*, and Ingmar Bergman's *Autumn Sonata* are not the only way she contributed to these films. Bergman was also the inspiration for the films in the first place. In a sense, *Notorious*, *Voyage in Italy*— and the larger quartet of films of which it is a part — and *Autumn Sonata* are about Ingrid Bergman. In the parlance of film theory, Bergman is one of the authors of these films. She is an auteur.

Auteur theory arose in France in the mid–1950s. François Truffaut's 1954 essay "A Certain Trend in French Cinema" is usually considered the first major statement of the theory. Truffaut argued that the worst films of certain gifted directors, such as Jean Renoir, would always be more interesting than the best films of other more conventional directors. To Truffaut, even though film-making is obviously a collaborative effort, significant directors impose a distinctive style on their films or involve themselves in projects with consistent themes. Consequently, when we view the films of these directors, we are drawn to think of them as a coherent body of work: books, as it were, written by the same author.

Truffaut's thoughts on auteurship were not labled auteur theory until 1962, when American critic Andrew Sarris used the phrase in his essay, "Notes on the Auteur Theory." To be called an auteur, according to Sarris, a film director must demonstrate a consistent technical competence and develop a personal style. Sarris also argued that the films of auteurs had common meanings, although he was vague about how we ascertain what those meanings are.[1]

Auteur theory has always been controversial. After all, during the reign of the studio system, distinguished directors were hired by studios to direct the films they were assigned, and even today, with independent production "packaging," directors can be brought on board projects that have already been considerably "developed." In these circumstances, it is difficult to see how directors have the scope and freedom to develop common themes from film to film or express a consistent personal vision. And of course, because filmmaking involves so many people — from scriptwriters and cinematographers to set designers, costumers, and make-up specialists — it is difficult to see how a director's body of work can possibly be so personal, stylistically or otherwise. Nevertheless, certain directors have managed to gain their freedom from studios and producers so that they are in fact involved in every aspect of the creation of their films and have the power of the "final cut." Hitchcock, Rossellini, and Ingmar Bergman are all commonly thought of as auteurs.

Obviously, then, we could consider actors to be auteurs if they direct themselves or write the scripts for the films they appear in: for example, we might think of actor-directors such as Charlie Chaplin, Ida Lupino, and Clint Eastwood, or actor-director-screenwriter Woody Allen as auteurs. But film theorist Richard Dyer argues something more subtle about the possibility of actors being auteurs: that actors, merely by acting, can make such a distinctive contribution to a film they become for all practical purposes auteurs.

To Dyer, influential stars are "semiotic constructions" whose contributions to films can be broadly divided into two categories: "Stars as authors," in which stars directly influence the nature of their films, and "Stars and authors," in which stars influence those involved in the production of films, usually directors, by having such powerful images or persuasive personalities that they virtually insist on determining the director's "concerns and 'characteristic patterns.'"[2]

In explaining "stars as authors," Dyer agrees with Patrick McGilligan:

> The auteur theory can be revised and reproposed with actors in mind: under certain circumstances, an actor may influence a film as much as a writer, director, or producer; some actors are more influential that others; and there are certain rare few performers whose acting capabilities and screen personas are so powerful that they embody and define the very essence of their films.... When the performer becomes so important to a production that he or she changes lines, adlibs, shifts meaning, influences the narrative and style of a film, and altogether signifies something clear-cut to audiences despite the intent of the writers and directors, then the acting of that person assumes the force, style and integrity of an auteur.[3]

McGilligan argues that Jimmy Cagney's films with certain directors have more similarities among them, a common subject matter, a sense of style, than the other films made by the same directors with different stars. This is the classic empirical argument for the star as an auteur.

It can also be argued that stars who carefully control their image or the conditions of their performances can be considered auteurs. Joan Crawford often insisted on certain roles and that she be photographed in a certain way. Fred Astaire designed his own dance routines.

But the most interesting and difficult cases to sort out are those which Dyer labels "stars and authors," cases in which actor-stars by the very nature of their image or personality influence producers or directors or screenwriters to such an extent that they seem to be a major force determining what the film is about, its very shape and form. Marilyn Monroe is the obvious example of a star with a limited range, but with such a powerful image that she took over many of the films she appeared in. And in certain of her best films — Billy Wilder's *Some Like it Hot*, for example, or John Huston's *The Misfits* — Monroe is the occasion for a study of her image. Wilder explores Monroe's sexuality in his gender-bending film, and in discussing his screenplay for *The Misfits*, Arthur Miller acknowledged that his purpose was to present Monroe as he saw her, as he thought she really was behind her blatantly sexualized screen image: an earth mother, a shy inarticulate intellectual with broad sympathies and interests. As a result of Monroe's powerful persona and the attention paid to that persona by thoughtful filmmakers and intellectuals such as Wilder and Miller, today, despite the very different circumstances in which her films were made, we often think of Monroe's films as a unified body of work, one indication of an auteur.

Bergman was a more accomplished actress than Monroe, and her life and image were, perhaps, even more complex. But like Monroe, with certain directors, Bergman as a star became an auteur: her very life, her aspirations and ambitions, her loves, the way she presented herself on screen and off, became the focus, the inspiration for *Notorious*, the Rossellini Quartet, and *Autumn Sonata*. Bergman not only stars in these films; she is the occasion for Hitchcock, Rossellini, and Ingmar Bergman to meditate on her life, her image, what Bergman meant to these men, and to us. In these films, Bergman contributes something rare to filmmaking: she is the occasion for these filmmakers to explore what Ingrid Bergman, the actor, and "Ingrid Bergman," the image, stand for and what both actor and image mean.

Hitchcock's *Notorious*

Alfred Hitchcock often confessed that he was especially attracted to northern European women, women from England, northern Germany, and

Scandinavia, whom he found much more exciting than Latin women because, he said, "sex should not be advertised." A northern European woman, Hitchcock told François Truffaut, is "apt to get in a cab with you, and, to your surprise, she'll probably pull a man's pants open."[4] This was one of Hitchcock's favorite fantasies: that women who seem to be outwardly cool and reserved are really a cauldron of passion inside. Hence, his fascination with cool blondes: Bergman, Grace Kelly, Doris Day, and Tippi Hedrin.

All of Hitchcock's biographers agree that Hitchcock had an "acute, unrequited passion" for Bergman. Says Patrick McGilligan, "They were kindred spirits. They shared the belief that Selznick contracts had trapped them in an 'absolute prison,' in Bergman's words. Both saw themselves as outsiders in Hollywood, and pined for the culture and sophistication they'd left behind in Europe. Both were refreshingly earthy personalities, with blunt senses of humor."[5]

Indeed, Hitchcock had a more particular fantasy about Bergman: according to Spoto, following the production of *Notorious*, Hitchcock often told a detailed story about how Bergman trapped him in his bedroom after a dinner party at his house on Bellagio Road and refused to leave until he had made love to her. Since both Hitchcock's wife Alma and Bergman's husband were at the party, Spoto doubts the story. McGilligan says that when Hitchcock told this story, it did not take place after a dinner party but, depending on his audience and the circumstances, in either his own home or Bergman's. No matter which place, when Hitchcock arrived, he found Bergman waiting to seduce him. Her enticements were hard for him to resist, but resist he did. According to McGilligan, Hitchcock always maintained that the incident only happened once and he never made clear when it happened, but like Spoto he thinks it most likely that it happened during the shooting of *Notorious*, if it happened at all. McGilligan is inclined to give the story some credence because actresses fall in love with their directors all the time, Hitchcock had lost some weight and could be devilishly charming—Bergman appreciated men who were not traditionally handsome; Rossellini, for one, obviously wasn't a matinee heart throb—and, after all, hadn't Bergman slept with her directors and co-stars before?[6] What McGilligan does not factor into his analysis is that during the filming of *Notorious*, Bergman was involved with Robert Capa, and may have still been seeing Larry Adler on the side. True, Bergman's previous romances had been restricted to co-stars and directors on the set, but now she may have already been juggling a husband and two lovers. And with Capa often on the set, it seems less likely that she would want to seduce Hitchcock.

Whatever the truth of the seduction story, Hitchcock always maintained that he made *Under Capricorn*, the second film after *Notorious*, just to work with Bergman again, that the subject of the film suited her better than it did him. He told Truffaut that he wanted to work with Bergman again because she was "the biggest star in America and all the American producers were competing for her services," that "to get Bergman would be a tremendous feat," "a victory over the rest of the industry, you see," that the very thought of being associated with Bergman publicly again, of being photographed with her at the London airport was "intoxicat[ing]." In retrospect, he thought "that was bad thinking, and my behavior was almost infantile."[7] This is not the language of a man talking about business decisions; this is the language of a school boy, explaining why he wants to carry Ingrid's books and walk her home from school.

There is no doubt that Hitchcock was deeply repressed. According to Arthur Laurents, talking about the homosexual subtext of *Rope*, Hitchcock was fascinated by sex, much like a young boy who knows nothing about it but who had heard from adults that it is naughty. Because of his strict Catholic upbringing, he also had a highly developed sense of sin. In his films, Hitchcock was always subtle and indirect about sex, perhaps to deal with the fact that he thought everyone else he knew had exciting sex lives and he did not. And because he felt left out, trapped outside the bedroom door, he withdrew into himself and was very circumspect about sex in his films.[8]

Hitchcock was raised in a strict Catholic home that was by all accounts loving and supportive. Still, certain events caused Hitchcock to bury his feelings and fear the unknown and unexpected. He had a strong mother, Emma, who regularly demanded that he come into her bedroom at night, stand at the foot of the bed, and recite his activities for the day. Hitchcock called it "confession." Hitchcock's father William once arranged with a friendly policeman to put young Alfred in jail, perhaps only for a few minutes, for being naughty. And one Sunday evening, Hitchock's parents put him to bed and went for a stroll in Hyde Park, an hour and a half away from home by tram and train. He woke up, called out and got no answer. Deathly frightened, he wandered the house, searching for his parents, calling out their names.[9]

As an adult, Hitchcock admitted his naivete about matters of sex. Once in Berlin, cajoled by UFA representative Graham Cutts to go with a group of people to a homosexual bar, the men found themselves propositioned by two women, who promised them a better time in a private room. The group took the women to a hotel, where the women made various offers. Not knowing just what the women were proposing, Hitchcock repeatedly said, *"Nein, nein,"* but the women ignored him. They slipped into bed and began to make love. Hitchcock was, says John Russell Taylor, "surprised but fairly uncomprehending."

Hitchcock's relationship with his wife Alma was formal and based on mutual respect. He was shy, hence their long courtship. They worked together closely and she always had a determining voice on his final scripts and final cuts. But the marriage may not have been passionate. McGilligan asserts baldly that Hitchcock was impotent, based primarily on later stories in which he claimed he was "chaste" and "celibate," and his popular joke that he had only had sex once — to conceive his daughter Pat — which he had to accomplish with a fountain pen.[10] It is standard practice in analyzing Hitchcock to argue that Alma was more of a mother than a lover. In fact, until her death, Hitchcock and Alma often traveled with his mother. When his mother died, Hitchcock had to deal with his anger, guilt, and resentment toward her, and by extension his frustrations with his wife. He sought solace from all these complex emotions in his fantasies about his female stars: women he adored but whom he dared not touch. His work has a strong motif of voyeurism: Jimmy Stewart watching the apartment windows in *Rear Window* and following Kim Novak in *Vertigo*, the sneaky camera going under the window to view Janet Leigh in her underwear and Anthony Perkins looking through the pin hole at Leigh undressing in *Psycho*.

In *Notorious*, Hitchcock, who had received Bergman's commitment to star in the film, consulted with Ben Hecht on the script. During the course of filming, he also saw that Bergman was deeply involved with Capa, who had managed to get an assignment to photograph the making of the film. And so the film became an occasion for Hitchcock to work out his feelings toward Bergman, to contemplate who she was and what she meant to him. In the process, he explored both her image and the reality behind the image. "Ingrid Bergman" the star becomes Alicia Huberman, a woman who leads a double life on many different levels. As a spy, she seduces and then marries a man, while concealing from him her true identity. As a lover, she conceals from her contact, the man she loves, her true feelings for him, just as a star and lover, Bergman hides her actual life and pretends affection for her husband.

Notorious also dramatizes Hitchcock's point of view about Bergman. It is about Hitchcock watching Bergman, who was then having an affair with Capa, and perhaps Adler, and still going home to her husband. It is a story about a man who has to share a woman with another man for professional reasons: Devlin has to share Alicia with Sebastian for the good of the country, just as Hitchcock has to keep his distance from Bergman for professional reasons but has to share her with her husband and lovers. Like Devlin, Hitchcock had always been afraid of women and needed to keep his love for Bergman unspoken and under control. And perhaps, if the seduction anecdote is true, Hitchcock dealt with his unrequited love by trashing the object of his affection and thinking of her as a prostitute, just as Devlin, despite his attraction to

Alicia allows her to become Sebastian's lover and then his wife, for which he despises her. Like Sebastian, Hitchcock recognized that he was not conventionally handsome and could not compete with men like Devlin, but he was jealous anyway. Even though he has been previously spurned by Alicia, Sebastian longingly aches for her and manages to articulate what Hitchcock never could: "You always affected me like a tonic," Sebastian tells Alicia. "I knew that if I saw you again I'd feel what I used to for you — the same hunger." Like Sebastian, who is torn between his love and allegiance to his mother and his love for Alicia, Hitchcock was torn between his love for his controlling mother-wife and his love for Bergman.

The problem with this psychoanalytic reading of *Notorious* is that it is based mostly on connections between Hitchcock's psycho-sexual life and the content of the film. It ignores the fact that the script of the film was the result of a long intense collaboration between Hitchcock and Ben Hecht. Hecht incorporated suggestions from Hitchcock but also producer David Selznick, and after Selznick sold the picture to RKO, Clifford Odets was hired to provide a rewrite before yet another Hecht draft. There is no evidence in the Hitchcock-Hecht collaboration that Hitchcock ever insisted on certain plot points or aspects of character development for biographical reasons, although Hitchcock did tell an RKO executive early in the development of the script that the story was about "a woman sold for political purposes into sexual enslavement."[11] We have no direct evidence that Hitchcock was thinking of Bergman at this stage in the development of the script, although we do know that after *Spellbound* he did want to make another film with her.

Nevertheless, Spoto has reason to insist that Hitchcock wrote certain scenes in *Notorious* all by himself and McGilligan argues that Hitchcock knew Bergman so well that "he could write her feelings and personality into the character of Alicia." French director-critics Eric Rohmer and Claude Chabrol go so far as to baldly assert with no evidence other than the films themselves that Hitchcock was so fascinated with Bergman he conceived of *Spellbound*, *Notorious*, and *Under Capricorn* as a unified triptych "that would throw light on the many facets of feminine personality."[12]

Rohmer and Chabrol may be extending the boundaries of textual analysis to the point of incredulity, but there is no doubt that that *Notorious* bears up remarkably well under the intense scrutiny of biographical criticism. *Notorious* is a film about seeing and being seen, about the odd voyeurism of a lover who cannot bring himself to stop the woman he loves from sleeping with another man but who is also fascinated by what she is doing. In a sense, he may love her *because* she is promiscuous and dangerous, someone he cannot have but can fantasize about. And so *Notorious* may also be about Bergman's wholesome star image, which we know now was based on a lie: she had a secret sexual life. The film gives us the occasion to ponder the basis for Bergman's appeal: in Wood's terms, whether Bergman was a star because she was so natural and nice, or because her sexuality was so constantly threatening to break out of its constraints. In *Notorious,* Alicia Huberman is more like Bergman herself than Ilsa Lunt, Sister Benedict, or Joan of Arc. Perhaps, the film suggests, that is the basis of her appeal. Framed by these larger psychological and social narratives, particular scenes and shots in the film can give us much to think about.

For one thing, there are all the close-ups. Joe McElhaney has calculated that there are 119 close-ups in *Notorious,* and 72 extreme close-ups, a total of 191 shots in a 101-minute film (66). Bergman is the object of this intense gaze much of the time. McElhaney argues that Hitchcock's use of the close-up was part of broader trend in American films in the late 1940s toward the real and the psychological. Hitchcock himself told Truffaut that in these pictures "eighty percent of the footage was shot in close-ups or semiclose shots."[13] All of this may be true, but it also provides Hitchcock with an excuse to film Bergman closely, to indulge his fascination.

The best example of this phenomenon is the long tracking shot of Alicia nuzzling Devlin as he goes off to get their assignment from the CIA director. This shot gave Hitchcock the chance to get up close and intimate with Bergman while claiming that he designed the shot in order to avoid the censors of the Production Code Administration, who demanded a time limit on kisses. The shot becomes a metaphor for Bergman's breaking the bounds of conventional love, and for Hitchcock's attempt to get as close to Bergman as he dared.

There are also the scenes of clandestine meetings between Alicia and Devlin after she begins her affair with Sebastian. Devlin's revulsion and pain in dealing with Alica is Hitchcock's. It is also ours. Who is this woman we so long for and adore?

And there is the rescue scene, Alicia lying in bed suffering the effects of poisoning, still beautiful in all her pain, shot in the Selznick manner to call attention to her stardom, Devlin bending over her, whispering that he has come to take her away, that he loves her, has always loved her, he was a fool to refuse to admit it to himself. The shot reminds us that Hitchcock is indulging in every male's fantasy: riding to the rescue of the damsel in distress. And the scene is a metaphor of how we reconcile our fascination with Bergman's beauty and the potentially sensational details of her sex life. We ride to the rescue and turn her back into a virgin/star. Our rescue restores her purity and goodness.

There is one final reason that it is not farfetched to think that *Notorious* is about Ingrid Bergman, the actor and star. Clearly *Rear Window* was, too.

The opening pan shot of L.B. Jeffries's apartment shows his photographs on the walls and the major magazine in which his photographs were published: the photos are shots of men at war and the magazine is *Life*. The romance between Jeffries and Lisa Fremont clearly alludes to the Capa-Bergman romance. The major subplot of *Rear Window*, whether Lisa can afford to give up her career in the New York fashion to traipse around the world with Jeffries, clearly alludes to Bergman's dilemma with Capa. The screenwriter for the film, John Michael Hayes, denies he had any knowledge of Bergman's affair with Capa when he was writing the script, but in the design and filming of Jeffries' apartment, Hitchcock found a way to suggest the connection, nevertheless.[14] For an extended period in the late '40s, Alfred Hitchcock could not get Ingrid Bergman out of his mind and used his films to record his fascination with both her personality and her image.

"The Rossellini Version of Me": The Bergman Quartet

Roberto Rossellini made four full-length original films with Ingrid Bergman — *Stromboli*, *Europa '51*, *Voyage in Italy*, and *Fear*. This does not count two other films Rossellini made with her: the short "Ingrid Bergman," part of a comic trilogy, and *Joan at the Stake*, a filmed version of the oratorio which Bergman starred in with music by Arthur Honegger, book and lyrics by Paul Claudel. The four full-length original films are so closely related in vision, theme, and technique that we can speak of them as a quartet. And one major theme of all four films is Ingrid Bergman herself.

Bergman's influence on the quartet has long been recognized. Leo Braudy notes that in *Stromboli*, Rossellini's camera "seeks out Bergman amid the rocky cliffs of Stromboli in an effort to respond to some subterranean mingling of actress and character, the mysterious knot of artifice and nature." In *Voyage in Italy* and *Fear*, Braudy seems to see an allusion to *Gaslight* and *Under Capricorn*: "Rossellini exploits that character that Ingrid Bergman often projects: the potentially insane erratic person, held in check only by her self-conscious will and by her reason."

Pierre Leprohon attributes a "psychological quality" to the films in the quartet because of Bergman's "presence," her "aura," but he does not articulate just what that quality is. He does, however, think that Bergman's "look, her voice, her gestures, her appeal" allowed Rossellini to express himself, thus making "a great contribution to his work."[15]

And Robin Wood notes the relationship between the characters in the films and Bergman's life and goes so far as to see a metaphoric connection between Rossellini's improvisatory technique, which put Bergman's acting skills to the test, and the spiritual torment inflicted on his wife by the scientist husband in *Fear*. To Wood, despite Bergman's denials, all of the films she made with Rossellini allude to her in some way. As Karin in *Stromboli*, she plays a "displaced person," just as Bergman had been "displaced" from America and her family. As Irene in *Europa 51*, Bergman plays a woman who neglects her child, just as Bergman herself neglected Pia to take up with Rossellini. As Katherine in *Voyage in Italy*, Bergman portrays a woman dealing with the breakdown of her marriage, just as she had in person worked through her divorce from Lindstrom and was now working on her deteriorating relationship with Rossellini. And as a different Irene in *Fear*, Bergman portrays a woman fighting desperately against the covert punishment of her angry and jealous husband, just as during the making of the film, the Rossellinis were on the brink of dissolving their marriage, one reason being Rossellini's jealous possessiveness. Moreover, to Wood, the reality-based "fiction" of the films can be interpreted as "a framework wherein Bergman might reveal herself without the self-consciousness that notoriously afflicts improvisation," Rossellini's primary directorial technique.[16]

In a 1974 interview with Wood, Bergman denies that the films she made with Rossellini were "documentaries on Ingrid Bergman," and when Wood asks her if the themes of the quartet, "a sort of quest for faith, salvation," were "very bound up with [her] presence," she replies, "Yes, maybe; I don't know."[17]

Bergman was not terribly insightful about much of her work, especially her work with Rossellini. In fact, the quartet of films she made with Rossellini are so autobiographical, so infused with references to her life and career, and what her image means in Hollywood culture that it may be easier to call Bergman an auteur of these films than for *Notorious*. In these films Rossellini meditates on both Bergman's life and career and on the notion of spirituality, on what it means to give allegiance to some higher power, some higher idea, than the things of this world. In doing so, Rossellini explores what spirituality means in the context of postwar Italy where artists and intellectuals were debating the future of society and torn between the secularism of the Socialists and the Marxist on the left and the conservative religiosity of the Roman Catholic Church on the right.

Bergman contributes to the quartet in two ways. First of all, the basic ideas of the films are drawn from her life and career. Her life and her Hollywood image are the inspiration for the situations in the films: the displaced northern European woman overwhelmed by "southern European" culture in *Stromboli* and *Voyage in Italy*; the women trapped in unhappy marriages with domineering or emotionally or spiritually empty husbands in all four films.

In exploring the nature of spirituality, Rossellini draws from his own past, from Bergman's past, and from their life together. The films explore whether it is possible to be spiritual in marriage or whether we need to flee from marriage in order to find God, to accomplish some real social good, and to live according to the high ideals of love, devotion, service, and forgiveness. In the first two films, *Stromboli* and *Europa '51*, escape from marriage and family seem to be the only hope for achieving any kind of spiritual life. The central character in each of these films runs away from her husband and family in order to save herself. In *Stromboli*, Karin, newly pregnant and trapped in a loveless marriage, tries to escape by climbing over the island volcano to a harbor on the other side, and on the volcano she confronts God, or her idea of God. In *Europa '51*, Irene, impelled by the suicide of her son, escapes from a marriage which has become routine and tries to live like a saint, befriending the poor and outcast.

Both of these films clearly allude to Bergman's Hollywood image as a wholesome woman who embodied sentimental notions of spirituality in such films as *The Bells of St. Mary's* and *Joan of Arc* and who escaped from Hollywood and her marriage to Lindstrom. They also allude to the life that Bergman and Rossellini are trying to create together in the glare of the publicity surrounding the scandal of their romance and marriage.

The last two films in the quartet, *Voyage in Italy* and *Fear*, explore whether spirituality is possible in marriage, especially in a materialistic culture, dominated by science and technology. In *Voyage in Italy*, Katherine, overwhelmed by the past of Pompeii, comes to realize, if only for a fleeting moment, the value of her husband Alex. In *Fear*, Irene, who has the same name as the central character in *Europa '51*, confesses to an affair and is reconciled with her scientist husband, if only briefly. More importantly, her husband Albert is moved to recognize the evil in his arranging to have his wife blackmailed for the affair and asks his wife for forgiveness, the act he had been trying to force his wife to commit.

Both *Voyage* and *Fear* echo the Bergman-Rossellini marriage, which was becoming increasingly frayed. In *Voyage*, Rossellini carried his improvisatory technique to the limit, deliberately unsettling Bergman and her co-star George Sanders. Rossellini was trying to force them in effect to not act at all but express their real discomfort and resentment for his camera. *Fear* then can be seen as Rossellini's meditation on the torment he inflicted on his wife during the filming of *Voyage*.

The second way Bergman contributes to all four films is through her Hollywood image. Rossellini uses that image as a form of ironic counterpoint to the drastically realistic situations of his protagonists. Rossellini frames Bergman in the standard Selznick glamour shot, undercutting the Hollywood image of Bergman to capture her *in extremis*. Contrary to Hollywood's sentimental treatment of Bergman's image as an honest, wholesome, natural woman devoted in romantic love, the female leads in Rossellini's films are cosmopolitan, devious, oblique, and seeking fulfillment outside of their marriages and often in spite of their husbands. Their spirituality is tormented, earned through pain and suffering, and totally outside the norms of social custom. In the first film, *Stromboli*, the Bergman character runs away from an abusive husband and a repressive society to confront God on a volcano. In the second film, *Europa '51*, the Bergman character becomes a modern St. Francis, and her behavior is so contrary to societal expectations that she is institutionalized. In the last two films, *Voyage in Italy* and *Fear*, the Bergman characters achieve a rushed revelation about the nature of love that is inherently ambiguous and deliberately unbelievable, causing us to wonder whether it is spirituality at all.

In all of the films in the quartet, references to the standard Selznick shot of Bergman and other allusions to the films she made in Hollywood — especially the noir plot and lighting and the Hitchcockian techniques in *Fear*— remind us that these films are not just about fictional characters: they are also about "Ingrid Bergman" the star, which in turn causes us to question just how spiritual that image is. Rossellini takes Bergman's image, which had been associated with the spirituality of romantic love, and converts it into another kind of spirituality: the spirituality of existential longing in *Stromboli*, the spirituality of self-abnegation in *Europa '51*, the spirituality of being "lost in history" in *Voyage in Italy*, and the spirituality of forgiveness in *Fear*.

At the end of these films, the Bergman characters are not bravely resigned to the loss of love, as her characters were in *Intermezzo*, *For Whom the Bell Tolls*, and *Casablanca*; they are not sure of their destiny as her character was in *Joan of Arc*. No, in these four films, Rossellini improvises variations on a new Bergman character, a character with a depth of spiritual suffering and insight that Bergman's previous characters could not even comprehend. But the echoes of the old Bergman are there and the ironies resonate throughout the films: in the process, Rossellini totally subverts the Hollywood association of "beauty" and "romance" with "spirituality" and calls into question Bergman's Hollywood image.

Stromboli

Stromboli is the film Bergman and Rossellini made during the scandal of their romance, and in many ways its themes and structure reflect Bergman's situation at the time. Bergman plays Karin, who is also blond, Nordic, reserved, in a film about freedom and the search for spiritual direction, escape, release. Karin is a woman trapped in an unhappy marriage with a domineering convention-bound husband, as Bergman was trapped in her marriage with Lindstrom. Karin is spiritually restless with her husband and isolated from his island community as Bergman was unhappy with her husband and the limitations of her Hollywood career. Karin longs to escape from the island, as Bergman longed to escape from Hollywood and make more aesthetically satisfying films. But the island of Stromboli where Karin is trapped is not only analogous to Bergman's Hollywood career; it is also analogous to Bergman's new home in Italy and her discovery of new limitations, new boundaries, with Italy and with Rossellini himself. The culture of the island of Stromboli becomes a metaphor for the life Bergman must learn to live with Rossellini and Italy, a life that will require resources she may not know she has.

In *Stromboli*, Karin is Bergman and an anti–Bergman. Unlike the public image of Bergman, Karin is not beautiful, wholesome, devoted, or conventionally spiritual. She is earthy, passionate, willing to give herself to any man who will help her achieve her goals. Rossellini deliberately makes her unglamorous, although occasionally he will photograph her in the Selznick style to remind us that his film is not just about Karin: it is also about Bergman, whether her old life was as glamorous and wholesome as her publicity suggested, whether she has really escaped to a better, more satisfying life making more meaningful films, whether the spirituality of her Hollywood films can really stand up under scrutiny.

Karin's strangeness is emphasized repeatedly in the film: she calls herself a member of "another race." Trapped in the maze of the Italian garden, she cries out in English, "I want to get out." She is associated with all things foreign, which the islanders link with America, a country for young people and where everyone drives a car. Karin complains to the Priest: "I am always outside. The house is full of old people who talk about America all day."

Rossellini is on record as saying that the major theme of *Stromboli* is "the struggle between Creator and creature. I found an actress who could bring the character to life."[18] Clearly, Rossellini means here that Bergman has the resources as an actress to capture Karin's temperament and to dramatize her rebellion against the social conventions oppressing her and her dramatic breakdown and confrontation with God at the end of the film.

The primary way Rossellini causes us to associate Karin with Bergman is by echoing the standard Selznick glamour shot. Karin is not glamorous, but she is beautiful and more sophisticated than her husband, less bound by convention, and searching for something beyond the satisfactions of day-to-day life. Rossellini plays with Bergman's beauty, goes out of his way to shoot her in ways which come close to making her seem ugly, but then he suddenly reveals her beauty in shots which capture her former glamour. He turns a Hollywood star into an Other; he makes her strange.

This technique is established the first time we see Karin. The opening tracking shot of women in a refugee camp establishes their plainness, their lack of glamour, the neo-realistic style. The camera then pans down to a high-angle shot of Bergman on a cot, looking down playing solitaire. Someone asks, "Karin, can you hear your lover?" and Bergman glances up and we see a Bergman we have not seen before: her smile is spread wide to emphasize her slyness, her nose is elongated. She is not attractive. Only when she stands do we catch a glimpse of her beauty in a fleeting echo of the Selznick shot — and then she immediately tosses off a casual, almost contemptuous good-bye and leaves to go meet her lover. The flat grainy light does not do her justice.

Rossellini uses a similar technique in a later scene when Karin and husband Antonio are on the boat to Stromboli. Karin is sleeping on the deck with her hands folded much like a corpse, and Antonio is on an elbow beside her. The camera captures them at a high angle, shooting up from a position near Karin's feet. The shot emphasizes Karin's breasts and nose from below and is distinctly unflattering. Cut to the lighthouse keeper, who is also on the boat, looking at Karin, and then back to Karin waking up. Karin sits up to announce that she is cold, and once again, we get a fleeting image of Bergman's beauty in the standard Selznick shot, as she turns to look out at the sea, this time not only from the camera's point of view but from the lighthouse keeper's, another indication that Rossellini was playing with the notion of how we should view Karin/Bergman.

Similar allusions to the Selznick shot occur in the Consular Office and during her final transformation on the volcano. But perhaps the two most obvious allusions to the standard ways of shooting Bergman are when Karin complains to Antonio after their first night on the island that she is different, that she belongs to another race, and when she sunbathes on the rocks. Karin's assertion of her difference from everyone else on Stromboli occurs at the end of a long continuous shot in which Karin finishes dressing by putting on and buttoning up a tight V-necked sweater, moving around the bed to go toward the camera, and sitting at a table to brush her hair and check her appearance in a compact. Sitting at the table, Karin is in close-up in the standard Selznick shot, her hair long and lush, reminiscent of Rita Hayworth and Anna Magnani, where she says, "I'm different. I belong to another race." Then in English: "I can't live in this filth." But the difference between this shot and a Selznick shot is that Bergman does not hold the three-quarter pose; she tosses her head and is often in profile and the shot has none of the Selznick shot's "effect lighting." Reflected light from the compact flashes across Bergman's face, and the natural lighting causes shadows to fall below her nose and on her neck. None of this is to the advantage of Bergman the beauty, the star, but the allusion to the Selznick shot and the use of English breaks the illusion of the moment and reminds us that this is not just Karin talking; it is also Bergman. Both are trapped in difficult circumstances. Both are different. Both may be contemplating, or have recently contemplated, escape.

The shot of Karin sunbathing is the most obvious reference to not just the Selznick way of shooting Bergman but the standard Hollywood treatment of female stars: it is pure cheesecake and occurs just after husband Antonio shows Karin why he has bought a ferret — to catch rabbits — whereby he allows a ferret to kill a rabbit before her eyes. In the low-angle shot, the camera pans along a rocky hillside showing the village houses against the sky and then comes down the hillside to reveal Karin sunbathing like Jane Russell in *The Outlaw*: with her blouse tied up under her breasts, revealing her midriff and her skirts high on her thighs. The shot is from some distance and has none of the Selznick shot's trademark lighting, but it does show the left side of Karin's face and captures some of Bergman's beauty: it is a direct allusion to Bergman's previous life in Hollywood and her status as a star and sex symbol. In this context, the allusion reinforces Karin's strangeness: Karin does not belong on these rocks, which is made even more obvious when she stands to walk down to the beach in her bare feet and has to limp and stagger to avoid cutting her feet, a realistic detail that undercuts the "perfect beauty" of the cheesecake shot. The placement of the shot also emphasizes Karin's strangeness. It comes after a scene of emotional turmoil when she has pummeled her husband for allowing the ferret to kill the rabbit. It comes just before the lighthouse keeper shows Karin an octopus and Karin falls against him in full view of the village women, lined up along the cliffs. In both scenes, Karin does not accept or act in ways acceptable to the cultural mores of Stromboli. The cheesecake shot reminds us that this is not just Karin rebelling against her circumstances: it is also Bergman. And it reminds us that it is not Selznick who is in charge of this film; it is Rossellini, who is going out of his way to shoot Bergman against all of Selznick's precepts.

Later, attempting to seduce the lighthouse keeper into helping her escape, Karin stretches out next to him on the beach, and the camera captures her in a high-angle shot on the left side of her face that parodies the standard Selnick shot. The high-angle shot again emphasizes Bergman's nose, not her most attractive feature, and when she turns to the lighthouse keeper, she exposes the right side of her face, in direct violation of Selznick's rules for shooting Bergman. All the while, natural shadows play over her face in ways that absolutely contradict Selznick's demand for "effect lighting." Again, this shot emphasizes Karin's naturalness, and again it reminds us that this is Bergman but not Bergman.

The final scene on the volcano does not refer to the standard Selznick shot of Bergman, but it does include several shots that refer to Bergman's

Hollywood image, including a moment when she stumbles while walking and then turns and throws herself on the ground in a way reminiscent of the earlier cheesecake shot on the rocks. Later, in her ascent Karin lies on the ground and we see her in close-up, her head on her arm horizontal to the camera, declaiming, "I'm scared. I'm scared." Then she rolls over, her head tilted sideways to the camera, and although the camera is shooting the right side of her face, it is composed like a standard Hollywood beauty shot.

From the heights of the volcano on Stromboli, Rossellini has given us cause to wonder what it means to be Ingrid Bergman the person, trapped in a failed marriage and a string of failed movies, throwing off her old life to begin life anew with a strange man in a strange culture. He has also given us cause to wonder what it means to be "Ingrid Bergman" the star, captured forever in what may be a superficial image of romantic love and devotion. In *Stromboli*, Rossellini also gives us cause to wonder whether we should associate beauty and romance with spirituality at all.

Europa '51

Europa '51 is the least biographical and autobiographical film in the Bergman quartet. There are some references to Bergman's life. As in *Stromboli*, Irene Gerard, the Bergman character, is clearly an immigrant who, her Communist cousin Andre tells us, came to Italy in 1947. Although Irene has a European accent, she is associated with America, which we are constantly reminded of by the presence of Irene's mother, who is visiting from America.

There are also allusions to Rossellini's life. The attempted suicide and later death of Irene's son is the turning point in her life, and the event echoes the death of Rossellini's son Romano, the son he had with his first wife Marcella. Romano died at the age of nine from an enflamed appendix that was not treated in time. Even at that age, he was the living image of his father: handsome, intelligent, charming. Rossellini could go off and leave his children for months at a time, but when he was with them, his affection could be intense. Romano's death affected him deeply.

Europa '51 also alludes to Bergman's first marriage. Because of her son's death, Irene begins to question everything in her life, including much of the society around her. She identifies instead with the poor and the downtrodden, and in the process she becomes increasingly alienated from her husband. Irene befriends in turn a working class woman, a prostitute, and a young bank robber. Each of her interactions with these people is a step on the road to a kind of communitarianism often identified with Saint Francis of Assisi. For the working-class woman "Passerotto"—or "Little Sparrow"—played by Giulietta

Masina, Irene agrees to take her place in a factory so that Passerotto can spend some time with her lover. For the prostitute, Irene goes in search of a doctor, something none of the prostitute's working class neighbors would do. And Irene counsels the young bank robber to give himself up, but she will not, even when pressured by the police, turn the young man in herself. In her increasing devotion to the poor and the marginalized, Irene becomes a living critique of not only the policies of the right-center Christian Democratic Party then in power in Italy, which was not sufficiently attentive to the plight of the poor, but also of the politics of the Socialist and Communist Left, who tended to be atheists and deny the power of religion as a social force. The cause of Irene's alienation from her husband — the death of her son — and her increasing commitment to the poor, at the expense of the social conventions of both sides of the socio-political spectrum of the time is a far cry from the cause of Bergman's alienation from her first husband: romantic love. Once again, Rossellini is providing an ironic commentary on Bergman's previous life, even though the irony spills over to his own life.

Europa '51 reminds us that Bergman gave up her former glamorous life for the "poverty" of Italy and Rossellini's lack of funding. She gave up making entertainment for making art; she decided to work for something higher than Hollywood could offer. Still, the film implies, making art is nothing compared to the rigorous anti-social compassion of a Saint Francis.

As in *Stromboli*, Rossellini makes these points using the Selznick shot: Irene goes to Andre to ask his help in getting a job for a poor woman. Andre agrees to help, but he can't deny his unconscious affection, even love, for Irene: he says, "Remember when you first arrived here in Italy — in '47, wasn't it? The things that have changed, and the things that have happened since then. In those days, you were rather selfish and frivolous. Now you're full of enthusiasm and concerned with the class struggle. Irene, dear, I really want to help you any way I can." Just as Andre says the words, "in '47, wasn't it?" Rossellini cuts from a two-shot to a brief three-second close-up of Irene in the standard Selznick manner, except of course for the "effect lighting" and the fact that the shot is not high-angle, reminding us of Bergman the star, so that the words that follow, "In those days, you were rather selfish and frivolous," have a whole other meaning. And what Irene is working for, something even beyond the class struggle, echoes not just through the film but through Bergman's career.

Later Irene goes to inform the working class woman that she has a job for her. At first Passerotto is enthusiastic, but then she conveys to Irene that she has fallen in love with a soldier and he will be in Turin during the middle of the week when she would have to be at work. The irony here is that Irene is working to help a woman who does not seem as concerned about her own welfare as Irene is for her. In any case, the woman wonders how she could manage both the job and the time away for her love life. She comes up with the idea that someone could take her place for a day. Who could that be? Irene doesn't know. Hey, the woman says brightly, you could go. Irene protests that she doesn't know how to do the job and she might get caught. The woman replies that all Irene needs to do is punch the time clock and do the job. When Irene objects that she doesn't know how to do the job, the woman dismisses the objection in terms that Irene cannot deny: "Neither would I, but you could learn, couldn't you?" To which Irene can only reply, "Probably." She utters this last phase in a Selznick close-up, in high-angle, her eyes down modestly, a perfect shot to capture her refusing the advances of a lover in her Hollywood phase, but here she is involving herself ever more deeply not in sex but in the problems of the poor.

There are also echoes of the Selznick shot in Irene's final meeting with the committee responsible for deciding whether she should be committed to an asylum or not, especially when she talks about her ideas of working with the poor day by day. In talking about her long-term plans she stands and paces the room. Many of these mid-shots capture the left side of her face, and she ends by saying, "When you are bound to nothing, you're bound to everybody. I have nothing more to say."

And so Irene is committed to an asylum, where the poor people she has befriended tearfully bid her goodbye. Because she has identified with the poor and become an outsider to mainstream morality, she is isolated and treated as if she were mentally unbalanced, and we are left to ponder not just Irene's isolation but Bergman's: the quality of her life before and after the scandal, the depth of her sacrifice in running off with Rossellini, the consequences of her behavior.

Voyage in Italy

By 1953, the year *Voyage in Italy* was filmed, the Rossellini–Bergman marriage had become seriously troubled. "It would be hard to guess whether there is any real happiness in the relationship," wrote co-star Sanders to wife about Bergman and Rossellini on the set of the film. "She was in tears a good many times." In a letter to former publicist Joe Steele, Bergman put on a brave face, mentioning only Sanders's "several nervous breakdowns due to not even seeing *one* word on paper," and the chaos accompanying she and Rossellini having the children with them, taking up an entire floor of the Continentale Hotel in Naples. Still, she mentions that she is writing during a break in shooting at the Naples Museum. It is cold and her hands are numb. Two months later in another letter to Steele, she recalls escaping the tension on the set by visiting the cast and crew of *Beat the Devil* several times at nearby Ravello — John Huston, Jennifer Jones, Humphrey Bogart, Peter Lorre, and Robert Morley: "I went up every night for dinner and laughs, as we don't have many laughs on our set." The shooting of *Voyage* may have been made more depressing because her old love Robert Capa came to visit, and she was reminded of what she was now missing, and a life that might have been.[19]

It is difficult *not* to see *Voyage in Italy* as an examination of the Bergman-Rossellini marriage. Rossellini got the idea for the film from Colette's novel *Duo*, published in 1934. In Peter Brunette's summary, the novel concerns the wife in a disintegrating marriage, who "refuses to apologize or feel guilty for an old love affair that the husband has discovered. Overwhelmed by this knowledge, the husband begins to moralize obsessively, finally losing control and taking his own life."[20] The potential for similar resentment and dismay in the Bergman-Rossellini marriage is overwhelming: Rossellini's constant womanizing, Bergman's previous husband and former lovers, although we do not know if she ever confessed to Rossellini the depths of her feelings about Robert Capa; Bergman's resistance to Rossellini's improvisatory methods, a constant reminder that he in effect took her away from a Hollywood she still admired and he detested. What can save this marriage? The film answers: only a sense of time and place and a miracle; or a series of brief temporary reconciliations when the couple recall their original attraction to each other and not the differences that have grown between them.

The film mostly expresses the point of view of the wife, Katherine Joyce. There is only one extended scene focusing on her husband Alex: his trip to Capri and his return to Naples, his picking up a prostitute. In these scenes, Alex has ample opportunity to express his discontent with Katherine by making a pass at his friend Marie or going to bed with the prostitute. Alex does neither. In fact, he is sympathetic to the prostitute's groping for solace at the loss of a friend due to the rigors of her trade. This may be Rossellini's idealized self-portrait. In real life, he showed less restraint.

But except for Alex's excursion to Capri, the film is Katherine's. From the beginning, she is constantly bored and irritated with Alex. She finds him insufferable as they quibble over insignificant details in the car on the way to Naples. After they arrive, she jealously follows his interactions with his female friends at a restaurant. As she explores Naples, visiting the Naples Archeological Museum and the fortress and caves at Cumae on her own, the Catacombs with a friend, Natalia , and Pompei with Alex, she is constantly reminded of the rich fecund life around her, the sweep of history, and the emotional poverty and insignificance of her own life.

The elements alienating Alex from Katherine suggest the Bergman-Rossellini marriage in a number of ways. Both Bergman and Rossellini had to accommodate themselves to their spouse's past, Bergman to Rossellini's ex-wife and mistresses, many of whom he still saw regularly, and Rossellini to Bergman's ex-husband and former lovers. This aspect of their life together is dramatized in a scene on the terrace of their residence in Naples, in which Katherine reminisces about the young poet Charles Lewington, who died shortly after reciting poetry one night outside her window. Katherine recites his poetry, an invocation to the "Temple of the Spirit ... compared to which mere thought seems flesh, heavy, dim." This drives Alex to say that Lewington's tubercular cough revealed more about him than his speech. Katherine asks what Lewington's cough indicated. Alex replies, "That he was a fool." Katherine reacts angrily: "He was not a fool. He was a poet!" Shrugs Alex, "What's the difference?"

This plot point clearly alludes to a similar scene in James Joyce's "The Dead," as Luciana Bohne was one of the first critics to point out, and after all, in *Voyage*, the couple's last name is Joyce.[21] At this moment in the film, the scene establishes that at least the Joyces have enough investment in their relationship that they can make each other jealous. Earlier, Katherine herself had become jealous at the way young women at a party paid attention to Alex. The richness and resonance of the scene, the allusion to "The Dead," may cause us to wonder at the depth of the Bergman-Rossellini romance, and indeed so many fraught modern relationships. In *Voyage in Italy*, Katherine/Bergman has feelings for a past lover more than her current husband, and Alex/Rossellini knows it. Naples is warm and sunlit, but the major image of "The Dead" applies: snow is general not just over Ireland but over the entire modern world.

One reason that Katherine and Alex are so frustrated may involve sex. Katherine did not want children, and as she drives through the city on the way to various tourist sites, she is overwhelmed by the images of pregnant women and women with their children in tow on the streets of Naples. In addition, Natalia, one of the couple they are staying with, tells Katherine that she is praying for a child. At the site of the Cumae, when the old guide demonstrates how the barbarians would have tied up a "beautiful woman" like her, his words, Katherine's response is "All men are alike." This remark combined with the couple's later discussion about whether they should have had a child intimates that they are not sexually compatible, just as Bergman and Rossellini were not.

The alienation of Katherine and Alex is best shown when Alex returns from Capri. While waiting for Alex, Katherine has been playing solitaire, but when she hears his car pull up, she immediately starts to put the cards away. A series of shots show Alex getting out of his car, entering the house, going down a hall and into a room, pausing at a door to listen for any sounds that

Katherine is still awake, and then turning out the light in order to get dressed for bed. These shots are crosscut with shots of Katherine sweeping up her cards, turning out the light, and snuggling down into her bed. While Alex, now in his dressing gown, goes to the bathroom to gargle, the crosscutting shots of Katherine are right out of the Selznick manual on how to film Bergman, this time at a slightly lower angle and with the shadows on the good side of Bergman's face and a small triangle of light under her left eye. Here, however, the shots do not emphasize Bergman's glamour but her anxious anticipation; she is listening intently to every sound Alex makes, and her eyes dart up and around. When Alex finally enters the room, Rossellini dramatizes the distance between the two people with Katherine in bed in the lower left of the frame, all in whites and grays, and Alex in his black bathrobe hovering behind her, so that she must talk to him without turning around. She asks when he returned from Capri. Alex confesses that he took the 5:30 ferry. Katherine asks what he did before coming home, and he says, nothing important. The awkwardness is palpable. Neither has the nerve to push the matter, especially when Alex says rudely, "Anything else you want to know?" No. Then: "Do I have your permission to go to bed?" Here once again the Selznick glamour shot is used to comment ironically on Bergman's romantic Hollywood image and the tension in her marriage.

The sequence at Pompeii brings the tension between the couple to the breaking point. They watch as the archeological team uncovers a grave, and to their great surprise — and to Rossellini and his crew — the remains are not of just one person, but two. At the sight of the dead lovers, their bones sculpted into the earth by the lava from Vesuvius, Katherine breaks down sobbing and turns away. She offers no explanation of why she found the dead couple so affecting, but we may assume that the image of being locked into nature, frozen in time, is a primary reason for Katherine to reconcile with Alex in the final scene.

In the car on the way back from Pompeii, the couple manage some mutual sympathy before Alex, perhaps afraid that Katherine is manipulating him again, reminds her that they have agreed to divorce. In the midst of their bickering, Katherine remarks, "Life is so short!" Alex replies, "That's why one should make the most of it." Suddenly, they are forced to stop by a large crowd attending a religious procession, the annual festival of San Gennaro, for which it is customary for Neapolitans to demand miracles. Katherine and Alex get out of the car to see what is happening. Rossellini shoots this scene with Bergman on the right, in a version of the Selznick glamour shot. Alex asks, "How can they believe in that? They're like a bunch of children!" Katherine replies, her face clouding over in mid-speech: "Children are happy.... Alex, I don't want you to hate me. I don't want it to finish this way." Bergman makes Katherine's unhappiness and her yearning for love palpable, and the Selznick shot provides the irony. The Joyces are not engaged in a conventional love affair; they are a middle-aged married couple. And not even in *Casablanca* and *Notorious* was Bergman the star reduced to begging for love.

Alex is not so easily seduced. He responds bitterly, asking what Katherine is getting at, what game she is now playing. He claims that Katherine has never even tried to understand him and asks bluntly what she wants. At this moment, Bergman exercises one of her trademark facial shifts: her hope and yearning cut away, replaced by anger and disgust. Her eyes glitter. "Nothing," she spits out. "I despise you."

Then in a sweeping crane shot Rossellini captures the crowd surging toward an old man stumbling forward at the edge of the formal procession, his palms up, the crowd chanting "*Miracolo! Miracolo!*" Katherine is caught by the crowd and swept down the street away from Alex, screaming for help. Alex plunges after her, as if he were a swimmer trying to ride the current. He reaches Katherine and brings her to him, and they embrace, the first time they do so in the film.

Leaning back, Alex asks what is wrong with the two of them, why they torture each other. Katherine confesses that she tries to hurt Alex in retaliation for his hurting her, but now she can no longer do that, she loves him so. To which Alex responds, "Perhaps we get hurt too easily." Sensing that they have achieved a kind of mutual sympathy, Katherine urges Alex to tell her that he loves her. But Alex balks and wants a concession, a promise that Katherine will not take advantage of him if he does so. Katherine's promise is immediate and heartfelt: she simply wants to hear Alex say the words, whereupon Alex says, not with a great deal of fervor, "All right, I love you."

In the context of the film as a whole, the implication of this scene is clear. The Joyces' tentative reconciliation, their provisional peace, is a kind of "miracle." In a culture accepting of miracles, the Joyces conjure their own personal secular version of a miracle. The exterior world, their daily working life together, may be the only thing still holding them together, as it may be the only thing holding Bergman and Rossellini together. But, Rossellini seems to be saying, "This too is a miracle."

In an interview, Rossellini said this about *Voyage*: "It is a very bitter film basically. The couple take refuge in each other in the same way as people cover themselves when they're naked, grabbing a towel, drawing closer to the person with them, and covering themselves any old how. This is the meaning the finale was meant to have."[22] When things are going badly, only immediate circumstances, minor miracles, keep people together. This was very likely the condition of the Bergman-Rossellini marriage in 1953.

Fear

The shooting of *Fear* in September of 1954 must have been difficult for Bergman. The previous May, Robert Capa the light of her life, the only lover she ever openly acknowledged, died from stepping on a land mine in southeast Asia. On September 9, former husband Petter Lindstrom remarried. And so Bergman was left to contemplate the choices she had made in leaving Lindstrom and not marrying Capa but instead marrying Rossellini. By the fall of 1954, the fights, the silences, the hostility between Bergman and Rossellini was so severe that her costar in *Fear*, Mathias Wiemann counseled her that Rossellini was tearing her up, that she would go mad if she went on with her marriage. Bergman expressed shock. She replied: she did not know how to leave Rossellini. Such a thing was "impossible!"[23]

Fear shows us is a leaner, almost gaunt Bergman, her features accented by the noir lighting. She looks haunted, driven.

Rossellini is on record as saying that *Fear* is about "the freedom in confession; it's about the importance of knowing how to confess, because it's in knowing how to confess that we achieve a certain humility and, above all, a grand spirit of tolerance." [24]

Many people associated with the film at the time took it to be blatantly biographical: Some thought that Bergman's success in *Joan at the Stake* made Rossellini "want to punish and dominate her."[25] Now we have reason to wonder if the film is Rossellini's meditation on how he treated his wife during the shooting of *Voyage in Italy*.

Discussing *Fear* is difficult because it was shot in two versions — one in German called *Angst* and one in English — and they are often quite different. *Angst* has a cutaway shot of Albert Wagner arriving for the final scene, which is really unnecessary and does not appear in *Fear*. *Angst* also lacks many of the lyrical tracking shots of the drive through the trees and point of view shots down the corridors of the opera house that are shown in *Fear*. The biggest difference between the two is that the performance in the opera house in *Angst* is *La Bohème*; in *Fear* a solo pianist performs Chopin's "G-minor Ballade." Apparently Rossellini did not contribute significantly to the postproduction editing, so we have no way of knowing if he preferred one version over the other. The critics agree that *Fear* is superior.

Like the other films in the quartet, *Fear* is about spirituality: in this case, the cruelty of suffering and the liberating force of forgiveness. The difficulty with the film is that the suffering inflicted on Irene Wagner, the woman Bergman portrays, is provoked by the same person who wants her to confess so that he can forgive her. That person is her husband, Albert, played by Mathias Wiemann. And so what Albert considers a moral act becomes wanton cruelty. Under the intense pressure of Albert's plot to force her confession, Irene ultimately refuses and decides to kill herself instead. When Albert realizes this possibility, he rushes after Irene. Entering his lab, he sees Irene holding a needle. He shouts her name and hurries to her, saying, "Forgive me," and then in her arms again, "Forgive me." Irene responds by crying out, "I couldn't tell you. I couldn't." Albert's reply is barely audible: "I know." And Irene kisses Albert in an outpour of feeling; "I love you. I love you. I love you." And the camera lingers on Irene, her head on her husband's shoulder. There is no doubting her sincerity, at least for the moment.

This ending is blatantly ironic. The near-maniacal scientist husband with his rigid standards of honor and justice, his willingness to torment his wife, to treat her like an object in his lab, in order to force her into confession and to ask for his forgiveness, what he considers a higher moral plane, now realizes the depths to which he has driven his wife and humbly asks her to forgive him.

The ending is so abrupt we might be tempted to think that Rossellini simply lost interest in the film and ended it as quickly as he could. And yet the ending is well prepared for. It is foreshadowed by a scene of the Wagner family in the country. Son Bobby accuses daughter Frieda of stealing his air rifle because she did not get one too. Albert forces Frieda to confess by lecturing her on having the courage to admit her mistakes. When Frieda protests that other members of the family and even the servants could have taken the rifle, Albert patiently argues that no one else in the household has any reason to take it. He goes on to reassure Frieda that Bobby will forgive her, and strongly implies that obstinacy in lying about a crime is almost worse than committing the crime in the first place. Frieda duly confesses and Albert sends her back to her room: her punishment is to lose a day of fishing. When Bobby mocks Frieda, Albert gives him a similar punishment. Irene protests the severity of the punishments, and Albert relents but he is unapologetic about his methods. He says, "I had to force [Frieda] to confess." Irene calls after the children that their father has forgiven them, and all is well again in the Wagner household.

The ending is also prepared for by the scene on the steps of the café in which Albert learns that Joanna, his accomplice in tormenting his wife, has told Irene everything. Upon hearing the news, Albert turns in alarm toward the camera to look off where Irene has disappeared, and his look suggests that he realizes that he has gone too far.

Despite the allusions to the troubled Rossellini-Bergman marriage, Rossellini makes sure that we think of Bergman the star when we contemplate Irene's fate, first in the use of the Selznick shot to remind us that this is "Ingrid Bergman" who is suffering so, and second in the way the film alludes to such

Hollywood standards as the mad-scientist film, film noir, and finally to the films of Alfred Hitchcock.

The first Selznick shot occurs when Albert pushes his test of Irene by asking her for the ring he knows she has given to the blackmailer as collateral. Irene has become increasingly distraught, and Albert is ratcheting up the pressure. The shot occurs in one long take in which Albert confronts Irene in the hallway, both of them in dark profile, where Irene first denies that she has lost the ring. When Albert says that he will get it from the safe, she lies and says that she has left it at a jewelers to be repaired. Albert then moves around her into the living room, so that he is in long-shot and Irene is in the left foreground. Assuming the role of the sympathetic husband, Albert asks, "Irene, what's the matter with you? You forget everything. You're so absent-minded. Why don't you tell me?" In saying this, Albert crosses behind Irene as she turns away from him and toward the camera, and Albert walks past her and then turns off camera to the left, putting Irene/Bergman in the Selznick shot over his right shoulder. Whereupon Irene replies, "It's nothing, really nothing. I'm only tired, so tired," and she breaks down sobbing onto his shoulder. This brief scene is a triumph of blocking, which is used to set up the Selznick shot and highlight Irene's emotional response, the collapse of her defenses. In doing so, the shot gives us a chance to see Bergman the star we know and love do her Hollywood stuff: the shift of mood, the breaking emotion, and again the irony: the shot alludes to a way of heightening her beauty and the spirituality of romantic love.

The second Selznick shot is more thematic: it occurs as Irene listens to her husband discuss his experiments with his colleagues at lunch. One of those colleagues suggests the uncertainty of what the group is doing. Albert replies, "I believe we must stick to fundamentals — life and death," and as he speaks the camera shows Irene in tight close-up, slowly turning to her husband when she hears these words. When a colleague describes in detail the failure of the latest trial, how the lab rat's heartbeat and respiration slowly faltered and then stopped altogether, Irene is lost in thought, clearly thinking about what it must be like to have her own suffering alleviated. "Without pain?" she asks. And the reply, "Yes, of course, at this point, pain no longer matters" catches her looking off left in the shot. Again, the shot reminds us that it is Bergman, not just Irene, who is suffering so.

Rossellini also reminds us of Bergman's past in Hollywood by paying ironic homage to Hollywood mad-scientist films. He shoots Albert's lab equipment and machinery in close-ups with heavy shadows and strong contrast that make them seem sinister. He films Irene peering into cages and through glass pens, equating her with the animals themselves, just another living thing for Albert to experiment with.

Albert is studying the effects of a new drug as an antidote to curare in laboratory rats, hoping to control the effects of narcolepsy. In an early scene the drug seems to be working: it improves the heartbeat and respiration of a rat that had been injected first with curare. But late in the film there are problems with the new drug: it too causes paralysis and kills one of the rats. Albert is the pure scientist, an absolutist about methods. A colleague suggests that the lab team tinker with the molecules in the new drug. Albert rejects that option out of hand: "We must interrupt [our experiment] and start over." Then: "I believe we must stick to fundamentals — life and death."

Fear also alludes to film noir: the high-contrast lighting with deep shadows, the psychological melodrama: a blackmailer, an evil husband torturing his wife. The suspense: will Irene be broken and confess or will she commit suicide? And *Fear* blatantly alludes to Hitchcock in its melodramatic suspense, in its use of point-of-view shots in the trip to the country and cross-cutting shots in the opera house, and in the long seven-minute shot in the office where Irene tries to control her mounting hysteria.

The final rescue scene is a play on the ending of *Notorious*. In that film, Alicia suffers for her country and for the fact that Devlin does not love her. In *Notorious*, Bergman's Alicia is systematically poisoned and kept prisoner because Devlin has allowed her to be put at risk in the first place, but when Devlin manages to invade the Nazi household where she is being kept and make his way to her bedroom in order to rescue her, she accepts him anyway. In *Fear*, Bergman's Irene is planning on poisoning herself, an act which her jealous husband Albert has promoted, but when he suddenly forgives her, she too accepts him. The ending of both films may be unnecessarily abrupt and perhaps unbelievable. In *Notorious*, the abrupt ending is a standard romantic convention of Hollywood. In *Fear*, the abrupt ending is the point of the film. It should cause us to question under what conditions we can and should forgive people, to ponder whether we are responsible for the behavior we need to forgive. The questions apply to the Bergman-Rossellini marriage, to all marriages, all relationships, and to Bergman's public: Did Rossellini need forgiveness for the way he manipulated his wife in front of the camera, especially in *Voyage in Italy*? Did Bergman need forgiveness for having run off with Rossellini, or was her public intimately involved in Bergman's decision to do so in the first place?

Like Hitchcock, Rossellini was so taken with Bergman that he could not keep his ideas of her out of his films.

Ingmar Bergman's *Autumn Sonata*

In his book *Images*, Ingmar Bergman acknowledges that he had Ingrid in mind for the part of Charlotte Andergast, the pianist mother, in *Autumn*

Sonata when the very idea of the movie came to him in March of 1976. Ingmar had just been through an extremely difficult period in his life. He had been accused of tax evasion by the Swedish government, and his sense that he was losing control of his life had triggered his tendency to paranoia and suicidal despair. He subsequently had a nervous breakdown. Sitting at home, pondering his lack of control and his previous attempts at suicide, he had a sense of machinery exploding and his identity being threatened. He could hear himself whining: the sound echoed in his ears like the moaning of a wounded dog. He got up from his chair to make his way to the window, and then lost all sense of what happened next. He could only say in retrospect that his wife had come home; his best friend and doctor Sture Helander appeared, and an hour later he was in the Karolinska Hospital psychiatric clinic.

Weeks later, home from the hospital at Sophiahemmet with a view out the window of his old childhood home, he controlled his agitation with Mogadon and Valium. Occasionally, however, he would rebel and go off his medication. Then his "suppressed anxiety" would shoot up like "the flame of a blowlamp," and he could not sleep at all. His demons raged at will. He thought he would be "torn apart by internal detonations." Back on medication, he prescribed an additional cure for himself: a regular schedule with each day divided into definite units, each unit filled with prescribed activities, alternating with periods of rest. The combination of drugs and routine seemed to work, and he became more clear-headed and able to analyze his situation: that his reaction to the charges of tax evasion were exaggerated, that against his natural inclinations he had reacted with "submission instead of anger," that he had declared himself "guilty without being guilty, craving punishment" so that he could "receive forgiveness and release as quickly as possible."

A week or so later he moved to Faro in northern Gotland, where the battle of the seasons, winter fighting off the coming of spring, contributed to his recovery. He felt calmer, but one day while taking his wife to the airport for a trip to Stockholm, he spotted a police car and felt seized by the old panic. Having dropped his wife off and returned home, he discovered fresh footprints and tire tracks in the snow outside his house. Convinced now that the police were closing in, he rushed inside, locked all the doors, loaded his rifle, and sat in the kitchen where he could keep an eye on the road and the parking space for the house. He sat watching, rifle in hand, for hours. Nothing happened. Night fell, and gradually he realized that he was behaving, in his own words, "like a dangerous lunatic." He unloaded the gun, locked it away, and cooked dinner for himself.

More time passed. Then at the end of March — on Wednesday, the 24th in *The Magic Lantern*; in *Images*, he says the outline for the film was written on March 26 — in his room, Ingmar heard the telephone ring and his wife answer it. He heard the phone drop to the floor and his wife's footsteps running toward him. She raced into his room in her blue checked dress with the news. The tax evasion charges had been dropped.[26]

That night, still unable to sleep, his imagination exploding with images, themes, and plot outlines, he went to his worktable and wrote out the plan for a film he first called *Mother and Daughter and Mother.*

The original notes in his workbook say this: "The night after the acquittal, when I cannot go to sleep in spite of sleeping pills, it occurs to me that I want to make a film about the mother-daughter, daughter-mother relationship, and I must have Ingrid Bergman and Liv Ullmann in the two roles, and no one else. Eventually, there may be room for a third character."

All of the essentials of the final screenplay are in this first plan: the arrival of the mother at her daughter's home, the gradually increasing animosity between them, culminating in what Ingmar designated as his major theme: "*The daughter finally gives birth to the mothe*r. Through this reversal they unite for a few brief moments in perfect symbiosis." The major difference from the later shooting script is that in this earlier version, a major source of contention between the women is not Eva's handicapped sister Helena, but a dead son named Erik. In this version, Eva tells her mother that Erik visits her often, that she can actually feel his touch. Charlotte becomes increasingly upset. She finds Eva's behavior alarming and tries to suggest as tactfully as she can that Eva and her husband Viktor should consider adopting or having another child. Later, Eva plays a piece for her mother on the piano, and Charlotte is complimentary. But "just to insure the purity of the piece," Charlotte plays it again herself, thereby letting Eva know that her interpretation was meek and ineffective.

Later that night Charlotte suffers from insomnia. Eva overhears her restlessness and joins her, thereby beginning "the grand unmasking." Eva tells her mother the truth about how she really feels: she has nothing but hatred and contempt for her. Eva's frankness inspires Charlotte to speak in turn about her own "bitterness, her loathing, her despair, her loneliness," about the indifference of the men in her life and the humiliation she has suffered because of their affairs with other women. In all this, Eva's confession has clearly been the occasion, has "given birth," as it were, to Charlotte's own revelation of her true self, her despair and loneliness. However, despite this brief meeting of souls, Charlotte leaves the following morning. She cannot bear the silence or "her raw feelings."

Ingmar insists that he does not understand the significance of this story and why he thought about it, nor why he thought of Ingrid for the role of Charlotte: "*Autumn Sonata* was conceived in one night, in a matter of hours, after a period of total writer's block. The lingering question is, why this: Why

Autumn Sonata? It contained nothing that I had been thinking about before."
Ingmar does say that he had long desired to work with Ingrid, but as far as
he can tell, that desire was not an inspiration for his screenplay. He had not
seen her since a screening of *Cries and Whispers* at the Cannes Film Festival.
At Cannes, Ingrid had stuck a letter into his pocket, reminding him that they
had earlier agreed to do a film together, an adaptation of Hjalmar Bergman's
novel *The Boss, Mrs. Ingeborg*. Ingmar claims that he has simply no idea why
the story of the mother and daughter came to him in such a coherent form.
In fact, he finds the outline more "finished" than "its final execution."[27]

Perhaps it is unintentional, perhaps he is being disingenuous, but Ingmar
himself raises the issue of why the role of Charlotte was so closely associated
with Ingrid and why Charlotte's life is so similar to Ingrid's. One reason is
the history of their relationship: Ingmar had had Ingrid on his mind for quite
some time.

In *My Story*, Ingrid gives her version of how the idea for doing *Autumn
Sonata* developed. Ingrid met Ingmar through her husband Lars. The first
time was at the Swedish Embassy in Paris on the occasion of Ingmar's production of Hjalmar Bergman's *The Saga*. Ingmar was not feeling well, but he
managed to accompany the group Ingrid was with to the theater. According
to Ingrid, the entire time the two of them barely said a word to each other.

A few years later, Ingrid and Schmidt had lunch with Ingmar in Stockholm. Schmidt had to go back to his office, so she and Ingmar stayed on at
the restaurant, chatting amicably for an hour or so. According to Ingrid, there
had been "instant sympathy" between them at the start of the lunch, and during the later conversation, Ingmar insisted that they do a picture together.
Ingmar even had an idea for the film: it would be based on Hjelmar Bergman's
book *The Boss Ingeborg*. Wouldn't it be amusing, Ingmar said, to have three
Bergmans, none of them related, all contributing to the same film? Ingrid was
happy with the idea and had thought herself about the idea of working with
Ingmar, but she had not dared to bring the subject up because she had heard
the legends about how Ingmar only made films with his small select group of
actors, a kind of repertory company, and his equally small select camera crew
and group of technicians.

But nothing came of the idea. The years went by and the two continued
to exchange occasional letters on the subject. During one of these exchanges,
Ingmar dropped the idea of basing the film on *The Boss Ingeborg* and promised
to write an original story for their film together. In another exchange, Ingrid
wrote Ingmar to congratulate him on becoming the director of the Royal Dramatic Theater, and playfully added that her only regret was that now he would
not have time to do their movie. Ingmar replied, "It's written on my forehead
in fire. The picture with Ingrid shall be done."

More years passed. Ingrid was invited to be President of the Jury at the Cannes Film Festival. Preparing to leave for Cannes, she discovered the ten-year-old letter from Ingmar, promising that they would do a film together. She copied the letter and wrote underneath, "It is not with anger or bitterness I give you back your letter, but just to show you how time marches on."

At Cannes, where his *Cries and Whispers* was being shown out of competition, Ingrid saw Ingmar surrounded by a mass of journalists and photographers. With some effort, she managed to work through the crowd and tell him that she was putting a letter in his pocket. He laughed and asked if he should read it right then. No, Ingrid said, read it when you get home, and Ingmar was swept away by the crowd.

Two years later, Ingrid got a phone call from Ingmar, and to the best of her memory, their conversation concentrated on minor issues because both of them were intensely interested in the project. Ingmar wanted to know if Ingrid would mind playing Liv Ullman's mother. Ingrid dismissed the concern: she had a daughter Ullman's age. Ingmar also wondered whether Ingrid would have any reservations about doing the film in Swedish, which would make the film less marketable internationally. Ingrid had no problem with that at all and was angry that people might have hinted to Ingmar that money would matter that much to her.[28]

And so both Ingrid and Ingmar agree that the idea of their making a film together was at least a decade old, and Ingmar's comment that the idea was "written on my forehead in fire" suggests that he must have at least mulled the possibilities of what such a film might be about. This in turn suggests that Ingmar's claim that he had no idea how or why the idea for the film came to him or why he thought of Ingrid in the role of Charlotte is deliberately evasive. For one thing, the aspects of Ingrid's life that are most like Charlotte's were common knowledge at the time. The well-publicized custody hearing with Lindstrom and the press coverage of Ingrid's constant battle with Rossellini over their children made clear that Ingrid was not the model of a devotedly attentive mother. She had always put her career first; she did not deny it. Ingrid's life resembled Charlotte's, and Ingmar had to have known that.

The published screenplay of *Autumn Sonata* contains a great deal of dialogue that did not appear in the final film. In a considerable amount of this dialogue, it is impossible not to imagine that it might apply to Ingrid and daughter Pia, especially when in response to Eva's accusations of neglect, Charlotte defends herself by arguing that for a time she broke off her career and stayed at home. To this, Eva replies that Charlotte's time at home may have been worse for the family than when she was away: Charlotte "cowed" her husband Josef and made life hell for the children. And Eva goes on, aiming for the jugular: Charlotte was unfaithful to Josef. Charlotte denies this, too, but curiously seems to argue that because she went off with her lover Martin for only eight months and because the situation was not "a bed of roses," she was not really committing adultery. Eva responds with a long speech in which she describes how she sat up late at night, trying to comfort her father by insisting that Charlotte would come back and reading him Charlotte's "long, tender loving, amusing, humorous letters," as if she were merely away on a long vacation. "We sat there like idiots," Eva says, reading the letters over and over again and "thinking that a more wonderful person than you didn't exist."[29]

Ingrid may also have been associated in Ingmar's mind with his own mother, who was distant and demanding. In *The Magic Lantern*, his episodic memoir, Ingmar documents his love-hate relationship with his mother. Violent and extremely jealous of his baby sister, he was consumed with attracting his mother's attention, with finding ways for her to exhibit her love. His main strategy was to feign illness, but since his mother was a nurse, she could easily see when he was "shamming" and quickly punished him, even in public. Having consulted a famous pediatrician and been warned about indulging her son's pretend symptoms, his mother became indifferent to his needs and adopted an air of "preoccupation" and aloofness. In response, young Ingmar modeled himself after her: he practiced "arrogance and a cool friendliness."

Ingmar has no specific memories of how this strategy played out, but he is certain that it attracted his mother's attention. When all else failed, Ingmar reverted to complaining about his health and refusing to go to school. However, he does recall one specific memory related to feigning illness: at some point, even though he was older than six, he refused to go to school. Day after day his parents dragged or carried him, yelling and screaming, to school. Often the exertion of putting on such a show caused Ingmar to actually vomit, become dizzy, or lose his sense of balance. Eventually his parents gave up and "postponed" his going to school, but in response, his mother took him for a visit to the pediatrician she had consulted before. Ingmar still recalls that the doctor had a large beard and smelled of cigars. After listening to his mother describe Ingmar's appalling behavior, the doctor turned and pulled down Ingmar's trousers, inspected his "insignificant organ," and then with a forefinger drew an airy triangle round his crotch and announced dramatically, "The boy still looks like a child *here*." Ingmar did not hear the advice the pediatrician gave his mother. But on this occasion, she was not harsh. She brought Ingmar home, dressed him in his faded yellow smock, served him hot chocolate and cheese sandwiches, and left him to play in the nursery. He had won this skirmish in the ongoing war for his mother's affection.

For the rest of their lives together, Ingmar and his mother engaged in this Oedipal struggle, the boy feigning sickness and indifference while inwardly crying out for affection, his mother feigning busyness and indifference because it was the right, the professional thing to do, demanding obedience for its own sake, what Ingmar came to think of as his mother's eternal game of blackmail: *Do it for me!*[30] It is not difficult to see why Ingmar might think of Ingrid as the actress best suited to play a version of his mother. From the published reports of Ingrid's various custody battles, Ingmar could easily infer that Ingrid too constantly asked of her children that they understand why she preferred acting to a life with them. She might very well have said, *"Do it for me!"*

Ingmar had always been fascinated with Ingrid's screen image. Burgess cites him in *My Story*, where he is clinically analytic about her. He had studied her early films in America, but not *Intermezzo*, and he clearly remembered being "fascinated" not so much by Bergman's body but by her face, especially her mouth, and her "strange radiance" and eroticism. Ingmar recalled one of the first times he met Ingrid. He was in a hotel suite in Stockholm with Schmidt, waiting for Ingrid to return from shopping. When she swept into the room, loaded with packages and "high colored" from the winter cold, he had the same response he had to viewing her on screen: "a strong erotic attraction and she was very beautiful."

Most importantly, Ingmar recognized that as an actress, perhaps Ingrid had not developed her full potential. His analysis of her role in *Joan at the Stake*—"fifty percent of Ingrid's performance was absolutely stunning, absolutely marvelous; twenty percent was acceptable, and thirty percent was absolutely catastrophic"—suggests that he considered himself the man to make her performances more complete, that he was the man to make her give all of herself to the role of Charlotte.[31] Ingmar recognized that Ingrid was capable of doing much more than her previous roles had demanded, that she had the performance skills necessary to convey the subtle play of emotion when the mother and daughter first meet, especially during the piano scene, and she had the range and the experience to do Charlotte's final emotional breakdown.

Ingmar may have recognized Ingrid's potential to play Charlotte, but during rehearsal he was constantly confronted with what he politely called "a kind of language barrier" between him and Ingrid. On the first day of rehearsal he discovered that Ingrid had "rehearsed her entire part in front of the mirror, complete with intonations and self-conscious gestures. It was clear that she had a different approach to her profession than the rest of us. She was still living in the 1940s." Moreover, well into rehearsal, he discovered that Ingrid had a tendency to take his suggestions and use them in the wrong way or in unexpected places.[32] Still, Ingmar persisted; he and Ingrid battled constantly, but eventually he got the performance he wanted.

That performance is in many respects the high point of Ingrid's career as an actor, and her performance resonates with us to this day because we can recognize it as a meditation on the psychological and emotional cost of Ingrid's public life: Was her career worth the cost? Is Ingrid tragic because she sacrificed her family life to the occasional demands of art, but more often to mere entertainment? Or is this the price we expect actors to pay for what they give us?

Nothing in the film causes us to question the value of Charlotte's artistry. The only questions are whether she had to forsake her children in order to become the pianist she wanted to be and whether she could have or should have resisted her love affairs for the sake of her family. The same questions obviously apply to Ingrid. Ironically, in this capstone to her career, Ingrid reveals the most about who she really was, the split between her public and private image.

This is a revelation that Ingrid resisted. At first she denied that she bore any resemblance to Charlotte. In fact, one of her best stories about the making of *Autumn Sonata* is about how she woke up after arriving at Ingmar's house. They had arranged for a 10:30 meeting, so Ingrid awoke in plenty of time, had breakfast, swam in the pool, took a walk in the woods, admiring the countryside, returned to her room to quickly review the script, and arrived at Ingmar's study exactly at 10:30. Ingmar was waiting. Without much of a greeting, Ingrid flipped open the script and asked, "How can a woman stay away from her children seven years?" Ingmar, prepared by Ingrid's earlier announcement during the trip from the airport that she often talked before she thought, burst out laughing. "I'm so glad you don't start on page one," he said.

Ingrid continued to protest, sometimes violently, that a career woman, even one as devoted to her career as Charlotte, would not stay away from her children for seven years. But it is not difficult to understand this excess as a form of denial and guilt. She allowed Burgess to include Ingmar's comment in her autobiography: "I found it a little strange that the things Ingrid protested against were characteristics which were very close to herself."[33]

The final cut of *Autumn Sonata* reflects Ingrid's resistance and is another reason for considering her one of the authors of the film. The filming of the final climactic confrontation between Charlotte and Eva came after Ullman and Ingrid petitioned Ingmar to change some of the lines. He had initially refused, but he did sanction their speaking the lines "against the work the way it is." Frustrated with the script, Ullman and Ingrid began shooting the scene. Ullman describes the scene at the end of a long day of shooting. She had a long monologue and then Ingrid was supposed to respond with the words, "Please hug me, please love me." Ullman finished her monologue, and the camera was turned on Ingrid, whereupon Ingrid announced very firmly that she did not want to say her lines as written and as rehearsed. Instead, she wanted to slap Ullman's face and stalk out of the room. Ingmar screamed in frustration: Ingrid was altering his script and changing Charlotte's motivation. Ingrid screamed back at him: no mother would tolerate what Charlotte had just heard from her daughter. Then the two realized that the crew was standing about, watching them, aghast. Ingmar waved everyone off the set except Ingrid. Through the door, Ullman and the crew heard the two of them still screaming at each other but with less and less intensity. Finally, there was something close to silence and the door opened, and the crew filed back on to the set. The shot was set up, and the camera was still on Ingrid, who was still supposed to say, "Please hug me, please love me." But in saying those words now, says Ullman, "Ingrid's face in that moment, her face was the face of every woman who has been forced to say, 'I'm here. Please like me. Please do this, please do that.' It was Nora of *A Doll's House*, it was anyone who, behind those wonderfully people-pleasing words, shows the anger. That is what she did. She showed a face for the daughter that was full of anger."

Ullman thought that Ingrid's underplaying those two lines was brilliant. Instead of making the scene sweet and sentimental, Ingrid "spoke for all of us women who have been brought up to be like this woman, so people will not think we have balls."[34]

Ullman generously gives Ingrid credit for the interpretation of the lines that finally appear in the film, but it could be argued that it was Ingmar's resistance and their major fight about the lines that produced Ingrid's interpretation,

There is one other reason why Ingrid should be considered a co-author of *Autumn Sonata*. She lobbied for a different ending: Ingmar had originally planned the finale of the film to be the mother leaving her daughter *sans espoir* [without hope], but Ingrid implored him to let the film express some sense of hopefulness. So Ingmar added the letter that Eva sends to Charlotte, and Ingrid says proudly, "He did it for me."[35]

This may be true. The final scene when Victor, Eva's husband, reads the letter Eva sends to her mother is not in the original plan for the film. In that letter, Eva writes that she now realizes she has wronged her mother, that she met Charlotte with "demands instead of affection," hatred instead of love. She asks for forgiveness because, after all, there is such a thing as mercy. Mercy is taking the "enormous chance of looking after each other, of helping each other, of showing affection." Eva wants Charlotte to know she will never let her disappear from her life again, that she will fight to keep their relationship alive.[36]

Gradually Ingrid came to accept that there was a great deal of her in Charlotte. In her memoir, she confessed that her friends were saying, "I hear you're playing yourself at last." In an interview after the film, she was much more open about the subject: "There's a lot of me in *Autumn Sonata*," she said, "and I was terribly nervous when my daughter Pia said she was going to see the film." Spoto also sees significance in the fact that Ingrid was acting the part of a pianist, as she had in *Intermezzo*, the film that she first left home to make: both films were about a pianist who lived to express her talent even if she had to sacrifice a normal life with a family. To Spoto, *Autumn Sonata* was the history of Bergman's relationship with Pia. In an interview published with the screenplay of *Autumn Sonata*, Ingrid too saw the connection with *Intermezzo*, that in each film she played a pianist, and declared, "My career has come full circle."[37]

Clearly, Leamer makes the necessary distinctions: There may be "something of Ingrid in Charlotte," but Ingmar took much about Charlotte's professional career in music from the life of Kabi Laretei, a Swedish concert pianist to whom he had previously been married for ten years. Charlotte is also clearly modeled after Ingmar's own mother, who was attracted to a man besides her husband, and surely Charlotte bears some resemblance to Ingmar himself, who was "an artistic egotist like Charlotte, molding actors to his purpose and will as if he were writing a novel." Although there is much of Ingrid in Charlotte, there are also many other people.

In addition, there are striking ways in which Ingrid is not like Charlotte at all. Ingrid was not as introspective as Charlotte, she had less knowledge of herself, and she was not as strong-willed. Nor was she ever forced to confront who she was as Eva forced Charlotte to do in *Autumn Sonata*.[38]

This is fair, although it ignores the details about Ingrid's potential contribution to *Autumn Sonata*. The sources of art are always mysterious. However, there is substantial evidence that Ingrid Bergman, the idea of Ingrid Bergman, was essential to Ingmar Bergman's conception of the film in the first place and that during the course of making the film, Ingmar Bergman, as Alfred Hitchcock and Roberto Rossellini had done before him, explored what Ingrid Bergman, the image of Ingrid Bergman, meant as a public personality and an actor.

Ingrid Bergman was an auteur.

EPILOGUE

Ten

The Art of Dying

"nothing in this life that I've been trying
Could equal or surpass the art of dying."
— George Harrison

Ingrid Bergman's death is even more the stuff of legend than the rest of her life. At times, it borders on mythology. She died on August 29, 1982, her 67th birthday. The cancer that she had at first denied and then fought so bravely for almost a decade finally claimed her. According to Leamer, Bergman knew that her end was near. Earlier in the month, at her insistence, she and Schmidt had flown to Stockholm so that she could see one last time her native city and Danholmen, Schmidt's island in the Baltic Sea. Bergman was so weak that she had to use a wheelchair to negotiate the airports.

Bergman saw the apartment where she had been born and where she had lived for the first years of her life. She walked past the Royal Dramatic Theater and sat on the very benches where she had sat to learn her lines as a student all those years ago. At Danholmen, she spent a great deal of time in the living room of the main house, looking out at the sea. At first, she was too weak to even step outside, but with Schmidt's help she forced herself to walk to the door and from then on by herself each day a few steps further, until eventually she could walk to the rock where she had so often gone by herself to look at the sea and learn her lines. There she asked Schmidt to have her ashes thrown over the water stretching out before her. He agreed to do so.

But Bergman's newly-found strength and heightened color did not last. Schmidt gave her a small dinner party with the Lundbergs, old family friends, who brought crayfish, which Bergman loved to eat. Bergman enjoyed herself, but after the party her health rapidly declined. Bergman knew she had to return to her apartment in London and the care of her doctor.

Schmidt left the island the day before her, perhaps because he could not bear to watch Bergman leave the island for the last time. Ever conscious of her image in the press, Bergman refused to fly back to Stockholm, where she might have confronted photographers. She insisted on taking a small fishing boat back to the mainland and then a car to her cousin Britt's apartment. With Britt, Bergman visited old friends and walked the theater district, where she had spent her childhood and adolescence. On the evening before she was to fly back to London, Bergman and Britt traveled to Malarstrand to visit Greta Danielson and her husband. Greta had been her father's lover after the death of his wife. Danielson knew that this was Bergman's last visit. "I am not afraid to die," Bergman told her. "I've had a rich life. I am content."[1]

Back in London, Bergman was cared for by Britt and Margaret Johnstone and Griff James. The children called, but Bergman insisted that they need not come to London. Still, she told Griff, "I said goodbye to everyone."

On the day before her birthday, as she was getting out of the bath, she felt an excruciating pain. The diagnosis was that her twelfth vertebra had collapsed: the cancer had spread to her spine. She had no hope of ever walking again. To ease the pain, Dr. MacLellan injected her with diamorphine, a form of heroin.

When Ann Todd called, Bergman told her, "I'm so tired, darling. I am so tired." Todd replied, "How lovely, Ingrid, how lovely. You just go to sleep."

On the morning of her birthday, Bergman took a number of calls from people who did not know how sick she was. During the day she breathed heavily, floating in and out of consciousness. Dr. MacLellan arrived and quickly learned that Bergman's lungs were now almost entirely collapsed.

Bergman insisted on putting make-up for the visitors she knew were coming for her birthday: Griff and Schmidt. Schmidt and her three caregivers stood around her bed. Schmidt had brought flowers. They toasted Bergman with champagne and brushed her lips with champagne, and she seemed to be at peace.

Schmidt left, and Britt and Margaret retired for the night. Britt, in a room adjoining Bergman's, also tried to sleep but found it difficult. Waking up well after midnight, she realized that she could no longer hear Bergman breathing. She went into Bergman's bedroom, took a mirror, and placed it on Bergman's lips, but she did not have to look at the results.

Britt told Isabella that on the night she died Bergman had a vision of her own mother, turned away from her, sitting at her makeup table. Bergman asked her mother if she had come to take her away. Her mother did not turn from facing the mirror, but Bergman thought she was as young and beautiful as she had been in the photographs taken by her father, the photos she had treasured as a child. Although her mother never looked at her, Bergman knew why she was there: she had been at Bergman's first birthday party and she had returned to be part of Bergman's last birthday, to make her more comfortable, and to ease her passing away from this life.[2]

On her bedside was a copy of *The Little Prince*, opened, Spoto says, to a passage she had marked: "I cannot carry this body with me. It is too heavy ... but it will be like an old abandoned shell. There is nothing sad about old shells ... I shall look as if I were dead, but that will not be true...."[3]

Isabella thought it was very typical of her mother to die on her birthday because she was such an "orderly," "tidy" person.[4]

In his obituary, Richard Schickel reports that on the day she died, Bergman claimed that she was a great actress because "she had acted on the last day of her life."[5] Schickel cites no source for this tidbit. None of the biographers mention it.

In an essay called "How to End It All," Hermione Lee ponders how biographers must decide how to deal with the death of their subjects. Given the intense involvement of most biographers with the object of their study, the natural tendency, Lee says, is to make the death fit the life, to make it meaningful, or to at least provide a sense of resolution: "We prefer not to read the subject's death, as perhaps it should be read, as without content, merely contingent, just the next fact in a series of facts.... We feel we must stage it and interpret it, or overinterpret it."[6]

Such tendencies are especially attractive, Lee goes on, for the biographers of writers. In dealing with the death of writers, biographers face the overwhelming temptation to try to imitate the writer's style or echo the writer's tone, to capture the spirit of the writer's work, to "make the moment of death somehow match up to, fulfill, or re-enact the *imaginative* life of the writer-subject." If this temptation is so great for biographers of writers, how much more of a temptation is it for biographers of actors, those self-conscious personas dedicated to dramatizing fictional lives with a subtle inflection, a look of the eyes, a telling gesture.

Most of the account of Bergman's final days given earlier is from Leamer's biography. Some of the details are confirmed by Chandler. Clearly both of these biographers think of Bergman's death as the culmination of her lifelong attempt to maintain order, to assert control, to manage her image. Even in death, Bergman was her own biographer, shaping her life to promote a vision of her character.

But in death, as with her life, there are other Ingrids.

As a child and young adolescent, Bergman knew death intimately. Her mother died when she was three. Bergman at first thought of her mother only as an "absence," but her image of her mother was shaped by her father's warm stories and his adoring gaze at the many photographs of her mother displayed about the house. Bergman's first real intimate contact with her mother occurred many years later when, going through the remains of her aunt Ellen's estate, she discovered a box of her mother's love letters to her father during their engagement. Reading about the intensity of their love in the face of strong opposition from her mother's family made her cry.[7]

Her father died when she was thirteen. She and Greta were at his bedside. Bergman remembers her father turning his head to look at Greta and then turning his head to look at her, and then he was gone.

Her Aunt Ellen died six months after her father, and because she was staying with Ellen at the time, Bergman was also at her bedside when she died. That night Ellen called her into her room. Her breathing was rough and raspy and frightened Bergman. Ellen told her that she felt extremely ill and that she should call Uncle Otto. Bergman rushed to the phone in a panic and called Cousin Bill, who lived around the corner. When she returned to the bedroom, Ellen asked her to read the Bible to her. Bergman did as she was told, but she did not know what she was reading. All she knew was that Ellen was getting worse and worse: her face seemed to blacken, and she began to rasp out the words, "I'm going to die," over and over. She wanted to know why help had not arrived.

Suddenly Ellen gasped, "Key — key." Bergman knew exactly what she meant. Ellen lived on one of the upper floors of her apartment building and rather than walk down the stairs to open the door, she usually threw the key out the window down to visitors, so that they could let themselves in. Bergman had forgotten that fact, and now realized in a terrible epiphany that her forgetfulness may have been the reason why Bill was taking so long: he couldn't get into the building. Rushing to the window, she saw that this was the case: there was Bill. He had been calling up to her, and she had not heard him. She threw down the key and ran back to her aunt. She took her aunt in her arms and held her, felt her gasping breath, stole looks at her face, which seemed by this time completely black. Bill arrived quickly with two nurses, who pulled Bergman away from her aunt, but Bergman recalls that it was too late, and perhaps the nurses could not have saved Ellen anyway.

Bergman confesses in the autobiography that the shock of Ellen's death, so soon after her father's, affected her deeply: it took her a good long time to recover.[8] Bergman told Chandler that for months after Ellen's death she dreamed about the episode again and again, replaying it in her dreams as if it were a film, but the ending was different. In Bergman's dream, she threw down the key much sooner, Uncle Otto showed up with Cousin Bill, and after some confusion, Ellen was taken to the hospital and survived. When Bergman woke up, she found herself not at Ellen's but at Uncle Otto's, and then she would realize that she had not saved Ellen after all. Bergman's family and friends all reassured her that even if she had remembered the key, Aunt Ellen probably would have died, that Ellen's death was not her fault. But deep inside, Bergman had her doubts, and from then on, she refused to enter Ellen's apartment. She only returned to the building with Lindstrom after they were engaged, to salvage from a basement storage room some furniture and utensils that they could use in setting up house.[9]

Given this history, it is remarkable that Bergman was as psychologically healthy as she was. It is easy to imagine another person with a similar history scarred for life, tentative, depressed, and fearful. Her outlook may have been shaped by her own good health. Before her cancer at the age of 57, Bergman had suffered very little from illness. Spoto reports that before the cancer, Bergman suffered only an episode of pneumonia, an appendectomy, and "a minor gynecological complaint." Otherwise, Bergman came down only with the usual colds and flu.[10]

Many of her lovers, friends, and colleagues died before her, some when she was in her early 50s: Robert Capa, of course; but also Gary Cooper, Humphrey Bogart, Spencer Tracy, Claude Rains, and David Selznick, to name just a few. And as a result, in her public statements, Bergman begins to talk about death maturely, optimistically, with a sense of perspective, long before she discovered that she had cancer in the fall of 1973. In the interview with Oriana Fallaci in 1968, on the occasion of her appearing in *More Stately Mansions*, Bergman talks about her friends dying and the process of aging. She finds the death of each friend a shock because she sees her "wrinkles in their wrinkles." These deaths remind her that even though she cannot see the effects of aging in the mirror every morning, she cannot ignore the fact that she is growing older. Indeed, meeting old friends from the past is like a slap in the face because they are not as young as they are in her memory. Still, Bergman does not regret the loss of her youth. Like Eugene O'Neill, who thought that getting old was natural, she recognizes that everything natural ages, trees age, animals age, and people should not be afraid of the natural, of dying. Aging may even be a sign of luck because it shows that you did not die young. Bergman's only fear, she says, is of becoming incapacitated and being forced to live her life in bed. Otherwise, she is not afraid to look old. She triumphantly tells Fallaci that she is 52 years old. She even tells her to write it down, to get it right. She is proud to be 52 because she is so happy.[11]

In 1974, a year after she learned that she had cancer, she said, "It is important to live one's allotted life-span to the fullest. It is too precious to waste. Life, be it long or short, is a gift to be cherished, and savored, and used well."[12]

In the years before she died, at least in public, she seemed accepting, reflective, positively elegiac.

She told Lawrence Quirk: "Life has been so good to me, on balance. It brought me three good men as husbands, four lovely children, all those awards, and the most satisfying career, creatively, that any woman could have. When people ask me how I can be so philosophical after some of the nasty harassment in former years by some segments of the press, I always reply along the lines of: 'Oh, but look at how the assets of my life have far outweighed the liabilities!' She added that she had learned, the hard way, that hurt and suffering promoted inner growth. 'Bad things help one appreciate all the more the good things that come. I believe in the law of compensation; that law has rewarded my richly.'"[13]

In a late interview with Charlotte Chandler, Bergman is equally accepting and reflective. Noting that someone once told her that people, especially women, can't have it all, she says defiantly, "Well, I did," even though she admits that she did make a mess of some of her life. She took risks and suffered the consequences. "Happiness," she says, jokingly, "is good health and a bad memory." She only regrets the unintentional things she may have done that hurt people. She regrets, for example, that she made Pia's childhood miserable. She does not regret "the loss of years" in which she made films with Rossellini rather than films to which she could have contributed more because, after all, during those years, she had three beautiful children. No, she has no major regrets. She would change little in her past and would not "give back any of the years of [her] life to be a year younger."[14]

In a letter to Donald Spoto, dated April 30, 1980, Bergman tells the story of visiting Alfred Hitchcock after he turned eighty years old the August before. Bergman recalls that Hitchcock took both of her hands and tearfully announced that he was going to die. She acknowledged his suffering and said that everyone dies sooner or later. She went on to share her own fear of dying because of a recent serious illness. Hitchcock seemed to find their shared pain consoling.[15]

Surely, considering her early frightening experiences with death, Bergman's final acceptance that she must die is a remarkable achievement. What is not clear are the sources of that achievement.

Often Bergman suggested that she found consolation in something approximating conventional religious belief. Burgess says in a third-person section of *My Story* that what Bergman had learned as a child from both her father and her aunts and uncles was to be honest, to tell the truth, and to follow the Golden Rule even more rigorously than Jesus had suggested: that she should treat others even better than she would treat herself. Still, there are indications that Bergman felt that religion was more than a moral code.

She says earlier in *My Story* that even before she moved to Italy, a Catholic country, she went to church quite often, especially before the opening of a show she was performing in. She usually went to Catholic churches because they were always open, unlike the Lutheran churches. Bergman would light a candle, then sit in a pew and pray that her show would do well.[16] In talking about her church attendance, Bergman uses the past tense. The implication is that Bergman no longer attends church often. Something has changed. And perhaps that change resulted from wrestling with the notion of the goodness of God. Burgess says that Bergman had never been an avid believer in God. She often wondered why God, since He was so powerful, did not do a better job of protecting the poor and the oppressed in the world, why He did not put an end to suffering and injustice.[17]

Later, in Bergman's second marriage, religion was a delicate subject with the Rossellinis and the Rossellini children. Rossellini himself was an atheist, but sympathetic to the claims of the church. Rossellini sensed, like Hamlet, that there was more in heaven and earth than most people dream about, and he certainly believed in miracles — that people get out of wheelchairs and walk, that blind people suddenly see — all the time.[18]

As a result, the Rossellini children were raised as Catholics and had been told that it was a deadly sin to pray with their Protestant mother. But Bergman, whatever her personal theology, never lost her need for intersession, her need to pray. With the children, she used to say a Swedish prayer and ask the children to join in. Once, however, they refused, saying that Rossellini had told them that she was a heathen. Bergman calmly denied the charge and tried to explain that both Protestants and Catholics believed in the same God: they just prayed to that God differently. She did not insist that the children pray with her; they could do so only if they wanted to. And so she began to pray by herself, and eventually all the children joined her.

During Isabella's operation to correct her spine, Bergman sought out a chapel where she could pray for Isabella's recovery. But in the middle of her meditation, she realized that she only prayed when things went wrong, and she wondered why. She decided that she did in fact pray when she was happy; she just did it in a different way. When she was happy, she did not go to a church; she simply thanked God in her mind or in a quiet whisper. And she remembered son Robertino when he was younger, asking who God was. Bergman was not quite sure what to say, but she finally managed to blurt out to her son that he should wait until he had a sick child of his own and then he would understand why people might want to fall on their knees and pray. Robertino looked at her quizzically and then replied that he would rather fall on his knees and pray to a doctor.[19] Robertino may have been more influenced by his father than his mother, or perhaps he sensed his mother's ambivalence about God.

Despite her need for prayer, Bergman claims elsewhere in *My Story* that she never had strong feelings about particular religions, and she follows this claim with an anecdote about Rossellini's frustration with the Catholic church for churning out saints. Rossellini, she says, believed in reason, although he admired people who have the determination to accept miracles. Rossellini thought that believing in miracles was already a kind of religion.[20] Clearly, Bergman is sympathetic to Rossellini's point of view here.

Still, she found talking about religion awkward, perhaps embarrassing, and often refused to do so publicly. In the autobiography, Bergman suggests that she was once blindsided by a question on religion from David Frost on his talk show, and from then on she decided that she would not talk about religion in public again. She and Frost had been discussing Bergman's role in *The Inn of the Sixth Happiness.* Bergman related that she had gone to Taipei to see Gladys Aylward, on whose life the film is based, but she had arrived too late; Aylward had died ten days earlier. But Aylward had not yet been buried and her friends were adamant that Bergman should see her in her casket. Bergman demurred, but Aylward's friends insisted, and only after considerable polite but pointed give-and-take did Bergman avoid looking into Aylward's casket. Having missed Gladys Aylward in life, Bergman had no desire to see the woman in death.

Having related this anecdote to Frost, Bergman paused, and Frost looked at her sympathetically. Then in a hushed voice, he asked, "You're very religious, aren't you, Miss Bergman?"

Bergman was flabbergasted. Schmidt and Pia were in the studio audience, and while Bergman writhed on stage, not knowing how to answer, she heard Pia laugh and predict that her Mother would say something ambivalent like "yes and no."

Totally at a loss for words, Bergman eventually blurted out, "More or less." And Pia was convulsed in laughter.[21]

On one other occasion, she was more blunt. During the question-and-answer session at the National Press Club luncheon in April of 1972, Bergman was asked her view of religion and how she faced the difficulties of life. Bergman announced peremptorily that she did not discuss religion. She was a Protestant and that was all she would say. As for how she handled difficult problems, she said this: "I try to face them with a laugh. I try to get a perspective by thinking of myself on a screen, to look at myself dispassionately and then laugh." Another reporter recorded the response this way: I handle "life's most difficult problems with a laugh and try to look at myself as though I was critically viewing a role on the screen — sometimes not good, sometimes ridiculous."[22]

Why this reluctance to talk about religion? Perhaps the peace and serenity she achieved late in life were earned through suffering that was too difficult to talk about: the early deaths of her parents, the failed marriages, Isabella's painful spinal problem, her own confrontation with cancer. Perhaps she paid a price for her serenity.

Isabella told Leamer that the evening before she went into the hospital for her operation to correct her scoliosis, Bergman took her to a church to light a candle and to pray. Bergman held Isabella's hand and left the church crying. On the street they were accosted by a beggar, whom they walked by dismissively. But the beggar followed them whining and pleading. Suddenly Bergman turned to the man, and in Leamer's dramatization "screamed hysterically": "Here! Here! Take it! Take it!" "She opened her purse and threw all her money at the beggar, every bill, every coin."[23]

When she forgot her lines during a performance of *Waters of the Moon* in 1978, she was distraught, but co-star Wendy Hiller consoled her, insisting that the audience had loved her and hadn't even noticed the dropped lines. To which Bergman responded, "You're right, Wendy. It's only a play."[24] This may have been an unconscious echo of Hitchcock's earlier advice to her when she was taking herself very seriously: "It's only a movie."

And of course there was her cancer, for which she went through the stages of grief. She agonized over her mortality more than she let on.

At first, she denied the possibility. Ironically, she was reading an article on breast cancer when she first discovered the lump in her breast. Immediately, she called Schmidt and he told her to go to a doctor the next day, but she did not. She wanted to wait for the end of the run of *The Constant Wife*. Months later, she consulted a doctor in London, who advised her to have the lump tested, but then she agreed to an extension of the play, and took the part in *Murder on the Orient Express*. It was not until the play was over and she went to New York to see her daughters that Bergman finally submitted to a full examination, where she was diagnosed with breast cancer. It was not until June of 1974, seven months after discovering the lump, that she had an operation to remove her breast.[25]

Then came the despair: Bergman told daughter Ingrid that she especially appreciated talking to Rossellini after her diagnosis: Rossellini, she said, gave her the courage to overcome her despair and deal with the cancer.[26]

As the illness progressed, there were also hints that Bergman may have contemplated committing suicide. Fiorella visited and learned while she was with Bergman that a friend had committed suicide. Fiorella told Bergman that her friend had died just as he had lived, and Bergman commented on the man's courage. Fiorella got the distinct impression that Bergman was thinking of suicide herself.

Once when Schmidt brought Bergman a new bottle of sleeping pills from Switzerland, he told Margaret to hide them because Bergman had told him that if she ever had enough of them, she might use them. And Isabella told Leamer that near the end of her life, Bergman was very sad and depressed and might have killed herself if she could. Bergman simply could not stand for people to pity her. The only thing holding Bergman back was the threat of another scandal. If Bergman could have arranged an accident, such as falling down the stairs or something similar, she would have done it. That was why caretakers Griff and Margaret were there all the time, and why Isabella herself visited every three weeks or so. But Isabella had to limit her visits because Bergman would have gotten angry, even violent, if she had known Isabella was monitoring her.

Twin sister Ingrid, however, did not take the talk of suicide seriously. True, Bergman would also berate her when she visited and stayed for more than a week. Bergman would constantly tell her to go home, but every now and then she would also say that if she became worse, she would jump out a window. Daughter Ingrid, however, doubted that her mother would actually do such a thing: she thought that Bergman loved life too much to give in to despair.[27]

With the public Bergman never gave the slightest indication that she was ever anything but content and happy. To the public she talked about acceptance and having a full life, and in public she displayed remarkable courage. She acted in A Woman Called Golda, despite the fact that her right arm ballooned with water during the day and had to be drained every night, especially for the scene in which she reproduces the image of Meir covering her face with two hands when she was elected.[28]

And perhaps Bergman's reluctance to talk about religion was that she knew her beliefs were not conventional and she did not wish to subject them to public scrutiny. There are indications that her suffering molded her conventional religious beliefs into something far from mainstream Protestantism. Her beliefs had always been tinged with astrology, and at the end of her life, Bergman seems to have developed something close to a cult of the dead.

Bergman insisted on marrying Lindstrom on the seventh day of the seventh month during a year with a seven at the end. But the film she was working on, Dollar, ran over schedule, so she had to get married on the tenth of the month.[29]

In discussing whether to take the doctors' recommendation to induce the birth of the twins who were long overdue, Bergman considers her horoscope and then decides against choosing a specific date. She does not want to confuse "the stars, the astrological signs, the moon, and the constellations," which should determine the twin's destiny on their own. If she chooses the date for the twins to be born, the heavenly bodies will be confused and the twin's birthday will be less meaningful. Roberto at first agrees, but then the doctors convince him to change his mind, and Bergman reluctantly gives in. When the doctors arrive to start inducing the twins on June 18, Bergman calls Rossellini to confirm that June 18 is a good day. He agrees that it is.[30]

Bergman did not only rely on astrology to promote good fortune. With Rossellini, she also used small Catholic rituals. Despite Rossellini's atheism, at important moments in their lives, Bergman would, with his permission, make "a little cross on his forehead" with her finger. It is not clear how seriously Bergman took these gestures to improve her life. Making the cross on Rossellini's forehead, Bergman dryly told Chandler, didn't help their films much.[31]

What is clear is that all her life, Bergman had a real sense of the dead. Early in her film career in Stockholm, she regularly got off the tram on the way to the studio because it passed by a small graveyard in which her parents were buried. She would go to a small bench near their graves, sit, bow her head, and say a prayer for her father and even talk to him.[32]

In the two windows of the living room in the house in Paris where she lived with Schmidt, Bergman placed two sets of framed photographs. In one went the photos of friends who were living, and in the other went photos of friends who had died. When a friend died, Bergman moved the friend's picture from one window to the other, until as the years went by, the photos in the window for the dead greatly outnumbered those in the window of the living. Isabella calls the look of the disparity between the two windows "ghoulish and depressing."[33]

During the shooting of *Autumn Sonata*, Ingmar Bergman noted that Ingrid kept some strips of film in a rusty tin box. He soon learned that the strips of film were from movies that Ingrid's father had taken of her as a child. The movie showed scenes of Ingrid as a toddler in her mother's lap and as a young girl singing and playing the piano and watering roses outside a greenhouse. There was even a scene of Ingrid dressed in dark clothes standing near her mother's grave. Ingrid seemed to value the film strips so highly that Ingmar borrowed them and made Ingrid good new copies.[34]

When she died Bergman had next to her bed a series of photographs: one of her four children, one each of Schmidt, her niece Fiorella (daughter of Zia Marchella), her mother Frieda, her father Justus, and her Aunt Ellen. Isabella Rossellini reports that Pia called her in New York from London, where Pia had gone to finish up Bergman's affairs, among other things, to clean out Bergman's apartment and put it up for sale. Said Pia, "You know those photos Mother keeps next to her bed? Grandma's, Grandpa's, and Aunt Ellen's photos are covered with traces of Mother's lips." Comments Isabella: "Like me and, I suspect, my twin sister Ingrid, Mother must have had secret ceremonies with her dead. She kissed those photos and whispered secrets. The connection to the beyond must have been strong...."[35]

And so it comes as no surprise that about her own death Bergman was self-conscious, self-promoting, and dramatic. Knowing she is not healthy, that she may not live more than a few years, Bergman ends her autobiography with some reminiscences of ceremonies in her honor. She in effect celebrates her own life. Despite her modest claim to be merely an entertainer, this is not an act of modesty. Bergman gives special attention to the Variety Club of America's television show in November of 1979 to raise funds for an Ingrid Bergman hospital wing for underprivileged and handicapped children. The show is on the old stage 9 of Warner Brothers Studios, where *Casablanca* was filmed. Paul Henreid is there, as well as Helen Hayes, Signe Hasso, and Joseph Cotten. While Teddy Wilson plays "As Time Goes By," Dooley Wilson having died years before, Bergman starts to hum along. Suddenly a voice behind her picks up the melody and starts to sing a bit louder than anyone else. The voice is Frank Sinatra's. Bergman is moved, and when Sinatra is done, she gives him a kiss, although the two have never worked together and hardly know each other. Bergman learns later that Sinatra volunteered to do the show because he had always wanted to sing "As Time Goes By" to Bergman herself in person.

With this anecdote Bergman ends her autobiography, except for one final note. In her last paragraph she eloquently expresses her joy at being able to act, to create make-believe worlds that entertain people from all walks of life. Theater stages and films sets bind people together like families, she says, and she is proud to have been part of so many families, who share their worlds of make-believe. She concludes: if in the future, some theater or film production should need an old witch, especially for the holidays, even though she is at the end of her life, she will be "ready and there."[36]

Two years after the publication of the autobiography and realizing that she did not have long to live, Bergman began to make arrangements for her death. She went through her wardrobe, organizing everything. She wrapped dresses in plastic, attaching to each a note indicating whom the dress was for. She grouped household items and other clothes, perhaps for posterity, according to which marriage they belonged. The notes read, "First Marriage," "Second Marriage," "Third Marriage."[37]

She arranged to go back to Stockholm and visit her old haunts. She took control of her death in ways that suggest, once again, Lena Geyer: Says the narrator of that book, "All her life she had made her choices — greatly, consistently, and stoically. She had learned to endure deprivation to achieve what she wanted — and she had wanted great things.... She made her choice when she gave up her love for the sake of her art; she made the same choice a second time when she condemned herself, in the fullness of her beauty and passionate maturity, to celibacy. She paid the enormous price exacted for that decision. She had the courage to rebuild her life according to her own standards, instead of sinking gratefully into luxury and ease that were only too eagerly offered her. Now she wanted one great thing more. She wanted to die bravely and to carry the burden of her suffering as resolutely as she had carried other burdens before."[38]

Despite her thought of suicide, Bergman seems to have decided, like Geyer, to carry the burden of her suffering resolutely. At the end, she did believe — perhaps she forced herself to believe — that there can be some sort of appropriateness, some sort of justice in death. Like the entire tale of Geyer's life, this is a very romantic notion. By all accounts, Bergman arranged her death with all the sense of order and propriety that she had brought to her life.

Given Bergman's tendencies to play a part, to control her image, to dramatize her life, given all the Ingrids that could have shaped the end of her biography, it is surprising that her biographers do not make more of the fact that she died on her birthday.

Still, true to Bergman herself, the endings of the biographies are not very Christian — rather, they imply a mingling with nature. Perhaps this is an unconscious recognition that Bergman's beliefs were not orthodox and may have been more like a worship of things as they are. Spoto ends by noting the fact that Bergman died in a time of year when sunshine reminds us of the waning days and the coming winter. He conjures a breeze from the Thames gently stirring the curtains and flowers in her room. Then Bergman's lips move silently and she gives one final long, gentle sigh, her breath mingling with the breeze. Starlight shines throughout the cloudless night.[39]

Leamer ends with a description of the memorial service at Saint Martin's-in-the-Fields Church in London with all the children there, Schmidt and the Rossellini relatives and John Gielgud and Wendy Hiller. The ceremony includes the reading of Shakespeare and Saint-Exupery. Bridgit Nilsson sings Beethoven. A children's choir marches down the aisle singing "This Old Man" from *The Inn of the Sixth Happiness.*

Then Leamer sings his own eulogy. Bergman, he says, "had ascended into myth." She lived on, however, in the memories of those who had loved her: in the adoration of Griff and Margaret, in the "emotional no-man's land" of Pia's ambivalent feelings, in Lindstrom's regret at the years he spent not telling the truth about his ex-wife, in Schmidt's suddenly taking on the role of curator of Bergman's image, loving her "in memory as he had not loved her in the flesh."

As part of his newly self-created role of curator of Bergman's image, says Leamer, Schmidt invites a small group of people to Danholmen the June, following Bergman's death. Schmidt and Isotta Ingrid and a Swedish priest take a small boat out into the sea and cast Bergman's ashes onto the water while those still on shore throw baskets of flowers into the waves. Leamer ends Bergman's written "life" with an image of a calm sea and baskets of flowers slowly drifting away from shore. The baskets pass a lobster fisherman, tending his pots. The fisherman does nothing to stop the drift of the baskets and slowly the baskets drift further away and disappear in "the endless sea."[40]

Bergman died as she lived. Her death does not resolve the ambiguity or the mystery of her life. In any case, her life is there, the fact of it. Perhaps that is all we should want of Bergman's life, of any life: its mere contingency, death as one more fact in a series of facts.

Bergman acted on the last day of her life, Schickel says. She had a vision of her mother, Britt says. Dying, she breathed one final long, gentle sigh that mingled with the breeze, Spoto says. Bergman's life was small and insignificant considering the vastness of the sea, Leamer implies. So and so, someone reported. Such and such, someone was told. It is said. Someone thought. It may mean. At the accumulation of such detail, Ingrid Bergman transcends her biographers.

Chapter Notes

Chapter One

1. Thor Severson, "Colorado's Senator Johnson," *Frontier*, April 15, 1950. Reported in the Appendix to the *Congressional Record—* Senate, 1950, Vol. 96, A3283–A3284.

2. "Licensing of Motion Pictures in Interstate Commerce," United States, Congress, *Congressional Record—* Senate, March 14, 1950, 3286–87.

3. "Licensing" 3281–3288.

4. There have been other biographies, but none of them has included the thorough research that we associate with major work. Curtis F. Brown's *Ingrid Bergman* (New York: Galahad, 1973) is a short summary of Bergman's career. John Russell Taylor's *Ingrid Bergman* (London: Elm Tree, 1983) is an introduction to the Kobal Collection of photographs of Bergman and posters advertising her films. Charlotte Chandler's *Ingrid Bergman: An Intimate Biography* (New York: Simon & Schuster, 2007) has higher aspirations but is mostly a compilation of interviews, interspersed with data from filmographies. It lacks comprehensiveness and does not offer a coherent interpretation of Bergman's life and career.

5. Severson, in *Appendix to the Congressional Record*, A3283.

6. "Bergman's Year," *Life* 19, November 12, 1945, pp. 127–30+; the Pageant survey is cited in "Licensing," 3285.

7. Qtd. in Tag Gallagher, *The Adventures of Roberto Rossellini* (New York: Da Capo, 1998), 452–53.

8. Donald Spoto, *Notorious: The Life of In-grid Bergman* (New York: HarperCollins, 1997), 13–14.

9. Spoto 29–30, 33.

Chapter Two

1. Spoto 399–400.

2. David Denby, "The Natural," *The New Yorker* 73, July 28, 1997, 72–75.

3. Ingrid Bergman and Alan Burgess, *My Story* (New York: Dell, 1980), 70; hereafter, referred to as MS. See also Leamer 31.

4. Leamer, on Bergman's relationship with Pia, 246, 250, 254–55, 267–71; on being a distant mother, 283; on conceding custody, 275; on arranging for Pia help take care of the Rossellini children, 473–78.

5. Leamer cites Lindstrom's judgment on this issue, 71.

6. Leamer 138; see also MS 210–12.

7. Mary Gordon, "Why I Love to Read About Movie Stars," *Ms.* 14.11 (May 1986): 22–23; Patricia Bosworth, "The Rich Mysteries of Ingrid Bergman's Life," *Working Woman* 11.4 (April 1986): 182–86. The quotation is on the last page; Anne Edwards, "Looking For Bergman: Leamer's Faultfinding Biography," *The Washington Post Book World*, March 8, 1986, C2.

8. Robert Skidelsky, "Only Connect: Biography and Truth," *The Troubled Face of Biography*, eds. Eric Homberger and John Charmley (New York: St. Martin's, 1988), 1–16. The quotations are from pages 3 and 13.

9. Isabella Rossellini, *Some of Me* (New York: Random House, 1997), 177.

10. Victoria Glendinning, "Lies and Si-

lences," *The Troubled Face of Biography,* eds. Eric Homberger and John Charmley (New York: St. Martin's, 1988), 49–62. The quotation is on page 52.

11. Richard Holmes, "Inventing the Truth," *The Art of Literary Biography,* ed. John Batchelor (Oxford: Clarendon, 1995), 15–25. The quotation is on page 17.

12. Two collections of essays written by biographers about biography are John Batchelor, ed., *The Art of Literary Biography* (Oxford: Clarendon, 1995), and Eric Homberger and John Charmley, eds., *The Troubled Face of Biography* (New York: St. Martin's, 1988).

13. Ira B. Nadel, *Biography: Fiction, Fact, and Form* (New York: St. Martin's, 1984), 180.

14. Virginia Woolf, "The Art of Biography," *Collected Essays,* Vol. 4. (London: Hogarth, 1967), 228.

15. MS 69.

16. Qtd. in Aljean Harmetz, *Round Up the Usual Suspects: The Making of Casablanca — Bogart, Bergman, and World War II* (New York: Hyperion, 1992), 91.

17. MS 138–39. The letter is dated January 12, 1942; MS 136.

18. Rossellini 14.

19. MS 353.

20. MS 356–58; Leamer 222.

21. Leamer 225.

22. However, Leamer admits that Bergman may have seen Pia twice in the early '50s. Lindstrom says that he brought Pia to Europe on two occasions and that Bergman saw her there. Pia confirms this account but her memories are so vague that Leamer doubts them (246); on Bergman blaming Rossellini, MS 362; for the letters, MS 360–61, 363–65; for Pia's letter, MS 367.

23. MS 368.

24. On not meeting Pia in New York, MS 415; Spoto 333; Leamer 249; on meeting six months later, MS 416–18.

25. Leamer 211.

26. On Isabella's bout with scolitis, see Spoto 363; MS 488, 492–97.

27. Leamer 285.

28. On Lindstrom's assertion: Leamer 71.

29. On the affair with Adolphson, Spoto 29–30; on Spoto's judgment about Bergman's affairs in general, 225.

30. On Houseman's testimony, Leamer 72. On Grady's testimony, Larry Swindell, *Spencer Tracy: A Biography* (New York: World,

1969), 172. On Tracy's testimony, Bill Davidson, *Spencer Tracy: Tragic Idol* (London: Sedgwick & Jackson, 1987), 80.

31. Leamer 96; MS 149.

32. On Bergman to O'Shea, Leamer 96; on Bergman to Roberts, MS 150.

33. On Wallace's testimony, Leamer 100; James Bacon, *Made in Hollywood* (New York: Warner, 1977), 60.

34. Jeffrey Meyers, *Gary Cooper: American Hero* (New York: William Morrow, 1998), 179–80, 183; Spoto 136.

35. Leamer 113.

36. Peck to Speck, qtd. in Gary Fishgall, *Gregory Peck: A Biography* (New York: Scribner, 2002), 98.

37. Peck to Darrach, qtd. in Fishgall 98. Darrach's article appeared in *People,* July 15, 1987.

38. Anthony Quinn, with Daniel Paisner, *One Man Tango* (New York: HarperCollins, 1995), 324–25.

39. Joseph Henry Steele, *Ingrid Bergman: An Intimate Portrait* (New York: David McCay, 1959), 39.

40. Leamer 67; MS 120–21.

41. On the dispute with Kottcheff, Spoto 365–66.

42. On the dispute with Quintero, MS 503–04.

43. Leamer 297.

44. On talking to the audience, Leamer 303; on acting in a wheelchair, MS 540–41.

45. Leamer 324.

46. Michael Sragow, *Victor Fleming: An American Movie Master* (New York: Pantheon, 2008), 477.

47. Leamer 33–36; MS 70–73.

48. Kobal 461, 467.

49. On Spoto's opinion of Bergman's filming in Germany, 59–60; Bergman's later admission, qtd. in Spoto 425.

50. Spoto 218.

51. MS 210–11.

52. Steele 112–14.

53. MS 210–12; Leamer 138; Spoto 217–18.

54. Spoto 239.

55. MS 523.

56. Rossellini 18.

57. Steele 34–36.

58. Rossellini 58.

59. Tom Shales, *Legends: Remembering America's Greatest Stars* (New York: Random House, 1989), 196.

Chapter Three

1. Irene Selznick, *A Private View* (New York: Knopf, 1983), 225.
2. Spoto 89.
3. January 21, 1940; qtd. in Spoto 88–89.
4. MS 87–88, 91.
5. Spoto 70.
6. On Selznick's claim, letter to Bergman, November 3, 1945, in the Selznick Archive of the Harry Ransom Center at the University of Texas-Austin, hereafter referred to as SA; see also Leamer 47. On the descriptions of Selznick, see Rudy Behlmer, "Editor's Forward," *Memo from David O. Selznick* (New York: Modern Library, 2000), xxvii, and Roger Ebert, "Introduction" to Behlmer ix.
7. SA: Selznick letter to MacNamara, March 22, 1946.
8. SA: January 13, 1947.
9. SA: Howard memo, May 18, 1939.
10. Behlmer 141–42.
11. Behlmer 143.
12. SA: Not in the published version of the memo.
13. SA: memo to Daniel O'Shea, February 23, 1945.
14. SA: memo to Daniel O'Shea, March 10, 1940.
15. SA: memo to Victor Fleming, January 22, 1941.
16. SA: July 28, 1942.
17. SA: memo to Shapiro, March 4, 1941.
18. Behlmer 144–45; the memo is dated June 22, 1939.
19. SA: memo to Strickling, December 26, 1940.
20. SA: memo to Birdwell, February 9, 1940.
21. SA: Memos from Birdwell and Brown to Selznick, February 12,1940.
22. SA: memo to Brown, February 16, 1940.
23. SA: Mishkin memos, dated from February 27 to August 8, 1942.
24. SA: letter from O'Shea to Benny, October 2, 1945.
25. SA: telegram from Wilkie to Steele, July 2, 1943.
26. SA: memo to Steele and Flagg, July 10, 1943.
27. SA: memo to Bolton, September 2, 1941.
28. SA: memo to Brown, February 6, 1940.
29. SA: memo from Brown to Selznick, February 9, 1940.
30. SA: memo to Brown February 16, 1940.
31. SA: memo to Birdwell, March 5, 1940.
32. MS 133; the lines from the play are in Eugene O'Neill, "Anna Christie," *The Plays of Eugene O'Neill* (New York: Random House, 1964), 14.
33. SA: memo from Bolton to Selznick, September 9, 1941.
34. SA: memo from Selznick to Bolton, September 13, 1941; letter from Selznick to Lindstrom, September 15, 1941.
35. SA: memo from Selznick to Shapiro, December 27, 1940.
36. SA: memo to Brown, February 5, 1942.
37. SA: letter from Barker to Selznick, quoted by Frances Inglis in a memo to Joseph Steele, May 4, 1943.
38. Thomas Carlile and Jean Speiser, "Ingrid Bergman: Young Swedish Star Brings a New Brand of Charm to American Screen," *Life*, July 26, 1943, 105–06, 108.
39. "For Whom?" *Time*, August 2, 1943, 55.
40. Donald Culross Peattie, "First Lady of Hollywood," *Reader's Digest* 43, September 1943, 40, 42.
41. S. J. Woolf, "In, But Not Of, Hollywood," *The New York Times Magazine*, December 26, 1943, 21.
42. MS 155–56.

Chapter Four

1. MS 186–87.
2. MS 187.
3. MS 190.
4. MS 115.
5. MS 131.
6. MS 136.
7. Steele 42.
8. MS 204–05.
9. Qtd. in Alex Kershaw, *Blood and Champagne: The Life and Times of Robert Capa* (New York: St. Martin's, 2003), 168.
10. Cornell Capa and Richard Whelan, eds., *Robert Capa: Photographs* (New York: Knopf, 1985), 204.

11. Martha Gellhorn, "Till Death Do Us Part," *The Short Novels of Martha Gellhorn* (London: Sinclair-Stevenson, 1991), 305–09.

12. MS 194.

13. Chandler 123.

14. MS 205.

15. Gellhorn 309.

16. Capa and Whelan 199.

17. Chandler 122–23

18. Steele 89–92; see also Spoto 209–212.

19. MS 205–06.

20. Gellhorn 310–11.

21. Bill Davidson, *The Real and the Unreal* (New York: Harper and Bros., 1961), 160.

22. Adler 113–14.

23. Leamer 120. There is one other version of the bathtub story in Richard Whelan, *Robert Capa: A Biography* (New York: Knopf, 1985), 241. In Whelan's version, the photo was taken by Capa's friend Carl Goodwin.

24. Leamer 121–22.

25. Adler 88; Spoto 205; on Adler's leaving for Europe in 1949, Leamer 150.

26. On Bergman's fear of Lindstrom, MS 180. On Lindstrom's denial, Leamer 135. On Steele's recollection, Steele 104.

27. MS 214, 217; Spoto 222; Steele 123.

28. MS 232.

29. Spoto 222–23.

30. Leamer 150.

31. MS 375 .

32. Steele 235.

33. Sragow 456.

34. Steele 137–38; Sragow, 459–60.

35. Sragow 462.

36. MS 218–25; Leamer 142.

37. On Fleming's appearance and personality, MS 222; on his death, MS 225.

38. Sragow 483–84.

39. On Lindstrom learning about the affair with Fleming, Spoto 232; on newspaper accounts of Bergman's wanting a child, quoted in Spoto 233.

40. On Bergman meeting Capa during *Under Capricorn*, Leamer 155; on Capa and Bergman parting in the winter of 1947, Whelan 249; on Adler seeing Bergman until 1949, Leamer 150.

41. On Capa's influence, MS 206; on the desire to make more realistic films, MS 225.

42. MS 233–34.

43. Steele 181–82.

44. MS 13–14, 238.

45. On when she saw *Open City*, MS 13–

14; on the evidence for the later date, Leamer 151–52.

46. Spoto 236–37; Leamer 152; Steele 161.

47. Selznick 374–75.

48. On only going to Italy to make a movie, MS 257; on first meeting Rossellini, 237–38.

49. Gallagher 308–09.

50. MS 240.

51. MS 244; Leamer 163–64.

52. MS 244.

53. Leamer 162; Davidson 162. (Yes, it is the same page number as the red carpet story in Leamer.)

54. Gallagher 309; MS 243.

55. Leamer 164.

56. Hedy Lamarr, *Ecstacy and Me: My Life as a Woman* (New York: Bartholomew House, 1966), 101–02.

57. MS 244, 249–50.

58. The letter of March 4: MS 249–50; the telegram: MS 251.

59. MS 251.

60. MS 257.

61. On Rossellini's bragging, Gallagher 308; on Lopert's comment, Leamer 168.

62. Steele's version of the letter is in Steele 232; Spoto's is in Spoto 266–67.

63. For Bergman's recollection of what she took with her to Rome, MS 250; Cohn's memory is qtd. in Spoto 267; Lindstrom's version is in Leamer 166 and cited in Spoto 267.

64. Selznick 375.

Chapter Five

1. Spoto 268.

2. MS 278.

3. Steele 171.

4. The list of mail is from MS 289. The number of letters is from Flanner 88. On the letters causing pain and being interrupted at dinner, MS 346.

5. On the 24-hour siege, MS 319; on the Italian free-lancers, Flanner 93–94.

6. The entire story of the siege at the clinic is from MS 326–29.

7. On Bergman's unhappiness, MS 24; on the newspaper reports, MS 259, 275, 286–90, 326–29.

8. "Ingrid Has a Baby," *Life* 28.7, February 13, 1950, 42; Janet Flanner (Genet), "Let-

ter from Rome," *The New Yorker* 26, April 8, 1950, 88.

9. Leamer 2; Spoto 297–98.

10. On the "waves of hatred," MS 331–32; on Lyon's support, Bill Davidson, *The Real and the Unreal* (New York: Harper & Bros., 1961), 143.

11. MS 287–88.

12. MS 346.

13. On the letters from Selznick and Hemingway, MS 291–93; on the letter from Gould, Steele 201–02; on the letter from the song writer, MS 286.

14. On the fan letters, Flanner 88; on the surveys, Adrienne L. McLean, "The Cinderella Princess and the Instrument of Evil," *Headline Hollywood: Century of Film Scandal*, eds. Adrienne L. McLean and David A. Cook (New Brunswick: Rutgers University Press, 2001), 180, 188; on the recent academic study, McLean 173–74.

15. Spoto 292–93.

16. Qtd. in "Licensing of Motion Pictures in Interstate Commerce," United States, Congress, *Congressional Record—*Senate, March 14, 1950, 3284.

17. "Bergman Has a Son at Hospital in Rome," *The New York Times*, February 3, 1950, pt 2: 27.

18. "Ingrid Gives Birth to Son in Rome; Rossellini at Hospital," *Washington Post*, February 3, 1950, 1, 23.

19. "Ingrid Has a Baby," *Life* 28.7 (February 13, 1950): 42.

20. "Stromboli Bambino," *Newsweek* 35, February 13, 1950, 32.

21. On Johnson's statement, "Admission of Aliens Admitting Acts of Moral Turpitude — Legal Aspects," United States, Congress, *Congressional Record*, March 20, 1950, 3624; on Selznick's statement, Behlmer 433.

22. Leamer 229; Spoto 316.

23. Steele 193.

24. Robert J. Levin, "The Ordeal of Ingrid Bergman," *Redbook*, August 1956, 84; Davidson 142.

25. On Bergman's summary of what Johnson said, MS 330–331; 522; on Johnson's hurtful remarks, "Licensing" 3285, 3286, 3288.

26. "Licensing" 3282, 3285.

27. "Licensing" 3284.

28. "Senator Proposes U.S. Film Control," *The New York Times*, March 15, 1950, 33.

29. On the R.K.O statement, "RKO Answers Johnson," *The New York Times*, March 15, 1950: 33; on banning and the number of prints, McLean, "Cinderella" 177.

30. "Censorship Threat," *The New York Times*, March 26, 1950, 101.

31. "The Purity Test," *Time* 55, March 27, 1950, 99–100; See also "Hollywood Labor," *The New York Times*, March 26, 1950, 101.

32. Thor Severson, "Colorado's Senator Johnson," *Frontier*, April 15, 1950, reported in the Appendix to the *Congressional Record—*Senate, 1950, Vol. 96, A3283.

33. On Wiley's response, Oscar Davis, "How Now, Senator?" *Washington Daily News*, April 24, 1950; on Johnson's response to Wiley, "Extension of Remarks," United States, Congress, Senate, Appendix to the *Congressional Record*, April 25, 1950, A2963–64. Davis's article is reproduced on A2963.

34. "Attitude of Executives of Motion Picture Industry," United States, Congress, *Congressional Record—*Senate, April 27, 1950, 5882.

35. "Rossellini Is Branded a Fascist by Senate," *The New York Times*, August 24, 1950, 15.

36. Leamer 156–59, 161 ; Spoto 258–63.

37. Steele 194–95.

38. Spoto 272.

39. MS 264.

40. Barbara Leaming, *If This Was Happiness: A Biography of Rita Hayworth* (New York: Viking, 1989), 160–201; Adrienne L. McLean, *Being Rita Hayworth: Labor, Identity, and Hollywood Stardom* (New Brunswick: Rutgers University Press, 2004), 90; McLean, "Cinderella," 170–71.

41. MS 294–95.

42. Spoto 273 .

43. Steele 188–89, 213.

44. Steele 236.

45. Steele 226.

46. "Ingrid Bergman Gives Birth to Baby Boy in Rome," *Topeka Daily Capitol*, February 3, 1950, 3.

47. "Licensing" 3285.

48. "Ingrid, Rossellini Reported Hoping for Catholic Wedding," *Washington Post*, February 4, 1950, 11.

49. "Rossellini Scuffles With Cameraman," *Washington Post*, February 5, 1950, 8M.

50. "Weak Condition of Ingrid's Baby Delays Baptism," *Washington Times Herald*, February 7, 1950, 3.

Chapter Six

1. Richard Schickel, "The Price of Redemption," *Time* 120, September 13, 1982, 82.
2. Qtd. in Francois Truffaut, *Truffaut on Hitchcock* (New York: Simon & Schuster, 1967), 189.
3. MS 13–14.
4. On being remembered, Spoto 212; on being Galatea, Steele 161.
5. For Rossellini's explanation of his directorial style, see *My Method: Writings and Interviews*, ed. Adriano Apra, trans. Annapaola Cancogni (New York: Marsilio, 1992), 56–57.
6. Robin Wood, "Ingrid Bergman on Rossellini," *Film Comment* 10, July 1974, 12.
7. Wood 12, 14.
8. MS 392–93.
9. Chandler 173.
10. Rossellini, *Some of Me* 43.
11. Chandler 285.
12. MS 447–51.
13. On turning down the part in *The Miracle Worker,* MS 512–13; on receiving other scripts, MS 462, 467, 473, 479, 509, 510, 519, 528.
14. MS 468–69.
15. MS 498, 500.
16. "Ingrid's Return," *Newsweek* 49, January 28, 1957, 63; "People," *Time* 60, January 28, 1957, 44.
17. Robert J. Levin, "The Ordeal of Ingrid Bergman," *Redbook*, August 1956, 36–39, 82–86; "Ingrid Bergman, the Woman America Can't Forget," *Coronet* 39, November 1955, 53–60; Bill Davidson, "Why Ingrid Bergman Broke Her Long Silence," *Collier's*, October 26, 1956, 34–41.
18. On the Alvin Gang, MS 407–12; Leamer 247, 312.
19. Spoto 335.
20. MS 443–46.
21. On the sold-out shows, MS 520, 522, 530; on the Hiller anecdote, Leamer 323–24.
22. Spoto 416; MS 575–76.
23. Leamer 211.
24. On Avanzo's analysis, Gallagher 369–70; on Lisandrini's comment, Gallagher 352.
25. Jean Renoir, *Letters* (London: Faber and Faber, 1994), 276; Gallagher 369.
26. George Sanders, *Memoirs of a Professional Cad* (New York: Putnam, 1960), 121–22.
27. Spoto 312.
28. MS 395–97.
29. MS 399, 401–03.
30. Leamer 251–54; Spoto 336–9; MS 423–28.
31. Steele 343.
32. On the court decision Leamer 275; on Bergman's comment MS 459.
33. MS 460.
34. MS 502.
35. MS 526.
36. MS 518–19; Spoto 381.
37. MS 544; Spoto 596–97.
38. Chandler 258.
39. MS 551.
40. Spoto 188, 433.
41. Dust jacket of Marcia Davenport, *Of Lena Geyer* (New York: Grosset & Dunlap, 1936).
42. Qtd. in Spoto 189.
43. Davenport 5.

Chapter Seven

1. Georges Gusdorf, "Conditions and Limits of Autobiography," *Autobiography: Essays Theoretical and Critical*, ed. James Olney, trans. Olney (Princeton: Princeton University Press, 1980), 44.
2. MS 175.
3. MS 180.
4. SA: letter to Selznick , January 20, 1943.
5. SA: memo to Steele, January 23, 1943.
6. On the background for the luncheon, MS 522–25; on Bergman's response to specific questions, Richard Coe, "Tribute to Ingrid Bergman," and Ruth Dean, "What Was It Like to Kiss Bogart?" in "Tribute to Ingrid Bergman," Congressional Record — Senate, Vol. 118, 92nd Congress, Second Session, April 19, 1972, 13371.
7. Levin 36, 38–39, 82–84. 36–39.
8. Oriana Fallaci, "Looking Back Over the 28 Years Since Her Arrival in America, Ingrid Bergman Recalls the Troubled Times When 'Hate Submerged Me Like a Tempest,'" *Look* 32, March 5, 1968, 26, 28.
9. John Kobal, "Ingrid Bergman," *People Will Talk* (New York: Aurum, 1986), 463–65.
10. A. E. Hotchner, "The Enduring Courage of Ingrid Bergman," *McCall's*, May 1982, 84–86, 156–58. rev. version: "Ingrid Bergman Has Only One Regret," *Choice Peo-*

ple: The Greats, Near-Greats, and Ingrates I Have Known (New York: William Morrow, 1984), 102–18. The quotations are from the article in *McCall's*, 156–57.

11. Levin 84.

12. MS 531.

13. Kobal 449, 450.

14. Coe 13371.

15. Leamer 211.

16. Leamer 312.

17. Spoto 403.

18. Leamer 335–36.

19. Spoto 423.

20. Judy Klemesrud, "Ingrid Bergman: No Regrets at 65," *The New York Times*, October 7, 1980, B16.

21. MS 335.

22. MS 522–25.

23. MS 538–44.

24. MS 502–05, 511, 514, 515–16.

25. MS 167–68; the Perkins version is in Leamer 272, and Spoto 352–53.

26. MS 70.

27. MS 362, 392–93.

28. MS 334, 338, 392–93; Leamer 212, 227–28.

29. MS 394, 392.

30. MS 508–09.

31. Adler 89.

32. Spoto 265, 278.

Chapter Eight

1. MS 166–67.

2. Richard Dyer, *Stars* (London: British Film Institute, 1979), 68–72, 142–49.

3. Stanley Cavell, *The World Viewed: Reflections on the Ontology of Film* (Cambridge: Harvard University Press, 1979), 33.

4. Robin Wood, *Hitchcock's Films Revisited*, rev. ed. (New York: Columbia University Press, 2002), 312–315.

5. Gill Branston, *Cinema and Cultural Modernity* (Philadelphia: Open University Press, 2000), 118.

6. Christine Geraghty, "Re-examining Stardom: Questions of Text, Bodies, and Performance," *Reinventing Film Studies*, eds. Christine Gledhill and Linda Williams (London: Arnold, 2000), 189–90.

7. James Naramore, *Acting in the Cinema* (Berkeley: University of California Press, 1988), 23.

8. Naramore 34–37; 52–59.

9. Most of the information in my discussion of screen acting comes from Naramore's book.

10. Naramore 23–24; Norman N. Holland, "Psychoanalysis and Film: The Kuleshov Experiment," *IPSA Research Paper No. 1* (Gainesville: Institute for Psychological Study of the Arts, University of Florida, 1986); Truffaut 214–15.

11. Naramore 25.

12. Irving Wallace, "Smorgasbord Circuit," *Collier's* 118, December 21, 1946, 95.

13. MS 70; Spoto 202.

14. Richard Dyer, "The Constant Stardom of Ingrid Bergman," *New York Times Magazine*, April 20, 1975, 5; Leamer 236.

15. MS 523–24.

16. MS 561.

17. Steele 29.

18. Qtd. in Leamer 273.

19. Leamer 286.

20. Qtd. in Lawrence Quirk, *The Complete Films of Ingrid Bergman* (New York: Citadel Press, 1991), 217–18.

21. Gallagher 402.

22. Laura Mulvey, "Vesuvian Topographies: The Eruption of the Past in *Journey in Italy*," *Roberto Rossellini: Magician of the Real*, eds. David Forgacs, Sarah Lutton and Geoffrey Nowell-Smith (London: BFI, 2000), 100.

23. Gallagher 304–05.

24. Adriano Apra and Maurizio Ponzi, "An Interview with Roberto Rossellini," *Screen* 14.4 (Winter 1973–74), 121; Reprinted in Rossellini, *My Method*, 153–6.

25. Gallagher 412.

26. Qtd. in J. Douchet, "Interview with Roberto Rossellini," *Arts* 739 (September 9, 1959): 6.

27. The dialogue in the final film version of *Autumn Sonata* does not necessarily follow the published script. I have basically quoted the dialogue in the published script but edited it to account for deletions but not paraphrases in the film: Ingmar Bergman, *Autumn Sonata*, trans. Alan Blair (New York: Pantheon, 1978).

Chapter Nine

1. Francois Truffaut, "A Certain Tendency in French Cinema," *Cahiers du Cinema* 31, January 1954; Andrew Sarris, "Notes on

Auteur Theory in 1962," *Film Culture* 27, Winter 1962–63, 1–8.

2. Dyer, *Stars* 174–77.

3. Patrick McGilligan, *Cagney, the Actor as Auteur* (South Brunswick: A.S. Barnes, 1975), 99; qtd. in Dyer, *Stars* 174.

4. Qtd. in Truffaut 224.

5. Patrick McGilligan, *Alfred Hitchcock: A Life in Darkness and Light* (New York: HarperCollins, 2003), 357.

6. Donald Spoto, *The Dark Side of Genius: The Life of Alfred Hitchcock* (Boston: Little, Brown, 1983), 292; McGilligan, *Alfred* 381.

7. Spoto, *Dark* 308; qtd. in Truffaut 185–86.

8. Qtd. in Spoto, *Dark* 304–05.

9. McGilligan, *Alfred* 7–9; Spoto, *Dark* 16, 18–19.

10. On the Berlin anecdote, McGilligan, *Alfred* 64–66; on being impotent 176–78, 653–54.

11. Spoto, *Dark* 283; Leonard J. Leff, *Hitchcock and Selznick* (New York: Weidenfeld and Nicolson, 1987), 177–209.

12. McGilligan, *Alfred* 376; Eric Rohmer and Claude Chabrol, *Hitchcock: The First Forty-Four Films* (New York: Ungar, 1979), 81.

13. Joe McElhaney, "The Object and the Face: *Notorious*, Bergman, and the Close-up," *Hitchcock: Past and Future*, eds. Richard Allen and Same Ishi-Gonzales (New York: Routledge, 2004), 66; Hitchcock qtd. in Truffaut 9.

14. Steve Cohen, "*Rear Window*: The Untold Story," *Columbia Film Review* 8.1, 1990, 2–7.

15. Leo Braudy, "Rossellini: From 'Open City' to 'General della Rovere,'" *Great American Film Directors: A Critical Anthology*, eds. Leo Braudy and Morris Dickstein (New York: Oxford University Press, 1978), 666, 668–69; Pierre Leprohon, *The Italian Cinema*, trans. Roger Greaves and Oliver Stallybrass (New York: Praeger, 1972), 132–33.

16. Robin Wood, "Rossellini," *Film Comment* 10, July 1974, 9–10.

17. Robin Wood, "Ingrid Bergman on Rossellini," *Film Comment* 10, July 1974, 13–14.

18. Roberto Rossellini, *My Method: Writings and Interviews*, ed. Adriano Apra, trans. Annapaola Cancogni (New York: Marsilio, 1992), 29.

19. Sanders 124, 125; Steele 311–12.

20. Peter Brunette, *Roberto Rossellini* (Berkeley: University of California Press, 1987), 156.

21. Luciana Bohne, "Rossellini's 'Viaggio in Italia': A Variation on a Theme by Joyce," *Film Criticism* 3.2 (1979): 43–52.

22. Apra and Ponzi 112; Rossellini 154.

23. MS 393.

24. Rossellini 57; Gallagher 435.

25. Gallagher 437.

26. Ingmar Bergman, *The Magic Lantern*, trans. Joan Tate (New York: Viking, 1988), 90–91, 93–94, 95–96.

27. Ingmar Bergman, *Images: My Life in Film*, trans. Marianne Routh (New York: Arcade, 1990), 326, 328–29.

28. MS 554–55.

29. Ingmar Bergman, *Autumn* 45–46.

30. Ingmar Bergman, *Magic* 9.

31. On Ingrid's eroticism, MS 557; on Bergman's acting, MS 558.

32. Ingmar Bergman, *Images* 329, 332.

33. MS 559, 562.

34. Chandler 281–82.

35. Spoto, *Notorious* 411. Spoto cites McKeon, "Bergman on Bergman" as his source; however, I could not locate the McKeon interview.

36. On the original plan for *Autumn Sonata*, Ingmar Bergman, *Images* 326; on the ending Ingrid may have inspired, Ingmar Bergman, *Autumn* 83–84.

37. MS 562; Mason Wiley and Damien Bona, *Inside Oscar* (New York: Ballantine, 1987), 556; Spoto, *Notorious* 409; Ingmar Bergman, *Autumn* 90.

38. Leamer 316.

Epilogue

1. Leamer 358.

2. Chandler 299.

3. Spoto 436.

4. Chandler 301.

5. Schickel 82.

6. Hermione Lee, "How to End it All," *Body Parts: Essays in Life Writing* (London: Chatto & Windus, 2005), 206.

7. MS 34.

8. MS 40–41.

9. Chandler 29–30, 33.

10. Spoto 391–92.

11. Fallaci 26, 28.
12. Quirk 14.
13. Quirk 14.
14. Chandler 209.
15. Spoto, *Dark Side*, 552.
16. Burgess in MS 522; Bergman in MS 454–55.
17. MS 53.
18. Chandler 176–77.
19. On praying with the children, MS 454; On Robertino's comment, MS 492.
20. MS 336.
21. MS 454.
22. Richard Coe, in "Tribute" 13371; Ruth Dean, in "Tribute" 13371.
23. Leamer 284.
24. Chandler 286,

25. Chandler 249.
26. Chandler 264.
27. Leamer 354–55.
28. Chandler 295
29. MS 68
30. MS 355.
31. Chandler 176.
32. MS 53.
33. Rossellini, *Some of Me* 19.
34. Ingmar Bergman, *Magic* 184.
35. Rossellini, *Some of Me* 27–28.
36. MS 575–76.
37. Rossellini, *Some of Me* 19.
38. Davenport 467.
39. Spoto 436
40. Leamer 360–61.

Bibliography

Adler, Larry. *It Ain't Necessarily So: An Autobiography.* New York: Grove, 1984.

"Admission of Aliens Admitting Acts of Moral Turpitude — Legal Aspects." United States. Congress. *Congressional Record.* March 20, 1950. 3624.

Apra, Adriano, and Maurizio Ponzi. "An Interview with Roberto Rossellini." *Screen* 14.4, Winter 1973–74. Reprinted in Rossellini, *My Method,* 153–16.

"Attitude of Executives of Motion Picture Industry." United States. Congress. *Congressional Record — Senate.* April 27, 1950. 5882.

Bacon, James. *Made in Hollywood.* New York: Warner, 1977.

Behlmer, Rudy, ed. *Memo from David O. Selznick.* New York: Modern Library, 2000.

"Bergman Has a Son at Hospital in Rome." *The New York Times,* February 3, 1950.

Bergman, Ingmar. *Autumn Sonata.* Trans. Alan Blair. New York: Pantheon, 1978.

_____. *Images: My Life in Film.* Trans. Marianne Routh. New York: Arcade, 1990.

_____. *The Magic Lantern.* Trans. Joan Tate. New York: Viking, 1988.

Bergman, Ingrid, and Alan Burgess. *Ingrid Bergman: My Story.* New York: Dell, 1980. "Between the Lines." *Redbook,* July 1956.

Bohne, Luciana. "Rossellini's 'Viaggio in Italia': A Variation on a Theme by Joyce." *Film Criticism* 3.2, 1979.

Bosworth, Patricia. "The Rich Mysteries of Ingrid Bergman's Life." *Working Woman* 11.4, April 1986.

Branston, Gill. *Cinema and Cultural Modernity.* Philadelphia: Open University Press, 2000.

Braudy, Leo. "Rossellini: From 'Open City' to 'General della Rovere.'" *Great American Film Directors: A Critical Anthology.* Eds. Leo Braudy and Morris Dickstein. New York: Oxford University Press, 1978.

Brunette, Peter. *Roberto Rossellini.* Berkeley: University of California Press, 1987.

Capa, Cornell, and Richard Whelan, eds. *Robert Capa: Photographs.* New York: Knopf, 1985.

Carlile, Thomas, and Jean Speiser. "Ingrid Bergman: Young Swedish Star Brings a New Brand of Charm to American Screen." *Life,* July 26, 1943.

Cavell, Stanley. *The World Viewed.* Cambridge: Harvard University Press, 1979.

"Censorship Threat." *The New York Times,* March 26, 1950.

Chandler, Charlotte. *Ingrid Bergman: An Intimate Biography.* New York: Simon & Schuster, 2007.

Coe, Richard L. Quoted in "Tribute to Ingrid Bergman."

Cohen, Steve. "*Rear Window*: The Untold Story." *Columbia Film Review* 8.1, 1990.

Curtis, Olga. "The Life and Times of Big Ed." *Denver Post Empire Magazine,* February 18, 1968.

Damico, James. "Ingrid from Lorraine to Stromboli: Analyzing the Public's Perception of a Film Star." *The Journal of Popular Film* 4.1, 1975.

Darrach, Brad. *People,* July 15, 1987.

_____. "Psycho II." *People*, June 13, 1983.

Davenport, Marcia. *Of Lena Geyer*. New York: Grosset & Dunlap, 1936.

Davidson, Bill. *The Real and the Unreal*. New York: Harper & Bros., 1961.

_____. *Spencer Tracy: Tragic Idol*. London: Sedgwick & Jackson, 1987.

_____. "Why Ingrid Bergman Broke Her Long Silence." *Collier's*, October 26, 1956.

Davis, Oscar. "How Now, Senator?" *Washington Daily News*, April 24, 1950. Reported in the Appendix to the *Congressional Record*— Senate, 1950, Vol. 96, A2963.

Dean, Ruth. "What Was It Like to Kiss Bogart?" in "Tribute to Ingrid Bergman."

Douchet, J. "Interview with Roberto Rossellini." *Arts* 739, September 9, 1959.

Dyer, Richard. "The Constant Stardom of Ingrid Bergman." *New York Times Magazine*, April 20, 1975.

_____. *Stars*. London: BFI, 1979.

Edel, Leon. *Writing Lives: Principia Biographica*. New York: Norton, 1984.

Edwards, Anne. "Looking For Bergman: Leamer's Faultfinding Biography." *The Washington Post Book World*, March 8, 1986.

"Extension of Remarks." United States. Congress. Senate. Appendix to the *Congressional Record*. April 25, 1950. A2963–64.

Fallaci, Oriana. "Looking Back Over the 28 Years Since Her Arrival in America, Ingrid Bergman Recalls the Troubled Times When 'Hate Submerged Me Like a Tempest.'" *Look* 32, March 5, 1968.

Fishgall, Gary. *Gregory Peck: A Biography*. New York: Scribner, 2002.

Flanner, Janet (Genet). "Letter from Rome." *The New Yorker* 26, April 8, 1950.

"For Whom?" *Time*. August 2, 1943.

Gallagher, Tag. *The Adventures of Roberto Rossellini: His Life and Films*. New York: Da Capo, 1998.

Gellhorn, Martha. "Till Death Do Us Part." *The Short Novels of Martha Gellhorn*. London: Sinclair-Stevenson, 1991. 295–339.

Geraghty, Christine. "Re-examining Stardom: Questions of Text, Bodies, and Performance." *Reinventing Film Studies*. Ed.

Christine Gledhill and Linda Williams. London: Arnold, 183–201.

Glendinning, Victoria. "Lies and Silences." *The Troubled Face of Biography*. Eds. Eric Homberger and John Charmley. New York: St. Martin's, 1988.

Gordon, Mary. "Why I Love to Read About Movie Stars." *Ms.* 14.11, May 1986.

Gusdorf, Georges. "Conditions and Limits of Autobiography." *Autobiography: Essays Theoretical and Critical*. Ed James Olney, trans. Olney. Princeton: Princeton University Press, 1980. 28–48.

Harmetz, Aljean. *Round Up the Usual Suspects: The Making of Casablanca — Bogart, Bergman, and World War II*. New York: Hyperion, 1992.

Holland, Norman N. "Psychoanalysis and Film: The Kuleshov Experiment." *IPSA Research Paper No. 1*. Gainesville: Institute for Psychological Study of the Arts, University of Florida, 1986.

"Hollywood Labor." *The New York Times*, March 26, 1950.

Holmes, Richard. "Inventing the Truth." *The Art of Literary Biography*. Ed. John Batchelor. Oxford: Clarendon, 1995.

Hotchner, A. E. "The Enduring Courage of Ingrid Bergman." *McCall's*, May 1982. Rev. version: "Ingrid Bergman Has Only One Regret." *Choice People: The Greats, Near-Greats, and Ingrates I Have Known*. New York: William Morrow, 1984.

"Ingrid Bergman Gives Birth to Baby Boy in Rome." *Topeka Daily Capitol*, February 3, 1950.

"Ingrid Bergman, the Woman America Can't Forget." *Coronet* 39, November 1955.

"Ingrid Gives Birth to Son in Rome; Rossellini at Hospital." *Washington Post*, February 3, 1950.

"Ingrid Has a Baby." *Life* 28.7, February 13, 1950.

"Ingrid, Rossellini Reported Hoping for Catholic Wedding." *Washington Post*, February 4, 1950.

"Ingrid's Return." *Newsweek* 49, January 28, 1957.

Kershaw, Alex. *Blood and Champagne: The Life and Times of Robert Capa*. New York: St. Martin's, 2003.

Kobal, John. "Ingrid Bergman." *People Will Talk*. New York: Aurum, 1986.

Klemesrud, Judy. "Ingrid Bergman: No Regrets at 65." *The New York Times*, October 7, 1980. Lamarr, Hedy. *Ecstacy and Me: My Life as a Woman*. New York: Bartholomew House, 1966.

Leamer, Laurence. *As Time Goes By: The Life of Ingrid Bergman*. New York: Harper and Row, 1986.

Leaming, Barbara. *If This Was Happiness: A Biography of Rita Hayworth*. New York: Viking, 1989.

Lee, Hermione. *Body Parts: Essays in Life Writing*. London: Chatto & Windus, 2005.

Leff, Leonard J. *Hitchcock and Selznick*. New York: Weidenfeld and Nicolson, 1987.

Leprohon, Pierre. *The Italian Cinema*. Trans. Roger Greaves and Oliver Stallybrass. New York: Praeger, 1972.

Levin, Robert J. "The Ordeal of Ingrid Bergman." *Redbook*, August 1956.

"Licensing of Motion Pictures in Interstate Commerce." United States. Congress. *Congressional Record—Senate*. March 14, 1950. 3281–3288.

Lindstrom, Pia, as told to George Christy. "My Mother, Ingrid Bergman." *Good Housekeeping*, October 1964.

McElhaney, Joe. "The Object and the Face: *Notorious*, Bergman, and the Close-up." *Hitchcock: Past and Future*. Eds. Richard Allen and Same Ishi-Gonzales. New York: Routledge, 2004. McGilligan, Patrick. *Alfred Hitchcock: A Life in Darkness and Light*. New York: HarperCollins, 2003.

_____. *Cagney, the Actor as Auteur*. South Brunswick: A.S. Barnes, 1975.

McLean, Adrienne L. *Being Rita Hayworth: Labor, Identity, and Hollywood Stardom*. New Brunswick: Rutgers University Press, 2004.

_____. "The Cinderella Princess and the Instrument of Evil." *Headline Hollywood: A Century of Film Scandal*. Eds. Adrienne L. McLean and David A. Cook. New Brunswick: Rutgers University Press, 2001.

Meyers, Jeffrey. *Gary Cooper: American Hero*. New York: William Morrow, 1998.

Mulvey, Laura. "Vesuvian Topographies: The Eruption of the Past in *Journey in Italy*." *Roberto Rossellini: Magician of the Real*. Eds. David Forgacs, Sarah Lutton and Geoffrey Nowell-Smith. London: BFI, 2000.

Nadel, Ira B. *Biography: Fiction, Fact, and Form*. New York: St. Martin's, 1984.

Naremore, James. *Acting in the Cinema*. Berkeley: University of California Press, 1988.

O'Neill, Eugene. "Anna Christie." *The Plays of Eugene O'Neill*. New York: Random House, 1964.

Peattie, Donald Culross. "First Lady of Hollywood." *Reader's Digest* 43, September 1943.

"People." *Time* 60, January 28, 1957.

"The Purity Test." *Time* 55, March 27, 1950.

Quinn, Anthony. *One Man Tango*. Written with Daniel Paisner. New York: Harper-Collins, 1995.

Quirk, Lawrence. *The Complete Films of Ingrid Bergman*. New York: Citadel Press, 1991.

Renoir, Jean. *Letters*. London: Faber and Faber, 1994.

"R.K.O. Answers Johnson." *The New York Times*, March 15, 1950.

Rohmer, Eric, and Claude Chabrol. *Hitchcock: The First Forty-Four Films*. New York: Ungar, 1979.

Rossellini, Isabella. *Some of Me*. New York: Random House, 1997.

Rossellini, Roberto. *My Method: Writings and Interviews*. Ed. Adriano Apra. Trans. Annapaola Cancogni. New York: Marsilio, 1992.

"Rossellini Is Branded a Fascist by Senate." *The New York Times*, August 24, 1950.

"Rossellini Scuffles with Cameraman." *Washington Post*, February 5, 1950.

Sanders, George. *Memoirs of a Professional Cad*. New York: Putnam, 1960.

Sarris, Andrew. "Notes on Auteur Theory in 1962." *Film Culture* 27, Winter 1962–63.

Schickel, Richard. "The Price of Redemption." *Time* 120, September 13, 1982.

Selznick, Irene. *A Private View*. New York: Knopf, 1983.

"Senator Proposes U.S. Film Control." *The New York Times*, March 15, 1950.

Severson, Thor. "Colorado's Senator Johnson." *Frontier*, April 15, 1950. Reported in the Appendix to the *Congressional Record—Senate*, 1950, Vol. 96, A3283–A3284.

Shales, Tom. *Legends: Remembering America's Greatest Stars*. New York: Random House, 1989.

Skidelsky, Robert. "Only Connect: Biography and Truth." *The Troubled Face of Biography*. Eds. Eric Homberger and John Charmley. New York: St. Martin's, 1988.

Smit, David W. "Marketing Ingrid Bergman." *Quarterly Review of Film and Video* 22.3, July–September 2005.

Speck, Gregory. *Hollywood Royalty: Hepburn, Davis, Stewart and Friends at the Dinner Party of the Century*. New York: Birch Lane, 1992.

Spoto, Donald. *The Dark Side of Genius: the Life of Alfred Hitchcock*. Boston: Little, Brown, 1983.

_____. *Notorious: The Life of Ingrid Bergman*. New York: HarperCollins, 1997.

Sragow, Michael. *Victor Fleming: An American Movie Master*. New York: Pantheon, 2008.

Steele, Joseph Henry. *Ingrid Bergman: An Intimate Portrait*. New York: David McKay, 1959.

"Stromboli Bambino." *Newsweek* 35, February 13, 1950.

Swindell, Larry. *Spencer Tracy: A Biography*. New York: World, 1969.

"Tribute to Ingrid Bergman." Congressional Record—Senate. Vol 118. 92nd Congress, 2nd Session. April 19, 1972. 13370–73.

Truffaut, Francois. "A Certain Tendency in French Cinema." *Cahiers du Cinema* 31, January 1954.

_____. *Truffaut on Hitchcock*. New York: Simon & Schuster, 1967.

Wallace, Irving. "Smorgasbord Circuit." *Collier's* 118, December 21, 1946.

"Weak Condition of Ingrid's Baby Delays Baptism." *Washington Times Herald*, February 7, 1950.

Whelan, Richard. *Robert Capa: A Biography*. New York: Knopf, 1985.

Whitcomb, Jon. "Encounter with Ingrid." *Cosmopolitan* 140, May 1956.

Wiley, Mason, and Damien Bona. *Inside Oscar*. New York: Ballantine, 1987.

Wood, Robin. "Ingrid Bergman on Rossellini." *Film Comment* 10, July 1974.

_____. *Hitchcock's Films Revisited*. Rev. ed. New York: Columbia University Press, 2002.

_____. "Rossellini." *Film Comment* 10.6, July 1974.

Woolf, S. J. "In, But Not Of, Hollywood." *The New York Times Magazine*, December 26, 1943.

Woolf, Virgina. "The Art of Biography." *Collected Essays*, vol. 4. London: Hogarth, 1967.

Worthen, John. "The Necessary Ignorance of a Biographer." *The Art of Literary Biography*. Ed. John Batchelor. Oxford: Clarendon, 1995.

Index